SAVING HOMEWATERS

SAVING
HOMEWATERS

The Story of Montana's
Streams and
Rivers

GORDON SULLIVAN

The Countryman Press
Woodstock, Vemont

Library of Congress Cataloging-in-Publication Data

Sullivan, Gordon.
Saving homewaters: the story of Montana's streams and rivers/Gordon Sullivan.—1st ed.
p. cm.
Includes bibliographical references and index.
ISBN 978-0-88150-679-2 (alk. paper)
1. Stream conservation—Montana—History. I. Title.

QH76.5.M9S85 2008
333.91'621609786—dc22

2007029999

Cover and interior photos by Gordon and Cathie Sullivan
Book design and composition by Karen Schober
Map by Jacques Chazaud

Published by The Countryman Press, P.O. Box 748, Woodstock, VT 05091

Distributed by W. W. Norton & Company, Inc., 500 Fifth Avenue, New York, NY 10110

Printed in the United States of America

10 9 8 7 6 5 4 3 2 1

To the memory of Gordon Ray, who took the time to teach me about rivers, trout, and wild places. And to all the conservationists who throughout Montana's history have fought to save our natural resources, especially my friend Jim Posewitz.

ACKNOWLEDGMENTS

I can't take full credit for this book. It is, after all, an attempt to tell the story of others—conservationists, fly fishers, and river advocates who have worked to save Montana's natural resources. The list begins with Jim Posewitz, a man of uncanny memory, followed by Paul Roos, Phil Gonzalez, John Bailey, Eric Bjorge, Justin Lawrence, Dave Blackburn, Craig Mathews, Mike Lum, Joe Dilschneider, Tim Linehan, Joe Kipp, Frank Stanchfield, Dan Shepherd, Brooks Sanford, Tim Tollett, and Hugh Zackheim. And to everyone else who fights for the rights of a river, I am grateful.

I am also indebted to my wife, Cathie, who from the very start believed in the project and constantly inspired me onward, as did Kermit Hummel from The Countryman Press, who extended insightful guidance, enduring patience, and trust. My editor, Beverly Magley, worked endlessly on the manuscript and had both the forcefulness and grace to inform me when the story was not being told.

For every writer charged with a large project, there is always someone standing in the shadows pointing a finger the right direction when things suddenly drift toward chaos. For me, that person was my good buddy Skip Gibson from Dan Bailey's Fly Shop.

Some influential people from the past also must be recognized: Dan Bailey, George Grant, and Art Whitney were all Montana conservationists who through their actions and undying commitment showed me the value of loving rivers and the wild places from which they come.

Last but certainly not least, a hearty thanks goes out to the generous and professional staff at the Montana Department of Fish, Wildlife & Parks, the Montana Historical Society, and Montana Department of Environmental Quality.

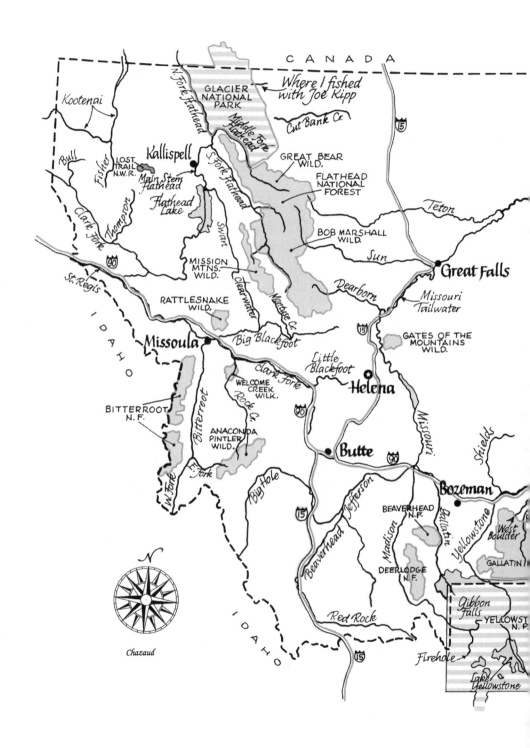

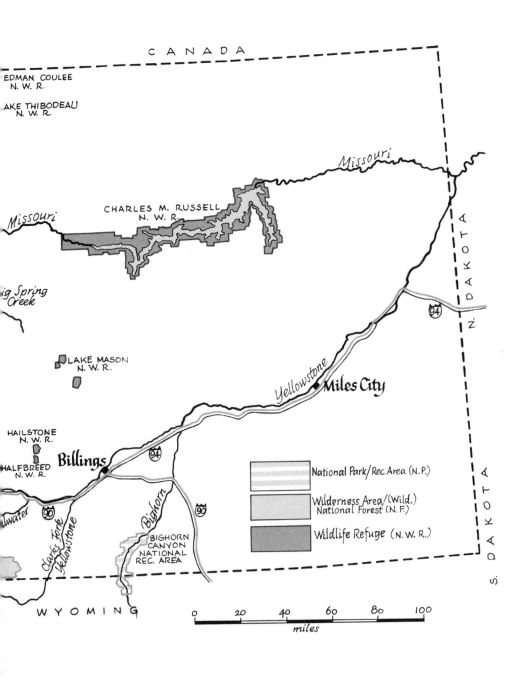

CANADA

EDMAN COULEE
N. R.

AKE THIBODEAU
N. W. R.

Missouri

Missouri

CHARLES M. RUSSELL
N. W. R.

ig Spring
Creek

N. DAKOTA

LAKE MASON
N. W. R.

Yellowstone

Miles City

HAILSTONE
N. W. R.

Billings

94

HALFBREED
N. W. R.

lwater

90

90

Clarks Fork
Yellowstone

Bighorn

BIGHORN
CANYON
NATIONAL
REC. AREA

S. DAKOTA

National Park/Rec. Area (N.P.)

Wilderness Area/(Wild.)
National Forest (N.F.)

Wildlife Refuge (N.W.R.)

WYOMING

0   20   40   60   80   100
miles

CONTENTS

INTRODUCTION

A few years ago, out of nostalgia if nothing else, I spent a week fishing the Big Hole River, a trout stream I had cherished as a youngster nearly half a century earlier. As I cast to familiar spots and dredged up old memories I was amazed to find the fishing even better than I remembered. Here was a river I had fished two, sometimes three times a week growing up, but had not revisited since I moved to the northwest corner of the state. In my absence, miraculously, the fishery had improved.

After enticing a big brown from an undercut bank, I retired my rod and sat on a trunk-sized boulder in the middle of the river to watch the evening shadows lengthen over the water. My mind began to wonder toward other Montana trout fisheries I had enjoyed through the years, rivers like the Madison, Boulder, Yellowstone, Bighorn, Flathead, and Swan. Perhaps I had been taking these waters for granted. What was it that made them special? How were they fairing amid ongoing threats from development, pollution, irrigation, and overcrowding? Who was looking out for them?

I realized that I had spent much of my fishing life casually passing through some of the most remarkable geography and history found anywhere in the West, yet I had not taken real stock of where I was, what I was doing, or the value of the trout fishing legacy passed down to me. So over the next two years I sat in the cluttered offices of biologists and historians, floated spectacular rivers with a host of master anglers, and kicked around in fly shops adorned with fur, feathers, and the secrets of the past as an extraordinary saga of river conservation took shape before me.

Saving Homewaters is my way of embracing Montana's legacy of sportsmanship and stewardship, a way of honoring every angler's homewater—that one special place to which we always return, where we feel most comfortable.

This is the story of our heritage as Montana fly fishers and conservationists. It begins over a century ago, at a time when the rivers were nearly void of trout and the mountainsides empty of game. The tale weaves through the hallways of a burgeoning state government, across mountain passes atop the Continental Divide, and through the tangled web of misguided industrial development and government policy.

Ultimately, it is a story about individuals who have cared deeply about Montana's rivers and the country around them. Again and again our waterways have been threatened under the guise of progress, and again and again determined anglers, outfitters, biologists, and political leaders have stepped forward to protect them. This often meant thwarting the will of some of the largest companies in the world, but as the anthropologist Margaret Mead said, "Never doubt that a small group of thoughtful, committed citizens can change the world. Indeed, it's the only thing that ever has."

I hope you come away from this book, as I did from my research, with a new respect for Montana's wonderful trout waters and what needs to happen next if we want to keep what we have in the Last Best Place.

A REMARKABLE HISTORY

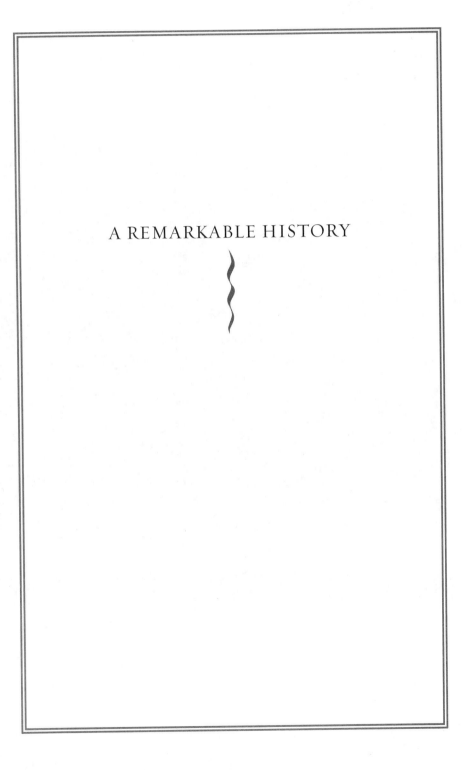

I

THE PROMISE OF IT ALL

}

*Like winds and sunsets, wild things were taken for granted until progress
began to do away with them. Now we face the question whether a still higher
"standard of living" is worth its cost in things natural, wild and free. For us of
the minority, the opportunity to see geese is more important than television,
and the chance to find a pasque-flower is a right as inalienable as free speech.*

—ALDO LEOPOLD, *A Sand County Almanac*

Grand are the images of Montana's recent past: the buckskin-clad fur trapper
trudging across fields of snow under mountains that reach all the way to heaven;
the dirt-hard placer miner squatting beside a raging stream, gold pan in hand, hoping for a big strike; the taciturn cowboy a-horseback out on the open plains with
longhorn cattle as far as the eye can see. In the final sorting out of our boom-and-
bust history, the only consistent aspect that remains today is the alluring promise of
it all—the wide open spaces, the wild rivers, and, of course, the shining mountains
above rolling prairie.

By the time President Lincoln signed the bill creating Montana Territory on
May 26, 1864, unregulated commercial hunting and fishing were efficiently wiping
out a long list of indigenous species previously plentiful in the wilds of the West. A
once healthy population of moose was all but a silent memory; trout, waterfowl,
and game birds barely held on.

A few early residents clearly recognized the problem. In one of their first acts of
business, the 1864 Territorial legislature passed a law stating "a rod or pole, line and
hook, shall be the only lawful way trout can be caught in any of the streams of the

territory." That same piece of legislation disallowed baiting hooks with any drug or poisonous substance, and made using dams, seines, or nets illegal for catching fish. As progressive as the new laws seemed at the time, it would be twelve more years before catching trout with explosives was outlawed.

A few years after removing dynamite from the tackle boxes of early anglers, the legislature began to deal with the unchecked polluting of rivers and streams. In 1881, Montana lawmakers first ventured onto the hallowed ground of industry as they drew a clear line between the decimation of the state's waterways and the unregulated activities of some of the state's largest and most powerful employers. An early act made it illegal to dump mill and mine waste, as well as sawdust, into precious public waterways. But twenty more years would pass before the legislature finally banned dumping coal washings and cyanide into the state's streams.

The nineteenth century was dominated by people intent on developing new towns, industries, and economies. In 1890 mining and smelting interests placed the first power dam across the Great Falls of the Missouri where, mere decades before, Meriwether Lewis had stood before its awe-inspiring kinetic energy and written, "I now thought that if a skillfull painter had been asked to make a beautifull cascade that he would most probably have presented the precise immage of this one."

Just one year before the dam was completed, when "Copper King" William A. Clark was asked by members of Montana's Constitutional Convention of 1889 to provide the body a justification for the billowing cloud of dark smoke that so often engulfed the mining town of Butte, he responded, "I must say that the ladies are very fond of this smoky city, as it is sometimes called, because there is just enough arsenic there to give them a beautiful complexion and that is the reason the ladies of Butte are renowned whereever [sic] they go for their beautiful complexions.... I say it would be a great deal better for other cities in the territory if they had more smoke and less diphtheria and other diseases. It has been believed by all the physicians of Butte that the smoke that sometimes prevails there is a disinfectant, and destroys the microbes that contribute the germs of disease...."

The age of corporate double talk had arrived in Montana, on the wheels of an industry that would lay ruin to some of the very rivers over which Lewis & Clark had gushed.

The environmental guidance in Montana came from a narrow core of leaders who seemed in touch with the more far-reaching conservation movement emerging on the national scene. These were the days following John Muir's thousand-mile walk from Louisville, Kentucky, to the humid shores of Florida in 1867. From that experience and others, Muir would draft a blueprint that opened the nation's minds to the concept of national parks and wilderness—a vision that soon would play an important role in preserving valuable landscapes in the West, including Yellowstone and Yosemite.

Adding to Muir's vision was ecologist-statesman George Perkins Marsh, who, in *Man and Nature*, ventured to ask his American compatriots compelling questions about our role in nature. Joining Marsh's publication was Charles Darwin's *The Origin of Species*, a treatise questioning our rightful place within the animal kingdom, and then his mind-boggling *The Descent of Man*. Also meeting the environmental awareness challenge head-on was Major John Wesley Powell, who explored geology, Native American ethnology, and, most important to the West, the impact of agriculture on the nation's arid interior. These controversial publications eventually found their way onto the reading tables of concerned Montanans, who subsequently built the early foundation of a real environmental ethic.

A gradually maturing perception of conservation was afoot throughout America. It found a strong public voice in the periodical *Forest and Stream*, produced and edited by George Bird Grinnell. Grinnell was intimately familiar with the growing plight of western states and had close ties to the Blackfeet Indians living near Montana's Rocky Mountain Front. At that time, the magazine's objective was to help the American people examine their suffering environment and embrace immediate reform. Grinnell's message repeatedly focused on the need to change well-established cultural patterns to protect valuable habitat so necessary for the future of all living beings.

The eloquent voices of Grinnell, Marsh, Muir, and many others rang loud and clear across Montana, which was tiptoeing into wildlife conservation with a few laws already on the books. Unfortunately, those laws suffered a very severe flaw—they lacked any system of reliable enforcement.

In late-nineteenth-century Montana, upholding the laws of the land fell under the jurisdiction of the United States Marshal. The marshal, however, was overly busy apprehending (and often lynching) desperadoes, stage robbers, card sharks, and swindlers—leaving little time or inclination to prosecute the dynamiters at work on Montana's streams, lakes, and rivers.

Regardless of the ineffectiveness of Montana Territory's conservation laws, the spirit of their message provided a seedbed for future growth. More importantly, these laws were enacted at a time when many indigenous species of fish and game animals were threatened with extinction. It was crucial that political leaders comprehend just how important these resources were to the electorate.

In late 1889, Montana waltzed and jigged its way into statehood on a flood of ragtime piano music punctuated by a barrage of shotguns, whistles, and clinking whiskey glasses. Once the party was over and the dust finally cleared, the daunting task of statesmanship began. The plight of wildlife and absentee enforcement of protective laws loomed high on the infant state's legislative list. In response to a growing public outcry, the state legislature empowered commissioners at the local level to hire a game warden to serve the needs of each county. Unfortunately, only four of twenty-six counties acted on the mandate, once again leaving the protective statutes on the books virtually toothless.

While various elements within Montana's fledgling state government battled for political supremacy, Theodore Roosevelt was busy hunting for some of the West's last big game species. Thus, he knew intimately the depleted condition of the West's fish and wildlife. Roosevelt was an avid outdoorsman, a hunter of great repute, and a lover of wildness. And more importantly, he seemed headed for a powerful position nationally, where he could devise a path for some of our nation's most progressive laws preserving land and wildlife.

Roosevelt was placed on the presidential ticket with William McKinley, winning election in 1900. The political bosses called him a "cowboy" and were at a loss to explain exactly what he brought as McKinley's running mate. However, they felt the cowboy vice president could be hobbled and fed as much political hay as he could possibly eat while staying out of the much larger picture. But Roosevelt carried a solid political base from his longstanding association with those who cherished hunting, fishing, and the more subtle rewards of nature. For example, Roosevelt was one of the original founders of the Boone & Crockett Club, an organization whose rolls included the names of many who would one day play key

roles in conserving land and wildlife: George Bird Grinnell, John Lacey, Jay Nor-
wood "Ding" Darling, and William Hallett Phillips, to name a few.

In his adventures afield, the vice president had clearly witnessed the state of
Montana's depleted fish and wildlife. This gruesome vision haunted Roosevelt, and
he spoke out frequently about ethical hunting, fishing, and sportsmanship. His progressive vision would finally spur Montana's future conservation leaders into more
aggressive action.

Of course, it is important to remember that Montana hosted a tough citizenry
that looked at fishing, hunting, and collecting firewood not as a matter of exercise
and pleasure, but as necessity. Here was a group who chose not to rely on the government for much of anything. Yet they were well aware that the U.S. Supreme
Court had ruled that the country's fish and game, as well as much of the West's
land, was a matter of public domain belonging to all the people, and that it was
managed merely in trust by the government.

At the time, fish populations in Montana waterways had dropped to danger-
ously low levels and were plummeting further. Remedies had to be immediate. In
1896, the U.S. Bureau of Fisheries built the state's first fish hatchery, on Bridger
Creek, just north of the booming agricultural town of Bozeman. The federal hatchery was capable of producing millions of cutthroat and rainbow trout, stock destined for many of the state's depleted rivers. They also raised and planted grayling,
brook trout, steelhead, and Lake Superior whitefish.

The Montana legislature also took the bull by the horns and created the state's
first Board of Game and Fish Commissioners. One of the commission's initial acts
was to publish a questionnaire in the state's newspapers, asking residents to identify
issues important to fish and game, and to help outline the role of future management.

The response was overwhelming, much of it directed toward public fisheries
and the need for a state-operated fish hatchery to augment the work of the federal
hatchery. But it would take an entire decade of bureaucratic and legislative games-
manship before Montana would actually start constructing the hatchery.

The newly appointed Game and Fish Commission registered frustration at the
slow progress, recorded in their second biennial report (1902–1904): "Was the
inactivity to implement new strategy to enhance and protect Montana's fish and

wildlife simply fate or was there some sort of unsettling scheme afoot in the new state government?" Only time would provide the answer.

Once again, action was swifter at the federal level. To aid in the struggle to protect the nation's wildlife, the landmark Lacey Act in 1900 at last provided some sharp teeth for future game law enforcement in Montana. The new federal law made it illegal to transport wildlife across any state border, which was a lethal blow to the commercial hunting industry. The Lacey Act provided the Montana Game and Fish Commission both the reason and the power to act, regardless of what hidden agendas might be brewing in state politics.

Taped to the back-bar of many country taverns in Montana is this quote, "Boy, there was sure a lot they didn't tell me about this job before I hired on." Those words were meant to apply to the hard and sometimes dangerous life of ranch hands. But as the twentieth century quietly slipped into Montana, that insightful quote may have best applied to Warden William F. Scott, the very first paid employee of the Game and Fish Commission. Despite his public backing, it still fell to this lone gent with the handlebar mustache and loaded sidearm to spread the shocking news that Montana was now enforcing game and fish laws, and that he was there to dole out costly citations.

Almost simultaneously, news unfolding in another part of the nation would have an enormous impact on Scott's job. Vice President Theodore Roosevelt, on a hunting trip in the Adirondacks in 1901, had just received the news that President McKinley had been assassinated. Suddenly Roosevelt was elevated to the most powerful office in the land. The United States of America had a "cowboy" hunter and conservationist as their chief executive.

Life changed abruptly for many who had gotten used to living off the bounty of America, either by raking in its pork at the big barrel of government or slaughtering its wildlife out on the western plains.

Although President "Teddy" Roosevelt would be quoted many times, one of his statements seemed particularly appropriate for Montana's new game warden: "I admire men who take the next step, not those who theorize about the two-hundredth step."

The fledgling Fish and Game Commission had taken its first huge step by hiring Scott to make once-stagnant conservation laws pack some real punch. This activism was an important turning point in the rough and tumble state of Montana. Nevertheless, it all came down to that lovely autumn morning in 1901 when Warden Scott spurred his horse into the sagebrush and buffalo grass to begin the difficult task of halting commercial hunting and fishing and repairing the damage.

Eventually, the new warden shared enforcement duties with the eight deputy game wardens allowed by the legislature. The meager state salary for Scott and each of those willing to assist him amounted to one hundred dollars per month, minus traveling expenses. To defray the expense of the new agency and keep it independent of undue political pressure—very important to its success—state lawmakers established a combined fishing and hunting license. The first licenses, issued in 1905, would cover an entire family for the cost of one dollar. The new fee was expected to cause a ruckus among Montana sporting families. Instead, thirty thousand families willingly tendered their dollar in the first year, a showing of unparalleled support for the evolving game and fish work.

When he first pinned on his badge, Warden Scott had made some strong promises to the Game and Fish Commission. Very shortly those promises would come due. But Scott was ready. Just a few years into his job, he was quoted in the commission's second biennial report as saying, "The slaughter has been stopped and the killing in violation of the law reduced to a minimum."

As an important footnote to his first report, the warden also solemnly warned that native game fish were in very serious trouble and required immediate attention if they were to survive; the resource would not last unless "restocked" to appreciable levels. Scott's admonition echoed the people's previous mandate to construct an additional hatchery.

Bolstered by Scott's report, Montana's newly created Department of Game and Fish embarked on a long and colorful campaign to save what remained of Montana's fish and wildlife and, remarkably, to replenish crucial populations to almost unbelievable proportions.

2

OUR GREATEST OPUS

}

I am not looking at the same land the firstcomers saw. The original surface of the hill is as extinct as the passenger pigeon. The pristine America that the first white man saw is a lost continent, sunk like Atlantis in the sea. The thought of what was here once and is gone forever will not leave me as long as I live. It is as though I walk knee-deep in its absence.

—WENDELL BERRY, *A Native Hill*

The air was promising snow when I pulled open the weighty brass door of the Montana Historical Society. It was early February 2006, and the resounding *thunk* of the door closing behind me echoed through the otherwise quiet museum. Ascending to the second floor, I met the glass eyes of an enormous white bison that stands six feet at the hump, posed majestically before a prairie landscape mural. This albino buffalo, known as "Big Medicine," was born in 1933 on the National Bison Range near the Flathead Indian Reservation. After its death in 1959, famed Montana artist Bob Scriber mounted it and presented it to the state as a memento of a troubled past. According to the late historian Dave Walter, the white buffalo carries a special meaning to native Montanans: "Northern Plains believers linked the white buffalo to the recurring legend of White Buffalo Calf Woman, signifying hope, the return of plenty and power and the unity of all peoples."

It seemed fitting that morning to be met by such a stately totem of Montana's character—a connection to the indigenous animals of our homeland. I had traveled to the state capital of Helena to review the first biennial reports drafted by Game Warden Scott for the Game and Fish Commission. I wanted to read, in the man's own words, how he saw things change in Montana after his epic ride to inform the scattered camps of market hunters that the slaughter would no longer be tolerated. I wondered if something in his words might help me better comprehend the attitude of the times.

The old books were layered between sheets of protective paper, stacked one atop the other. The pages, yellowed and frayed, smelled old as I opened the first tome. Here, between my fingers, were pages printed at about the time my own forebears arrived in Montana, pages upon which were recorded the thoughts of men willing to step to the head of the pack and have their actions chronicled during their time in power.

The first biennial report was drafted in 1900, the year before the commission received authority from the Montana state legislature to hire a paid game warden. It included the first questionnaire the commission submitted to the public through the state's newspapers. One of the twenty-eight questions was, "Do you believe game animals, birds, or fish should be sold under any circumstances?" The answer to this question is best portrayed by the next fifty years of accomplishment. This was a time in which not only were several big game species replenished throughout Montana, but serious attention was paid to habitat preservation and game management.

The second biennial report, drafted and submitted two years after Warden Scott was hired, includes a collection of gripping photographs of our outdoor heritage—hunters afield, birds flushing over pointing dogs, and the grand mountains overarched by the Big Sky. One that caught my eye depicted a market hunters' camp, those hard, bearded men posed in front of long rows of deer carcasses outstretched before a backdrop of open prairie. Other photographs featured gutted trout and whitefish strung like a long necklace between vertical poles, each strand containing hundreds of fish, all profitable fodder for a demanding market.

The text of the second report is from Scott himself, no doubt drafted after the wildlife slaughter across Montana had slowed. With casual tone, the warden takes his readers on an imaginary east-to-west train ride across Montana. I hear his voice, the words clicking in the perfect rhythm of train wheels as he describes the wild geography rolling by. In scene after scene, Scott depicts agrarian lands stretched out for hundreds of miles between towns along the route like Billings,

Livingston, Butte, Missoula—their bellowing smokestacks, balding hillsides, and silt-darkened streams all marks of the state's quickly advancing industry.

"Few people realize that the fish and game of a State is one or [of] its most attractive and profitable resources," Scott wrote. "This is due principally to the fact that they have given the question little or more thought.

"It is true that almost every person enjoys to either hunt or fish, and embraces every favorable opportunity to do so; but the matter of game and fish protection, or its value, is very seldom considered.

"This, in our State, comes from enjoying 'abundance and plenty' and the greater proportion of the people seldom think of the future, but only enjoy the present, with little thought that in a short time their source of pleasure will come to an abrupt end unless some provisions are made and enforced to protect the game and fish. We should not wait 'until the horse is stolen and then lock the door.' We should profit by experience of the older States, who are now enacting and enforcing the most stringent protective measures to lengthen the existence of the small remnant of game they have left."

At the time of this report, others around Scott were also intent on rebuilding the state's sport fisheries. Leadership and support came from a growing interest in local rod and gun clubs. Some, like the thousand-member Butte Anglers Club, organized in 1902, got involved early in conservation and replenishment. That historic club went at their projects with a level of intensity that matched the frustrations of the times. In the field, sportsmen felt the need to save trout fishing in Montana and personally acted on that premise by planning to stock state waters. After all, this was a "can do" population. If the state wasn't going to respond to the problems delineated by their own game warden and a standing mandate from the people that was already half a decade old, sporting groups would act for them.

Copper King William A. Clark and other leaders of the mining industry realized the power of the public's commitment. Investing in some form of support was a tribute to their astuteness as capitalists, if not future politicians. By 1905, Clark had built Montana's second hatchery at the beautiful Columbia Gardens and had donated funds so the Butte club could operate it.

Columbia Gardens, an amusement park also built by Clark, appeared to be the perfect place to locate one of Montana's first privately operated trout hatcheries.

From this very spot, nestled beneath the Continental Divide, flowed the still-pristine headwaters of the Clark Fork River, primary tributary of the Columbia River. However, just a few short miles downstream of the hatchery, the mining industry was already in the process of turning the Clark Fork River into a biological "dead zone" by their daily discharge of heavy metals and arsenic-laden mine and smelter waste into the headwaters.

To resident trout fishers, the hatchery was not just a series of holding tanks, it was a piece of heaven itself. From those tanks came fine, healthy trout for restocking local waters. The hatchery operated for decades, supplying tens of millions of trout to the waters of southwest Montana. The nearby Big Hole River was a favored water for releasing fish from the Gardens hatchery.

Warden Scott's second report also proudly recognized an advancing conservation movement afoot in Montana, a movement spawned at the highest level of federal government and already flowing like a much-needed tide throughout the entire country. He specifically highlighted, in great detail, the immense influence President Theodore Roosevelt was having on the youth in rural states like Montana: "There is a healthy moral tone springing up in the intelligent and manly boy throughout the country to-day that must eventually redound to the country's credit, and which is traceable in a very large degree to the example set them by their noble President. He has shown them in his interesting writings, by his every-day official conduct, that instincts of a sportsman are thoroughly compatible with those of the chief magistrate of the nation....No one can be a sportsman without close communion with nature; this joy indescribable purifies both body and mind; and from so happy a combination only good can follow."

The footsteps of environmentalism, even though halting in their early stages, made a distinct imprint on Montana during the first decade of the 1900s. These steps did not stop at the door of a meager pack of market hunters. Instead, they proceeded throughout the entire social landscape of Montana and eventually tramped right to the heavy oak doors of some of the state's most powerful industries and agricultural groups.

Serious concerns over industry's effects on wild habitats were expressed plainly in the biennial reports. This level of frankness in a government report is all the more amazing when you consider what was happening in Montana at this time.

The decades of boom and bust were waning, each new economy falling by the wayside. The state was just beginning to embrace a somewhat longer-term stability built on deep-vein mining, irrigated agriculture, government employment, railroad expansion, and logging. Then a state agency emerged, pointing fingers at the very golden goose that was supposed to put a full piggy bank at the door of every resident and a fresh trout in the basket of every fisherman. The social tension of the times must have been extreme, with the Game and Fish Commission and Scott caught in the middle. The mining, agriculture, and timber interests literally ruled state politics; nevertheless, the conservation movement was soldiered by outspoken leaders willing to paint a much different picture.

In response to a stack of letters addressed to his office, J. A. Henshall, Superintendent of the U.S. Fish Hatchery in Bozeman, was quoted in the third biennial report: "The fouling of water by smelting of ores and its disastrous effect on fish is patent to every resident of Butte. To the washing of coal and to the mining of ores is also to be attributed a great loss of fish life. Where the fish food is not entirely destroyed by the soluble substances, the insoluble matter is deposited on the spawning beds, smothering or killing the eggs and newly-hatched fry; sawdust and coal dust are destructive in this way...

"By the vigilance of game and fish wardens the minor evils of illegal fishing, illegal sale of fish, and dynamiting can, to a certain extent be prevented, as punishment for those offences is provided for by statutory enactment. But there is another agency of fish destruction in Montana, so appalling and widespread, that in comparison with it all the other causes mentioned sink into utter insignificance. It is the wholesale destruction of fish both large and small, by means of irrigation ditches.

"No one, except the ranchers and those who have investigated the matter, can have a realization of the awful loss of fish life, of the wanton sacrifice of millions of God's creatures left to gasp out their little lives on the meadows and grain fields all over the state of Montana. Often the stench arising from the decaying trout—the loveliest object on God's footstool—is intolerable; 'it smells to Heaven.' And yet the past legislatures of the state have utterly ignored any attempt to prevent it."

Dr. Henshall expressed further outrage over the loss of fish by promising to discontinue stocking fish in any river from which unscreened irrigation systems originated. Serious disputes between anglers, conservationists, and farmers and ranchers would reach slugfest proportions in the next century, although this seldom led to any solutions.

By the time of the third biennial report, hardrock mining for silver, zinc, and copper had effectively replaced placer-mining gold as the raw material for a boom economy. Mining techniques had changed dramatically, from handwork by individual prospectors to the labor-intensive work of heavily financed companies like the Anaconda Company. At the same time that mining was gobbling healthy riverine habitat, the agriculture and livestock industry was gaining serious momentum. Irrigation from free-flowing rivers provided the only answer to low annual precipitation. The agricultural equation for most areas in Montana has always been simple: the entire effort will fail without irrigation.

In effect, the battle to save Montana fish species and important aquatic habitat had just begun.

The state faced the difficult task of rebuilding wildlife and aquatic resources that had been nearly decimated. And like prizefighters in the ring, big industry and conservationists stood on opposite sides, ready to duke it out for supremacy. On one side, the fledgling fish and game agency was fronted by a tenacious commission and a small community of dedicated scientists. Across the ring stood the politically powerful financial titans of industry and agriculture—two of the largest contributors to environmental problems in Montana. The devastating work by market hunters and anglers just a few years earlier would prove a modest problem when compared to the pollution and alteration of Montana's rivers and streams at the hands of these more modern invaders.

As I read the reports, it became clear that the most crucial element that kept the commission and the new agency alive back then—that is to say, kept the well-oiled lobbying efforts from unduly influencing them—was that the primary source of funding came from licenses sold to the general public. It was the sporting public, actual Montana voters, who kept things on an even keel back in those unsettled times. This public was dead serious about its rights to hunt and fish, often to the displeasure of industry and agriculture.

There were plenty of Montanans who simply wanted more fish to catch, big game to hunt, and birds to flush. Even the least informed, however, were beginning to understand the close relationship between habitat and wildlife populations, a lesson that already had been learned the hard way in the East and Midwest. For those interested only in quantity, the idea of conservation mostly meant restocking prime game and fish species. Others with a wider view wanted to restore vital habitat and the broader spectrum of abundant, healthy, indigenous wildlife experienced by Lewis and Clark. Regardless of motivation, the license purchasers of Montana were willing to back the new agency for both the privilege of hunting and the overall survival of wildlife.

The real cultural debate over preserving the environment and wildlife for their intrinsic value, as opposed to the use humankind could make of them, would not come for at least six more decades. Early in the twentieth century, the battle was waged on a strictly utilitarian platform. Hunting, fishing, and enjoying the outdoors were part of a sturdy heritage of frontier living, a concept tightly woven through the roughneck ways of the West.

Montana joined a growing environmental movement that was surging forward nationally, a movement that blended the earth and biological sciences with the power of grassroots campaigns waged on behalf of wildlife, habitat, and ethics.

3
TAKING STOCK, TAKING ACTION

If an angler has certain obligations to the State, the State has equally definite obligations to the angler. The government of a young State is primarily a trustee appointed by the people to look after all natural resources, whether they are to be developed by private or by public ownership. The trusteeship implies, above everything else, that the resources shall be managed in such a way as to provide maximum benefit not to individuals, but to the people as a whole.

—RODERICK HAIG-BROWN, *The Western Angler*

Throughout the nation great things were happening environmentally and culturally, which, in turn, nourished many of the progressive efforts being waged on behalf of fish and wildlife in the West. Huge efforts mounted on behalf of public lands and waterways resulted in substantial habitat improvement. Encouraged by a developing conservation ethic, federal lawmakers had created the Forest Reservation Creative Act back in 1891. The act ultimately increased the country's forest reserves from 43 million acres to an impressive 190 million acres. This vast new forest reserve eventually was guided by Gifford Pinchot.

Even before his election as vice president or his subsequent elevation to the presidency, Teddy Roosevelt, along with other members of the Boone & Crockett Club, was instrumental in altering important federal environmental policy that set things in motion in the West. The time was ripe for change, a solid core of leadership was in place, and the sense of opportunity seemed to spread like a breath of fresh air through Montana.

In 1908, President Roosevelt chaired one of the most important meetings ever convened on behalf of fish and wildlife, the Conference of Governors. To the East Room of the White House, he invited a number of governors to meet face to face with the leadership of many of the nation's most active conservation groups and societies. The president's agenda was simple: get the entire group to collectively embrace conservation as not merely a political topic but as an underlying organizational ethic, and pass it on through the various elements of political machinery at work within each of their states and associations. A reliable dialogue established through the conference did, in the end, advance a sense of unity between the different participants.

In Montana, grassroots rod and gun clubs like the Butte Anglers Club were one of the keys to the growth of this new dialogue. Sporting clubs in many other states were developing a powerful voice as well. These organizations had usually operated with a defined local agenda in Montana, but many were increasingly willing to look outside their narrow geographic region in order to participate in larger statewide management decisions.

The same year that Roosevelt chaired the Conference of Governors, Montana finally acted on Warden Scott's longstanding concern over fish populations. That year the Commission broke ground for the first state-owned fish hatchery, located right in the lap of the copper-smelting kingdom of Anaconda.

Tucked under the Continental Divide, the town of Anaconda was, among other things, the living oeuvre of Marcus Daly. The mining tycoon, yet another of the famed Copper Kings, owned the town of Anaconda. On the foothills of the great divide, Daly built the town from huge profits taken from his mines in Butte. He saw the beautiful setting in which Anaconda was located partly as a personal haven designed pretty much to his specifications, but also as an important component of his bulging mining and smelting kingdom.

Daley built the world's largest copper smelter to process the rich copper ore arriving from the mines of Butte, some thirty miles to the east. The immense operation stood like a belching dragon on a hillside above the company town. The smelter's massive smokestack and soot-coated buildings jutted skyward, silhouetted against snowcapped mountains. The stack rose hundreds of feet into the air and now is preserved as a state park, a reminder of days gone by.

Daly's copper dynasty eventually became a holding of Standard Oil, Amalgamated Copper, with J. D. Ryan at its helm. It was under Ryan's reign that the land for Montana's first state-operated fish hatchery was donated. The hatchery was located on Warm Springs Creek at the opposite end of town from the giant smelter. The Anaconda hatchery was a beautiful facility, a diamond in the rough located in a mountainous setting already impacted by the deep scars of industry. The hatchery drew its chief source of life from the very heart of a rugged landscape, a domain that one day would be designated the Anaconda-Pintler Wilderness.

So the first privately owned fish hatchery was built and donated to the Butte Anglers Club by William A. Clark and the first state-operated fish hatchery was donated by Clark's chief competitor and archenemy, Amalgamated Copper. It was no small irony that both of these acts of "philanthropy" occurred during a time when the copper industry dumped mine waste by the ton into the headwaters of the Clark Fork River.

THE HATCHERY ERA

Situated between the Anaconda-Pintler Wilderness and the Flint Creek Range, Georgetown Lake collects icy runoff from some of Montana's most rugged mountains. Following the opening of the state hatchery in Anaconda, millions of wild trout eggs were collected from the lake annually, allowed to mature at the hatchery, and transported by rail to dozens of streams, rivers, and lakes throughout western Montana. Aided by the pure tributary streams flushing from the Continental Divide and the Anaconda-Pintler Wilderness, as well as the high, cool elevation of the mountain nursery, the state's first agency hatchery thrived, adding to the bounty provided by the private hatchery at Butte and the federal operation in Bozeman.

Native cutthroat eggs taken from Georgetown Lake, plus imported rainbow, brown, brook, and grayling eggs, were nurtured by the millions at the Anaconda hatchery. Impressed by the hard work and success of the state's first hatchery, Amalgamated's Butte, Anaconda & Pacific Railroad made the "copper trust's" next donation: a converted passenger car. State employees had some fun naming the car "Thymallus" and watched proudly as it rattled across iron tracks laid on the very edge of some of Montana's grandest trout streams, carrying a precious cargo of young fish.

The state next proposed a facility at Somers, located on the northern shore of yet another wilderness-fed lake, Flathead. This second state hatchery was approved and built in 1912.

To put the newly emerging hatchery program into perspective, the same year the Somers hatchery was built, the Anaconda hatchery stocked over four million trout and grayling eggs in Montana rivers. Combined, the two state-managed facilities soon added tremendously to the bounty already being stocked by the federal facility in Bozeman, as well as privately owned hatcheries springing up throughout the state. At last, an enormous effort to restock state waters was under way, and visionaries like Warden Scott could sit back and await the results.

The number of hatchery fish planted in Montana waters was astounding. By 1914, the two state-operated hatcheries had produced more than twelve million trout, grayling, and Lake Superior whitefish. By itself, in the years 1903 and 1904, the federal hatchery produced more than a million trout and four million grayling.

The brook trout eggs used in the stocking program originally were imported from Rhode Island and Pennsylvania. These strains proved hardy enough to survive in high wilderness lakes and backcountry streams, although the cold water and battering runoff stunted their growth in many highland settings. As stocking efforts expanded by leaps and bounds, millions of brook trout were poured into giant buckets and lugged into remote wilderness areas aboard heavily loaded pack animals, a scene common to early mountaineers and sportsmen hiking the winding mountain trails along the Continental Divide.

In the early days of hatchery stocking, few records were kept. As a rule, a local rod and gun club, private citizen, or property owner simply placed an order for fish. This order generally arrived at some predetermined railhead, with the final destination remaining unquestioned for many years.

Local sporting groups played a prominent role in the placement strategy. As might be expected, the most popular rivers and streams were first on the list, but as trout numbers grew, so did enthusiasm to expand the program. Eventually, any likely looking water was viewed as a potential stocking site. Barren lakes, ponds, and small mountain tributaries were stocked with gusto and without much regard for the detrimental effects that nonnative species like rainbow, brook, and brown trout might have on a natural ecosystem or what native fish might remain in these remote fisheries.

Some of the same trains used to transport trout and grayling fingerlings to local streams also offered quick transportation to anglers interested in spending the day riverside. These "fishing trains" allowed anglers to jump off at their favorite spot, no questions asked. On the return trip, the engineers slowed at the dropoff points, and tired fishers were retrieved and returned to their home station. One of the most famous fishing trains operated along the trout-rich waters of the Big Hole River, particularly downstream from the present town of Divide. A second renowned train traveled north of Helena, along the trouty waters of the Missouri River between Wolf Creek Canyon and Great Falls.

Trains and trout enjoyed a romanticized connection that added greatly to the already extensive folklore of trout fishing under the Big Sky throughout that era. Fishing stories that appeared in local newspapers were relayed from clerk to customer in fly and tackle shops, often finding a third outlet on the printed pages of the nation's best sporting magazines.

One such story would eventually appear in *Field and Stream* magazine in 1935, submitted by Butte angler Charlie Cook. In the story, Cook maintained that on one summer's evening, while drifting a Dr. Mummy fly under an overhanging willow on the Big Hole River, a monster brown trout came to the surface and enthusiastically engulfed his quietly drifting fly. The trout was what Cook and his companions called a "Loch Leven," their name for introduced brown trout. That trout was probably reared and planted by either the Butte Anglers Club or the state hatchery in Anaconda. Regardless of its origin, clearly it had been in the Big Hole for a long time before Cook finally got its attention, because it weighed in at a jaw-dropping 11.25 pounds. According to the account in the magazine, the catch was made outside the ranching town of Melrose (probably in Maiden Rock Canyon).

The yarn won Cook first prize in a national contest sponsored by the historic magazine. It also embellished the wonders of Montana's Big Hole River, a magic that continues today.

The critical relationship between the maturing Department of Fish and Game and grassroots rod and gun and angling clubs was treated with the highest regard among state employees and hatchery workers. There existed almost a brotherhood, a bond inspired by the good work of replenishment and rebuilding fish stocks. Pride abounded, and for a long time even the railroad workers joined the mix.

But nature was to deal a serious blow to the growing programs. On the debilitating heels of drought, in 1910 wildfires ravaged the forests of western Montana to such an extent that their impact was mentioned in the department's biennial report: "On the Bull River fifty blacktail deer were found dead in one bunch.... Trout Creek, Bull River and Beaver Creek...also ran hot during the fire, thus killing all the fish of these streams.... The St. Regis River and Fish Creek...also ran hot, destroying all fish. The loss of human life is known to have been seventy-two persons in the section...".

Despite this setback, rivers and streams once scarce of trout were beginning to reflect the outstanding resource first reported by Lewis & Clark a century before. Backcountry lakes, silent for decades, once more resounded with the splash of rising trout. More accessible sites like Flathead Lake were stocked with new species such as lake trout and Lake Superior whitefish.

As more stable jobs emerged across the state, sportsmen and anglers enjoyed increased leisure time to pursue their hobbies. And as more state hatcheries were added to the system, the interest of sportsmen continued to grow. It would not be long before a serious sense of expectation replaced casual interest. Rivers were expected to net trout, the fulfillment of an angler's day, and it fell to the state hatchery program to put fish where they could be quickly added to the creel.

4
RIGHTS OR WRONGS: WATER AND AGRICULTURE

Sycamores grow by running water; cottonwoods grow by still water. If we know the simple mysteries, then think of all the complex mysteries that lie just beneath us, buried in the bedrock: the bedrock we have been entrusted with protecting. How could we dare do anything other than protect and honor this last core, the land from which we came, the land that has marked us, and whose essence, whose mystery, contains our own essence and mystery?

—RICK BASS, *"On Willow Creek"*

One hot afternoon along Montana's Hi-Line, I shared the little bit of shade outside a machinery dealership with a wheat farmer who had arrived in Montana as a young boy in the late 1920s. He was drinking water from a dented water jug, one of those familiar green and white Colemans that were forever rolling around in the back of every ranch and farm truck when I was a kid. The old gent was dressed in bib overalls and a pin-striped white shirt, yellowed under the armpits and soiled around the open collar. It had probably been worn for years of Sunday services before being reduced to the status of work shirt.

As we sat in the small square of shade behind the dealership, I asked how the wheat had come up that year. He answered slowly, "Well, I'd have to say the crop wasn't as good as some, better than a few years back but not near up to local projections, which of course included a suspicion this damn drought might break this season."

Drawing a breath and taking another swig of water, he continued. "Now six years back, now, there was a season to remember. Rains came just in time, let up just in time, and stayed away long enough at the end of things to let us get a good crop in the wagons before all hell broke loose.

"Ah hell, that's the way things are up here," he said. "And they'll stay that way until we find some way to grow wheat indoors—and only the big shots have enough time to sit and ponder that dream."

After he left, I remained in the shade and wondered what it would be like to gamble your whole life on rain, especially when you live at the northern edge of a part of America that has, over the centuries, earned the title "Great American Desert."

Two concerns quickly crop up in relation to annual precipitation in Montana. The first is what effect the lack of spring rain has on the flow of rivers and streams, and whether it can be made up for by seasonal snowpack. The second is one of the most dreaded words among trout fishers: irrigation.

Throughout my lifetime, the terms "in-stream flow," "irrigation draw," and "water rights" have been as integral to trout fishing in Montana as "trout rod," "felt soles," and "Royal Wulff." The first three have more to do with the life of a river, the health of its trout and insect life, than any other single factor affecting our state waters. To truly comprehend this, it is helpful to start with a short history of farming under the Big Sky.

LAND FOR THE TAKING

Situated just east of the massive front wall of the Rocky Mountains lies the edge of the Great Plains. Through the eons, moisture-bearing clouds, the result of evaporation on the Pacific Ocean, drift east to the Rockies like huge ivory ships. Too heavily laden to climb over the high peaks with a full load, the other side often gets nary a drop of rain. Climatologists call this effect a "rain shadow." In layman's terms it means simply that the stark alpine country receives adequate seasonal rain, while the tillable plains go without.

The first people to live here understood this well; they told stories of mountain-dwelling gods and their control over the frail land below the mountains. Jim Hill, founder of the Great Northern Railway, and his staff of railroad promoters and agricultural experts knew it too, but somehow they failed to mention it to the thousands upon thousands of homesteaders they lured here.

Not counting the especially moist northwestern corner, the annual level of precipitation throughout Montana is barely adequate to sustain farming of any great measure. This not only includes places like the Big Dry and the eastern counties of Rosebud, Garfield, Prairie, Blaine, and Phillips, but also—surprisingly—Beaverhead, Madison, and other counties in the western half of the state. Yearly precipitation in the southwest Montana town of Dillon, pressed between the Red Rock, Beaverhead, and Big Hole Rivers, is only ten inches. So when folks talk about the effects of drought, that chatter isn't only emanating from around the kitchen tables of farmers or anglers in Chinook. It might just as easily originate at a table in Melrose, located within earshot of the Big Hole.

Anyone who went west in the latter years of the 1800s, including Jim Hill, soon enough realized the implications of scarce water and fickle rain. The railroad was one of the first to hoard water coming from the western mountains, for use in their steam-driven locomotives. This same railroad enterprise also figured out a promotional scheme designed to get people throughout the world to believe that Montana's portion of the Great Plains suddenly contained enough water to sustain as many families and as much stock as could be carried to it—by Mr. Hill's railroad, of course. Thus was started one of Montana's darkest eras, one that utterly destroyed the once fertile shortgrass prairies of the northern Great Plains and placed far too much stress on the state's streams and rivers, sending thousands of innocent dreamers into the ranks of the truly poor.

The railroads and other groups across the country hustled homesteaders with elaborate brochures and handbills that stretched the truth about Montana's precipitation records like a rubber band. The promotional material quoted college professors of the day, as well as agricultural experts such as Professor Thomas Shaw, who helped the "honyonkers," as they came to be called, make up their minds, lay down the fare, and come out West before all the "good" land was spoken for. In his controversial book *Montana: High, Wide, and Handsome*, Joseph Kinsey Howard quotes from a Shaw brochure of the times directed at dreamers considering a move to the northern plains.

"Hurry, honyonker, hurry!

"As stated previously, these lands comprised 1,400,000 acres. Giving each man who files 160 acres, this area will furnish 8,750 farms. At first thought it might seem to be many months before all these farms would be taken. If any cherish such a view they will be greatly disappointed. It is questionable if a single farm will be left unfiled upon one month after the opening of the lands for entry....

"Hurry, honyonker, and do not investigate too closely!"

Howard went on to paint a more accurate picture of the annual rainfall and thus the farming potential awaiting newcomers on the Northern Plains: "To be sure, no records of rainfall had been kept 'for any lengthened period' at Culbertson: once a cowtown, careless of statistics, it was just being reborn. But in Glasgow, a hundred miles west, the records had been kept since 1894. There the 15–16 inches which you were told were 'average' had only been recorded three times in fifteen years; precipitation had been 12 inches or less ('rarely,' said the brochure) seven times in fifteen years.... Bozeman, Montana has an average annual precipitation of about 19 inches. Sixty miles west as the crow flies the average is 11 inches. That is Montana."

For his more honest version of the story of farming and other enterprises in early Montana, Howard's book was banned from sale in many places in the state, and in some it was only available "under the table." In the maverick mining town of Butte, a setting used to controversy, a reader could buy a copy from bartenders moonlighting in the literary business.

The Free Homestead Act of 1862 was very much in keeping with the foundation under which America was formed: the land belonged to the people. It naturally followed that new, "empty" land should be made available to those who would take the risk to settle on it. The first round of homesteading legislation that applied to the Great Plains was split between two very crucial factors: the limit of 160 acres and the requirement that a family live on the homestead to "prove up" for five years. This federal legislation came just as Montana was targeted by the placer gold rush, when few had farming interests.

When the indigenous fish and wildlife started to become scarce, however, and huge herds of cattle were driven to Montana, the need for very large sections of grazing land became apparent. The Desert Land Act, passed in 1877, caught the attention of cattlemen because for the minimal sum of one dollar and twenty-five cents per acre, they could effectively own 640 acres (one square mile) of rangeland. This law required a person prove up on the land for three years and promise to bring water to it in the form of irrigation, a process that received broad interpretation by enterprising stockmen of the West. In painting a picture of the questionable irrigation practices, Wallace Stegner wrote that a fellow could act on his promise, "Or he could drive around from claim to claim with a barrel and a bucket and pour a little water on a parcel of desert land and later accommodate the boss of some cattle company by swearing that he had brought water to that claim." Under the auspices of the Desert Land Act more than three million acres of public land in Montana passed into private hands, including some valuable bottomland along many of our rivers. This act set the foundation for Montana's pattern of bottomland irrigation, and established the water rights that now claim historic use of river water.

Most cattlemen of the day merely wanted the free range. For a small sum, they not only could lock up the range, but also the water rights from which their stock were watered. A few cattlemen made good on their deal with the government, especially when it came to the valuable bottomlands that surrounded Montana's flowing waters, the sites of many of our best trout fisheries today. The Desert Land Act's stipulation to irrigate effectively created the massive riverside hayfields of yesteryear that now are morphing into rows of summer homes or twenty-acre ranchettes.

Despite its apparent failure in other states on the Great Plains, the rush for free Montana farmland got a huge boost with the 1909 passage of the Enlarged Homestead Act. This time the boom days did not hinge on nonrenewable natural resources like gold, timber, fur, or copper. Instead, the new boom centered on the little savings homesteading families had, and the ageless dream of making an honest living on your own piece of ground. Drawn like prairie pronghorns to a waving flag, farming families came by the thousands, lured by the promise of free land, a new life, and prosperity.

As Stegner wrote in *Beyond the Hundredth Meridian*, "Those who were defeated, and up to 1900 two-thirds of those who tried were, were by the normal course of events in peonage to the banks. A mortgage was more common on a western farm than a good team. The Homestead Act and other laws made no provision for government loans and did not insist, as they might have, that abandoned claims be returned to the public domain for the benefit of other homesteaders. The land of the failures went to the banks, and thus onto the market, and often into the accumulating domains of speculators or large ranch companies. In the end, the Homestead Act stimulated the monopolizing of land that its advocates had intended to prevent."

Decades earlier, John Wesley Powell and his team of federal scientists, in a document entitled "Arid Region," had attempted to warn the nation about the physical limitations that arid regions imposed on farming, but their advice fell on deaf ears. In 1878, Powell presented for congressional consideration a plan to survey and establish districts and townships around their closeness to water resources. He advocated the democratic premise that no single entity should be able to monopolize an indigenous water resource simply by filing a claim on its rights. The report went so far as to declare that the minimum size of a farm in regions such as the Great Plains should consist of no less than 2,560 acres and must have access to adequate water. This was in direct contradiction to the 160 acres awarded by the Homestead Act or even the 320 acres awarded under the Enlarged Homestead Act.

Ten years after the land rush started, about 40 percent of Montana's plains had been turned over by the plow. Thirty-seven million acres of once-fertile prairie grass that had carpeted the high plains for millennia and provided nutritious forage for millions of wild animals first was nibbled to roots by vast herds of domestic cattle and sheep. Then ambitiously it was turned wrong side up.

The state's population exploded from 376,053 to 548,889 and wheat acreage ballooned from 258,000 acres to a whopping 3,417,000 acres between 1909 and 1919, the decade that accounted for most of the homestead migration to the high plains. The loss of native rangeland coupled with the quickly mushrooming population placed great stress on rivers, streams, wildlife habitat, and native fish and game, just when hopeful early signs of a recovery were beginning to show after the damaging work of commercial market hunters of the prior decades.

Good rain fell during the early years of the land boom. Crops came in at decent volumes and fairly stable markets managed to keep the price up, especially between 1910 and 1918. Then the natural climate cycle brought drought.

Dry years and rain years come in regular cycles on the high plains, almost like the rhythms of the moon or the call of returning geese to the wetlands of their birth. A few good years blessed by consistent rain, good crops, and bank-full rivers always are followed by a long stint of hot, unrelenting drought. In fact, it is drought above anything else that best defines the physical landscape and its flora and fauna.

Montana's climatic extremes effectively ended the homestead boom. The 3.4 million acres that had been planted in wheat by 1919 dried up in a checkerboard of barren ground. Mortgages on the small farms fell to foreclosure and soon many farmers were bankrupt, essentially due to the inadequate size of the farms and the lack of available water. More than 60 percent of the farming families lost everything, their fate sealed by the dry, hot summers or the unendurably cold winters—or both.

Imagine sitting on a homestead, your entire life's fortune spent. You have only a bag of seed, bought with money earned by clearing snow from railroad tracks or maybe working in the deep copper mines of Butte. You're surrounded by soil dry as bleached bones, with a bank mortgage due. Each day huge storm clouds appear like clockwork over the rugged mountains on the western horizon. They spin and whirl above the granite peaks, dropping torrents of rain miles away while the remaining land is left dry, waiting. And so are you.

IRRIGATION MAKES ITS MARK

The long era of drought caused other serious problems for the state. Fires raged in western forests, leaving their dark signatures on thousands of acres of scorched timberland. Great swarms of grasshoppers filled the air above the weathered plains. Professional varmint hunters and trappers had already collected the bounty on most of the coyote population. Absent these predators, what grass was left went to the exploding population of prairie dogs. Sky-darkening dust storms swept in waves across the high plains, eroding the deeply tilled topsoil, clogging the air, and further draining the life out of the land.

The dry years dropped the normal level of every major river. Many of Montana's smaller streams went totally dry, turning into long ribbons of parched sediment and sun-baked cobbles. Aquatic life that evolved here for millennia experienced massive die-offs. A lucky few species went into hiding, with only a marginal chance of return. By the time the drought lifted in the mid-1920s, more than fifty million dollars had been lost by farm families who had little to begin with.

Those who outlasted the ordeal learned that water had to come from the rivers and streams. The paramount sentiment developed, and continues today, that the agriculturalist and stockman are first in line for water. Never mind that this notion arose on the heels of mass public deception by commercial promoters. The disaster that prefaced it had been forewarned by Powell and lived through by thousands of unfortunate homesteaders, but even today few will publicly admit that the plains of Montana are no place to run a farm without taking major amounts of water from public rivers. Sadly, trout and wildlife have all too often been trumped by irrigators when it comes to water shortages caused by drought.

The dust storms of the 1920s sent a loud and anxious call forward to government officials for federal assistance to construct and maintain irrigation systems. It was a call that would not grow quiet for the next century, and is not likely ever to fade. For in Montana, even for those who do not make a living farming, raising cattle, or trying to control the frequent wildfires that engulf our state, the reality of drought plays a serious part in our lives. Trout suffer greatly during dry times, not because nature hasn't provided enough water—after all, fish and other aquatic life survived for millions of years before "civilization" came to the lands beneath the Rocky Mountains—but because today there simply are too many users of the water.

Massive concrete dams like the Tongue, Yellowtail, Canyon Ferry, and a long list of others, originally were proposed to the Montana public as flood-control projects that could also supply much needed irrigation to farm and ranches.

From the turn of the last century through the 1940s and 1950s, the state's water was divided up and historic rights were filed on as much of it as was possible under the slippery heading of "beneficial use." For decades this term primarily meant agricultural or municipal use, with a limited amount of industrial use thrown in for good measure. Only water that could be justified as having a so-called beneficial use could be considered for water rights.

An entire way of life, as well as a significant piece of Montana's economic puzzle today, balances on those historic water rights. As John Wesley Powell so artfully pointed out in his presentation to Congress, the real gold of the arid West could not be carried off in a rough leather pouch. The real gold was and always will be water, and the true value of western land would always be weighed by the presence or absence of water. Stockman and agriculturist alike realized the value of water long before the general citizen, and early on they devised a rudimentary system of water rights to protect their investment in the West. Of course the system provided the most protection to those who filed first, hence the phrase "first in line, first in right."

What placed a man ahead of his neighbor in water rights had as much to do with the speed of his horse as anything else. All that was necessary back in the early days was for the fellow to arrive at the county seat, fill out a short form, and identify both the stream in question and the beneficial use intended for the water to be withdrawn—and get it filed before his neighbor did. It was that simple.

By the time most farms and ranches really got going in Montana there were any number of federal acts to assist the aspiring yeoman in his claim for individual parcels of land and, consequently, water. These included the Homestead Act, Timber Culture Act, Desert Land Act, Pre-emption Act, and Timber and Stone Act, along with railroad grants and Indian and soldier scrip (certificates granting private ownership of public lands)—all schemes devised to successfully divide up the wilderness lands of the West. And then there was the public sale of lands lost by farmers who had already gone bust. In the early days of Montana water law, it was just as lucrative for a man to go into the business of acquiring land, filing for water rights, and then presenting the land for resale as it was to try to make a fruitful living from the land. The "beneficial use" of water by stockmen and farmers was largely unquestioned, and took preference over all others.

Powell's warning regarding the importance of water and the potential for its abuse inside the existing system fell on ears already deafened by the whispers of land speculators who were out to make a killing. The irrigation draws that were soon established sacrificed the in-stream flow of Montana waterways both large and small.

Although principles in fisheries management continued to slowly evolve through the years, this issue of maintaining adequate in-stream flow has remained problematic right through to the present day.

5

AGAIN THE BOTTOM FALLS OUT

}

Life is like a game of cards. The hand that is dealt you represents determinism;
the way you play it is free will.

—Jawaharlal Nehru

Although the game and fish restoration and restocking programs begun in Montana a century ago were impressive, wildlife management was chiefly a matter of ensuring that game animals and fish were available for sportsmen. At the time, wild animals were narrowly characterized as either game or predator. Only when a species fell into the category of "game" did the public feel it merited agency protection. For a species placed in the latter category, the approach was simple: control it or, preferably, eradicate it. Funding to ensure the eradication of predators was readily available and dispensed freely. Thus, two very effective approaches to manipulating wildlife populations existed simultaneously in Montana: protection for coveted species, and eradication for the rest. Each policy was aggressively pursued by the Montana Fish and Game Commission, and subsequently by the Department of Fish and Game.

Consistent with the public's view of predator versus prey, the native bull trout came up on the wrong side of the ledger. Many sportsmen and fisheries managers considered bull trout not worth the effort of saving, deeming it a predator fish that ate its way through other trout populations.

In the early 1920s, the Fish and Game Commission and its management agency began to reconsider their own direction, a struggle revolving around the need for accurate biological science, especially regarding fisheries. The commission's biennial reports revealed a growing sense of urgency that focused on issues such as the holding capacity of rivers and streams, the impact different species of trout had on one another, and the growing need to redesign or even rethink the very popular stocking program.

Some scientists, among the few that there were, had the reasonable suspicion that uncontrolled stocking of nonnative trout in Montana rivers could be leading to ecological havoc, especially on whatever populations of native trout still survived. A comprehensive picture of stream ecology, fish mortality, population morphology, insect entomology, and creel counts was sorely needed. Without this data, managers were more or less operating in the dark. Department and hatchery managers acknowledged the need for a more scientific approach, and in 1924 they agreed to begin the search for a qualified fisheries biologist.

Time would prove the wisdom of this new approach, but with private hatcheries and sporting groups stocking individual waters almost at will, any new scientific paradigm was destined to cause some serious conflicts within the department as well as with those license holders who were happy to have plenty of trout to catch. Private individual anglers typically felt as confident about their own knowledge of healthy rivers and good trout fishing as about anything that might come from state bureaucrats. After all, these were the days when fishers adhered to a twenty-five-pound daily bag limit on wild species like bull trout to help protect the restocking efforts.

Understandably, no one with a state badge wanted to step forward and start explaining that the private hatcheries and sportsmen's efforts might no longer be needed. It took a remarkable twenty-three years before the decision to hire the state's first biologist would be acted on, a nerve-racking period for those who felt the growing need to approach stocking Montana's rivers from a more scientific angle.

The state's license holders represented about the only financial support the department and the commission had, and sporting clubs considered themselves an equal partner in the successful replenishment of the state's waterways. To take an entirely different management approach would have meant the loss of support from the sporting public, and state officials were acutely aware of this. Compounding the dilemma was the pride of those hatchery workers who had brought back a broken fishery from the brink of extinction, making it a reliable resource—one their friends and neighbors appreciated greatly. But Montana was well on its way to becoming a "put and take" trout fishery. Without accurate numbers or studies, nobody knew for certain what role native trout played in this scenario. To change things in midstream, based on a suspicion, seemed pointless.

Nevertheless, the Fish and Game Department edged closer and closer to believing it had to manage by biological science, and the sporting clubs were slowly squeezed out of the mix. Anyone who fished in Montana at the time probably felt it coming, and most resented it.

All of us who fish today and have seen rivers deteriorate for one reason or another have little doubt that the more we get involved in altering a streambed, either physically or biologically, the more we need to pay attention to managing its future health. Reservoirs and tailwaters are perfect examples, but in the 1920s biological science was new and still tentative; state employees had gathered much of what they knew about fisheries management from the operation of hatcheries.

The proposed shift toward relying more heavily on biological science also set the stage for a battle over water pollution. The ongoing degradation of Montana's waterways seemed a secondary consideration to sportsmen of the day, but as the years went by, a direct connection between fishing success and pollution would become evident.

The Fish and Game Commission, now under the direction of T. N. Marlowe, realized that the future health of Montana streams and rivers depended on what they did next. They knew that they couldn't just summarily change their emphasis without causing an outcry. They first needed to convince the fishing public of the validity of this new approach. This would require a massive public education program.

The most critical tool the commission employed for public education was Montana's first conservation magazine, *Montana Wild Life*. The importance of the publication cannot be overstated. The articles were insightful, informative, interesting, and intended to solidify the support of sportsmen for changing the management paradigm.

Montana Wild Life, published from 1928–1933, was one of three state-issued periodicals produced at strategic times by the Fish and Game Commission; the others were *Montana Wildlife* (1952–1970) and *Montana Outdoors* (ongoing since

1971). Each came at times marked by serious public tension regarding management decisions. They did their jobs to perfection, with articulate and courageous writers explaining the issues clearly enough to gather public support behind the hard work of resource management. These publications undoubtedly altered the direction of management in Montana.

This use of *Montana Wild Life* was exceedingly important for a state like Montana, where tremendous geographic distance separated prairie, mountain ranges, and rivers. A land with so much remoteness could hide a lot of abuse from the eyes of the public majority, and the era of the well-traveled fisher had not yet arrived. Trout fishers, especially, stuck close to home and had little knowledge of what was happening elsewhere. The magazine drew a tighter circle around the massive resources of the state and enabled sportsmen to consider a much larger area with regard to resource conservation. It was an important lesson that still resonates today: Fishers and hunters alike always must be informed about the resources on which they rely and the management strategies they are asked to support.

A CRISIS LEADS TO CHANGES

Many other states faced similar wildlife and fishery issues. Unfortunately, even as conservation edged into wider public awareness, the entire country was once again forced to direct its attention elsewhere. For in 1929 the Great Depression began to clench the economic neck of the nation. Farm prices dropped to rock bottom, followed by cattle prices, mineral prices, and virtually everything else Montanans produced or harvested to feed their families. By the mid-1930s more than one-quarter of the state's residents stood in relief lines, battered by the harsh reality of sudden poverty. Many of the farms and ranches that had withstood the ravishing effects of the previous drought now failed quickly, putting even more Montana families on the move or on public assistance. With work across the state scarce or nonexistent, available tax revenue plummeted and the base of state government began to crumble. One of the victims of the depressed times was *Montana Wild Life* and its growing model of public education.

Montanans had gone through tough times before, but the onset of the Great Depression was something totally different, more widespread, with more hunger and more loss. It left a mark on virtually every walk of life. Families who relied on mining and wood products had to look elsewhere for basic sustenance. Many depended on wild game and fish to help them survive the crisis.

To make matters worse, another wave of drought hit the Great Plains in the early 1930s, bringing wind that again sent gigantic dust clouds adrift, rising like massive pillows over the plains. The winds peeled away valuable topsoil in unparalleled quantities. In Montana, game birds and trout suffered severely as the lack of precipitation dried up many of the smaller streams and left others void of any life. Those who lived through the drought and dust called it the "dirty thirties" or the "dustbowl years."

A startled nation was forced to question its land-use policies, finally remembering the cautionary words of John Wesley Powell and George Perkins Marsh. It was from this time of national despair that Aldo Leopold drew much of the inspiration for the ideas he later articulated in his famed "land ethic," which steered a growing conservation movement in the decades to follow. This emerging paradigm centered around maintaining the value of land and using it correctly to ensure its future wholesomeness. Man's approach to, and use of, the land, as proposed by Leopold, might be best inspired by acknowledging our own vulnerability, our reliance on the health and productivity of the land we have chosen to put into production, along with the natural elements, such as water, on which we rely to keep the land wholesome.

Leopold saw all things in nature, animate or inanimate, as linked by the process of community: "Civilization is not, as they often assume, the enslavement of a stable and constant earth. It is a state of mutual and interdependent cooperation between human animals, other animals, plants, and soils, which may be disrupted at any moment by the failure of any one of them."

It was clear that something on the high plains of Montana and other states had failed horribly, and it would take decades of work if ever the symbiotic relationship between human animals and other animals, plants, and soils would recover.

The long days of the Great Depression stimulated the most important surge of environmental thinking in the twentieth century. Leopold and others moved away from the traditional, utilitarian concepts of land use. The new paradigm involved a more biocentric view of the landscape upon which we live and rely, highlighting the close association that exists between life, water, and land. Leopold's book *Game*

Management, published in 1933, would serve as a reliable reference for game managers well into the future.

As a solution to the staggering unemployment gripping Montana, President Franklin D. Roosevelt announced plans to construct the largest earthen structure in the world across the free-flowing Missouri River, Fort Peck Dam. Some ten thousand workers drew paychecks during the years of its construction. Fort Peck was the first of ten dams that eventually shackled Lewis & Clark's great river and changed its natural mystique and aquatic life forever.

Another leg of the reform brought by Roosevelt's New Deal in part answered the historic call for irrigation. Works Progress Administration (WPA) projects bloomed like islands of new grass throughout Montana. Stock-watering ponds and irrigation reservoirs were constructed on many of the state's secondary waterways. Extensive channels were dug and diversions installed. Given the seriousness of simply surviving the times, little thought was given to any permanent damage this work might cause fisheries.

The completion of new dams and reservoirs inspired an increase in private fish stocking. Once again, the species and place of stocking could be determined by anyone willing to take the time and spend the money to make it happen.

But in the height of the nation's economic collapse, in a gutsy and critical move, Montana's fish and wildlife managers for the first time in history publicly challenged private stocking on public streams and rivers. This decision to speak out may have saved Montana's waters and native trout for the future. It took tremendous courage to wage such a battle in the face of a public that had, by all accounts, lost faith in the workings of government. However, a good share of the state fish and game employees had taken reduced hours just to keep the agency alive during the long depression, and they were committed to facing the challenge of unregulated private stocking. Standing as one, the managers in 1934 supported legislation that made unauthorized stocking illegal and strongly recommended that control of Montana's water be granted to the Water Conservation Board, a milestone decision that ultimately protected our waterways.

Throughout our state's colorful and dramatic history, special leaders have stood up, spoken out, or just plain acted. The Fish and Game Commission's decision to outlaw private stocking and effectively put private hatcheries out of business took more guts than we contemporary trout fishers might ever comprehend. But the decision followed their conservation mandate to the letter.

Our fisheries are what they are today simply because our predecessors took them seriously, watched over them closely, and did what was necessary for the future—regardless of public opinion.

6

THE BEST OF HARD TIMES

{

We end…at what might be called the standard paradox of the twentieth century: our tools are better than we are, and grow better faster than we do. They suffice to crack the atom, to command the tides. But they do not suffice for the oldest task in human history: to live on a piece of land without spoiling it.

—ALDO LEOPOLD, *The River of the Mother of God and Other Essays*

Around the same time that Aldo Leopold was advocating for a new land ethic after watching the dust swirl on the Great Plains, other national conservationists were also inspired to act. This included famed cartoonist Jay "Ding" Darling, who not only spoke out on behalf of threatened wildlife and vanishing habitat, but acted aggressively on his tenet. In 1934 he assumed one of the nation's key positions as the head of the Bureau of Biological Survey.

Darling's passionate interest in migratory birds, both songbirds and waterfowl, was already well-known across America through his nationally syndicated cartoons and drawings. His new post under President Roosevelt allowed him to make huge strides on behalf of unprotected species that often were overlooked in the larger mix of things. It also helped him appeal to others in similar positions of power to join the crusade.

The drought years of the 1930s had dealt a serious blow to fish and birds of all species. Darling and a growing team of followers realized the urgent need to protect not only individual species, but also the vital habitat upon which their survival depended.

From his place in leadership, however, he also could see a federal revenue system struggling in the wake of serious economic decline. Darling recognized that the funding to protect migratory birds and other seriously threatened species had to come from an independent source removed from the coffers of state or federal government. With the support of other active conservationists around the country, his group had a congressional bill crafted to mandate that every waterfowl hunter above the age of sixteen purchase a special stamp for each hunting season. With the passage of that federal legislation, the "waterfowl stamp" was born. It's still in use today to protect birdlife and wetland habitat. A good share of the revenue generated by the bird stamp was to protect wetlands. This eventually created another cornerstone of our country's conservation legacy, the National Wildlife Refuge System.

After their significant accomplishments on behalf of migratory birds, Darling and his followers urged members of Congress and sportsmen across the country to support a more scientific approach to wildlife and fisheries management. The resulting landmark Cooperative Wildlife Research Unit Program and the Federal Aid in Wildlife Restoration Act (or Pittman-Robertson, named after the two senators who sponsored the legislation) eventually were enacted into law. Their influence was almost immediately felt across the country, and flowed to the heart of the complex issues facing Montanans. The Federal Aid in Wildlife Restoration Act bridged some gaps that existed between implementing new biological science versus continuing the more traditional and less costly reactive approach to wildlife management. Pittman-Robertson funds would prove vital to furthering new strategies in wildlife and habitat management. More importantly, the act utilized a nontraditional funding strategy that would be effectively employed by conservation advocates again in the future.

The backbone of Pittman-Robertson was a federal excise tax levied on the retail sale of firearms, ammunition, and archery equipment—a thriving business in America at the time. According to law, the sizable receipts were earmarked for wildlife restoration and hunter safety. Administered by the U.S. Fish and Wildlife Service, the monies pumped new life into wildlife management. The funds were doled out to individual states on a matching basis. The downside of the new approach for states like Montana was that it set a new precedent: The supportive relationship between license holders and the state management system was weakened due to the use of outside funding. No longer were wildlife managers entirely accountable to the immediate public they served. As time went on, the results of this separation would become increasingly apparent—no more so than in the transition from unregulated, prolific stocking of fish in Montana waters to a sound, broad, ecological approach.

Be it now judged healthy or unhealthy, productive or unproductive, the restocking of Montana's rivers always will be considered one of the state's great civic and moral accomplishments—one we should continue to celebrate with each wild rainbow trout brought to net or rising brown trout. But stocked trout were meant for one fate: to be caught. And because hatchery trout were not supposed to last long, the put-and-take system revealed practically nothing about the ambient quality of the water resource.

It is conceivable, even agreeable, to stock trout in some places where the water is of such poor quality that it can only sustain fish for a limited time—in effect, trout not taken by anglers are expected to perish shortly. It might be unfair to say, but it seems that in states where put-and-take trout fishing has been the norm, fisheries managers have, in large part, given up on controlling and enhancing the quality of their water. Yet in Montana, the water quality in most rivers in the 1930s had not diminished to the point where trout could not grow and mature over time. To be sure, the state faced some huge pollution problems in that era, but on many waters things were not irreversibly bad, perhaps in large part because most of our watercourses originate in high, remote wildernesses or in protected parks and wildlife refuges. This effectively provided wildlife managers of the day the opportunity to return some of our rivers and streams to the status of native fisheries.

BRINGING SCIENCE TO WILDLIFE MANAGEMENT

On July 1, 1947, C. K. Phenicie walked through the heavy doors of the Fish and Game office in Helena, rolled up his sleeves, and went to work upsetting the public applecart that had been happily rolling through the watery hinterlands of Montana for almost half a century. Phenicie's sketchy job description was reminiscent of that of William F. Scott, Montana's first game warden, who had put a stop to the commercial slaughter of wildlife. Like Scott, Phenicie was a determined man, educated, scientifically minded, and committed to the task, however tough it might turn out to be. Here was a newcomer to the state and to the department, an outsider, who would change the way hundreds of state employees had been doing things. He also would change things on Montana's rivers and streams, disrupting the expectations of tens of thousands of citizens. This job would be seen as wildly unpopular both inside and outside the department—yet it proved to be the salvation of many of Montana's most important rivers. Under his tutelage, "biological science" would become a commonplace term understood by the populace.

Predictably, sparks flew between those who staunchly held to put-and-take and the new wave of science-minded fisheries employees, but eventually the long custom of casually stocking streams and rivers drifted silently into the past. Phenicie became the first in a long roster of fisheries biologists who would, at one time or another, play critical and controversial roles in the management and future of trout fisheries. The way was now open to a future enhanced by steadily advancing biological science—an advantage that one day would provide wildlife biologists the ammunition they needed to make powerful statements regarding the impacts of industrial development.

But the public's growing awareness about the health of our streams and rivers was forced to take a back seat when, in December 1941, a cloud of black smoke rose over Pearl Harbor and the nation was drawn into World War II. By 1942 more than forty thousand patriotic Montanans had signed up for the war effort, exchanging their fly rods and big game rifles for government-issued weapons and uniforms. Another thirty-five thousand residents who had survived the hard years of the Great Depression now left for the big wages and family security offered in the West Coast factories that were ramping up for the war effort.

Remarkably, while the war raged overseas and Montana emptied its population, work in the Department of Fish and Game went on at a healthy clip. When the war finally ended and families were reunited, a frenzy of trout fishing began in earnest. Stricken by the massive devastation and tragedy they had witnessed overseas, the men and women who returned to Montana viewed their peaceful homeland and all it offered in a much different way. Family life centered around outdoor activities and enjoying all that had been protected during the war. This monumental time marked the beginning of the Baby Boom, when families expanded and young kids learned to fish and hunt beside parents who had learned the real price of freedom. Fishing, camping, national park visits, summer vacations, warm summers on mountain lakes, and weekend travel were all on the rise, and as a result, more expectations fell on the shoulders of natural resource managers statewide.

In 1950, fisheries managers were handed one of their most powerful tools ever: a substantial source of funding. Much like the Federal Aid in Wildlife Restoration Act that had directed federal tax revenues to wildlife restoration, the Federal Aid in Sport Fish Restoration Act (Dingell-Johnson) passed by Congress was to be used as a tool to aid in the revival of fisheries across the country. The act allowed a three-to-one federal match for all fishing license receipts received by each state desiring funds. The federal funds were generated by the fast-growing sporting industry, again through an excise tax, this time levied on fishing and boating equipment.

The sale of Montana hunting and fishing licenses had exploded to 285,000 by 1950, an increase of 131,000 in less than a decade. The new law provided a substantial revenue boost for the state fisheries division and enabled it to hire a full-time biologist for each of its five administrative districts. The addition of this level of biological support greatly enhanced the day-to-day management of fisheries, at the same time enabling critical ecological and biological studies. The baseline data collected would prove to be an invaluable tool in future battles over water use and water quality.

Although the new source of funding did create a solid foundation for more scientific management within the state, it also perpetuated reliance on federal money. In retrospect, one can see that the availability of those outside funds continued to erode the close relationship between local sportsmen and those in charge of managing public resources.

Based on scientific findings, the Fish and Game Commission in 1953 adopted a new set of stocking criteria statewide. The terms included the following:

- No fish would be planted closer than a quarter-mile from portions of streams closed to public access.

- Except for experimental plants or reestablishment of species, only grayling, rainbow, or cutthroat trout would be planted in Montana streams.

- Rainbow and cutthroat trout planted in streams would not be less than six inches long.

- Lakes should be planted only where spawning was nonexistent or inadequate.

- Fish should be liberated only where a reasonable return to creel was assured.

- Fry and fingerling trout would only be used where practical.

- Fish of all sizes should be liberated at such times and in such manner as to ensure the greatest possible return to the creel.

- Fish should be planted where fishing pressure warranted and where fish populations were being reestablished.

Some changes in the new management strategy were subtle, possibly designed to nudge the program away from put-and-take and toward a time when fish populations might generate naturally, stimulated by introduced species already in the rivers and streams and whatever stock remained of the native population. Anglers who had gotten used to following the stocking trucks to the edge of the river weren't excited about this new direction, but popular or not, it would someday be the backbone of management as Montana grew into one of the best trout fisheries in the Lower Forty-Eight for all species, native and nonnative alike. Had a less aggressive management approach been taken in the 1950s, it is quite possible our present-day cutthroat population simply would have disappeared or would now exist at no appreciable level.

The Department of Fish and Game had to juggle two very slippery balls. One was meant to keep the fishing public happy, and the other to protect existing habitat and whatever population of native trout still remained in Montana waters.

Keeping anglers satisfied remained one of the state's critical objectives even as concerns increased over industrial pollution, stream alteration, dewatering by irrigation, and poor livestock practices. This situation would fester until a final stand could be taken on behalf of stream ecology.

PROOF AT LAST

Reports from new scientific studies started to slowly seep in, further opening the eyes of managers. One of the early ecological studies conducted in 1954 on the tributary streams of the Gallatin River attempted to assess the long-term impact certain agricultural practices had on trout populations and stream bionomics. The results of the Gallatin study clearly showed that removal of streamside brush by property owners had reduced the weight of existing trout by more than 40 percent, while the decimation of undercut banks on the tributaries was credited with a weight reduction approaching 33 percent. The study proved that healthy riverbank ecology would increase trout weight overall, a message of good tidings for fly fishers, but one not so well received by area stockgrowers whose cattle had unlimited access to public waterways.

Other biological work crucial to Montana fisheries indicated that once a brown trout population had been firmly established on a receiving stream, the endurance and adaptability of this species made further planting unnecessary. Contemporary fisheries scientists deem this species to be extremely adaptable to new water and new terrain, simply because they are believed to learn five times faster than rainbows. Their supposed higher level of intelligence even helps them fit into degraded habitat better than most trout species, and browns also can adapt to warmer water. That same fish intelligence caused problems for the put-and-take angler, however, because brown trout also learn to avoid the hook and have a wonderful ability to use their habitat to fend off fishing pressure.

As a result of the study, Montana's last scheduled brown trout release on a river occurred in 1954, on the Blackfoot River. In the years that followed, brown trout were stocked only under special conditions on some select streams, when an entirely new population needed to be established. At the time, this study was challenged by many trout fishers and rod and gun club members who were reluctant to believe brown trout could acclimate so quickly to Montana streams. But today blue-ribbon streams like the Big Hole, Bighorn, Madison, Rock Creek, Ruby, Beaverhead, and Red Rock feature vibrant populations of brown trout—all the prodigy of fish stocked prior to 1954.

Additional studies conducted that same year focused on the controversial impact of logging practices in northwestern Montana. Heavy logging in the Kootenai National Forest had released tremendous sediment loads into area rivers, including the Kootenai, Yaak, Bull, and Fisher. This sediment made its way to the larger rivers through a web of tributaries. It greatly impacted the upstream migration of a number of trout species, including native cutthroats, bull trout, and the very rare native redband rainbow. But any studies linking the timber industry to river decimation and trout loss were openly and aggressively disputed by logging-dependent communities like Libby, Troy, and Eureka.

Through many of the early statewide studies, biologists determined that Montana's wild stream habitat was changing steadily due to any number of abuses. Hundreds of miles of indigenous habitat were seriously compromised, altered, or rendered lifeless by generations of unchecked industrial and agricultural operations. Fortunately, many Montanans read the early work of state biologists and defended clean water and healthy aquatic life.

Based on these findings, the Fish and Game Commission had no choice but to draw a line in the sand that would pit them against a well-funded consortium of powerful mining interests, with agriculture and stockgrowers fast on their heels. All the impending targets were supported by strong and effective lobbyists and plenty of capital.

And so, for the second time in its history, the Fish and Game Commission used public education in order to gain support for another controversial undertaking. The campaign was launched in 1952 with the reintroduction of a state conservation magazine, this time entitled *Montana Wildlife*.

In science, there is a time-tested axiom that generally states "information and data equals power," a presumption that would prove itself time and time again as Montana moved through the minefields that lay ahead. Soldiered by a staff of newly hired, energetic biologists and supported by federal funds, fisheries managers steadily compiled a scientific database that brought Montana's waterways and their problems into much sharper focus. Their strategy was to identify precisely what made a healthy stream function and to compare those characteristics to sites already damaged by polluters.

Fostered in part by the early research of those biologists and pressure from an informed public, in 1955 the Montana state legislature took an aggressive step to address habitat loss. It enacted the nationally pacesetting Water Pollution Control Act. This stringent law at last provided some strong muscle for the Fish and Game Commission to begin to tackle water pollution problems that related to habitat loss. Inspired by additional public support, the commission created a key position in state government, a pollution control biologist—yet another controversial hiring in the business quarters of Montana.

Zealous promoters were focused on increasing tourist dollars at the same time that the Fish and Game Commission was putting federal funds to work on Montana rivers. Public relations experts for years had been bragging about the thirty thousand miles of "well-stocked" trout waters crisscrossing Montana. Eye-catching brochures touted the plentitude and pleasure to be found on Montana trout streams. The ads endeavored to paint all of the state's rivers and streams with the same broad brush.

As scientific information on individual streams rolled in, however, reality just did not match the promotions. Water pollution clearly was impacting fisheries. Big dam projects, irrigation diversions, and channel alterations resulting from proposed highway construction hung like a dark cloud over many of the state's rivers. Some fisheries managers felt one of the first and most important steps was to develop a method to measure the "value" of each stream from both an economic and a recreational perspective. A reliable ranking system could establish the "worth" of a trout fishery. That worth could then be balanced against any projected damage that might come as a result of large construction or alteration projects.

The classification committee's mission was to develop a system that would attempt to put a price tag on sport fisheries as well as assign some importance to the social legacy of trout fishing that had long been a part of the Montana lifestyle. An important component of their mandate was to build a system that could be used by future planners whenever and wherever projects might impact public waterways.

Shortly after the committee completed its work, the U.S. Fish and Wildlife Service began distributing the information in a brochure entitled "A Classification of Montana Fishing Streams." The publication identified the state's streams and rivers with a color-coded system, ranking each according to their relevant value: blue being a class-one stream or a waterway of national and statewide value; red a class-two stream or a waterway of statewide value; yellow a class-three stream or of value to large districts of the state; and gray a class-four stream having value only to smaller districts. The final designation was a class-five stream that carried no color but denoted a waterway having restricted local value.

A colored map identified each stream's ranking. The prestigious term "blue-ribbon trout stream" actually comes from that committee's ranking system. The eye-opener was how few Montana streams were awarded the prestigious blue-ribbon classification—only 410 miles. Class-two streams accounted for 1,072 miles, class three came in at 2,437 miles, and class four added up to a whopping 5,004 miles.

The sections that received the top ranking on the early map included the Missouri from Three Forks to Townsend and from Wolf Creek to Ulm. Extensive sections on the Madison and Yellowstone also were designated, as was the Big Hole from Divide to Twin Bridges, and Rock Creek outside Missoula. Some of the lowest rankings went to waterways that flowed adjacent to or immediately downstream of our major cities. The 1959 map presented a fairly dismal picture of Montana's trout fishing resources, but the picture was still impressive compared to what had existed before the restocking efforts a half century earlier. The committee's assessment showed just how far the state had to go to live up to its own promotions.

The new classification system would prove invaluable as Montana turned its attention to major interstate highway construction and the new large-scale mining and dam projects ready to come off the drawing boards. The question was, would the state's trout fisheries be protected and improve, or would they worsen as cities grew, industries became more powerful, and more and more irrigation water was drained from troubled waterways?

7

A TORRENT OF ADVOCACY

I've always had a special connection to the Henry's Fork. The river runs through my family's roots. They say that we're all made up of 96 percent water. I can't help but feel the water in my body came from the Henry's Fork. I've shared the best times on this water, and I'm scarred from the battles I've fought trying to save this river.

—MIKE LAWSON, *Spring Creeks*

For years the word "dam" has struck fear in the hearts of fly fishers and conservationists. As Montana slowly moved through the twentieth century, promoters of dam building grew more aggressive, presenting their arguments in what federal bureaucrats call a "cost-benefit ratio." Here was a system of sharp-pencil analysis that was supposed to balance a project's economic benefit against environmental and cultural blemishes left as a result of damming pristine and free-flowing rivers. In the 1950s and 1960s, as dam after dam was promoted to Montana residents, the cost-benefit argument was used repeatedly to try to convince the masses that dams were a good thing, and that construction would infuse immediate revenues into surrounding communities. They did not dwell on long-term environmental or cultural impacts.

I lived through those times, and observed that dam-building ran as much on colossal "federal ego" as it ever did on actual economic justification. In the late 1950s, the U.S. Bureau of Reclamation and the Army Corps of Engineers surveyed more than one hundred individual dam locations within only the Jefferson River drainage—which included the Beaverhead, Big Hole, Ruby, and Red Rock tributaries. It was clear to any angler in this period that these agencies literally wanted to control every river in Montana. And their use of cost-benefit analysis probably would have enabled them to achieve their goal had it not been for the intervention of sportsmen and conservationists who saw things differently.

The Bureau of Reclamation's power stems from the 1902 Newlands Act, which had as its prime objective the creation of irrigation projects across the semi-arid West. As time went on, however, the bureau's objective shifted appreciably. Hydro-electric power assumed major importance in the federal agenda. Further shifts in the bureau's management philosophy came as a result of the growth of industry and urban centers in Montana, with their quickly increasing need for an adequate supply of water. Containing Montana's waters became yet another reason to build a big dam, in addition to flood control, navigation enhancement, and silt and pollution control. Secondary considerations, far down the list, included protecting or enhancing fish and wildlife habitat and outdoor recreation opportunities.

In the early part of the century, the bureau relied primarily on irrigation and hydroelectric generation for supportive arguments. Passage of the Flood Control Act in 1944 changed the paradigm that drove dam building. Control of, and final use of, the water resources originating in the entire state of Montana became subject to federal review. For example, the Missouri River Basin encompasses an enormous slice of the state, including the Bighorn, Tongue, Milk, Marias, Shields, Yellowstone, Gallatin, Madison, Gardner, Big Hole, Jefferson, and Beaverhead Rivers, among others. Authorization of the Missouri River Basin Study under the Flood Control Act resulted in the Missouri River Basin Project, which in a historical context might be considered nothing short of a frontal assault on the rivers, streams, creeks, and springs that feed the Missouri River.

Prior to the establishment of the project, twenty-one storage dams, reservoirs, and adjoining irrigation systems, pumping stations, and diversion dams were located in the drainage. Between 1949 and 1965, the Bureau of Reclamation constructed twenty-seven new multipurpose dams and reservoirs under the umbrella of the Missouri River Basin Project, with dozens more proposed for the future.

A DAM IN PARADISE VALLEY?

Federal agencies such as the Army Corps of Engineers had talked about damming Montana's Yellowstone River at the Allenspur narrows as early as 1902, and the engineers never stopped dreaming about it. But once Dan Bailey moved to Montana, the federal agencies had a new adversary to contend with when it came to blocking the nation's longest remaining free-flowing river.

On a trout stream, Dan Bailey, one of Montana's foremost conservationists and anglers, carried a perpetual smile, but when engaged in a struggle to protect a favorite water, he assumed the look of a gladiator ready to do battle. Dan Bailey's Fly Shop in Livingston quickly established itself as one of the most important contact points for the growing army of fly fishers traveling through Montana. Between the fly fishers he met locally and his loyal list of contacts in the fishing and media world, Bailey managed to build a syndicate of support for Montana rivers and streams.

In the late 1950s, yet another round of whispers about plans at Allenspur came to the Yellowstone. Bailey went about the hard work of gathering support for what would turn out to be a battle to save the river and beautiful Paradise Valley through which it flows. I was a kid of only eight at the time, in my first year of fly fishing. On a humid summer evening, my uncle and I drove from the West Boulder River to Livingston to meet Dan on the Yellowstone during the first phase of heated disputes over the proposed placement of the Allenspur Dam a few miles south of Livingston. Such a placement would have backed up the river for more than thirty miles, flooding all the bottomland and destroying almost a hundred miles of wonderful trout water, some of it blue-ribbon. My uncle, a conservationist in his own right, wanted to commit his support to Bailey's growing army of like-minded sportsmen and conservationists willing to engage in the fight to save the river.

On the Yellowstone River that evening, I listened to the two men talk about the future of the river. Over the course of just a few hours in the presence of one of Montana's leading conservationists, the seed of advocacy was planted in my young head. I realized for the first time that "we, the people" actually hold the key to our own fate and what remarkable success conservationists have had throughout the history of Montana.

Surrounded by a swarm of caddisflies, the two accomplished fly fishers worked the big water of the Yellowstone and brought trout to the surface with uncanny precision, while I stayed on the bank close behind. Every now and again they drew closer, stopped casting, and talked about the proposed dam and how money would be needed to continue the fight and, for that matter, for the many more fights that would come in the future as additional Montana rivers were threatened.

As I look back on that evening, I realize how historic it was in my family's life and how fortunate I was to have been introduced to a conservationist like Dan Bailey. I learned about the most powerful tool at our disposal: grassroots activism. I only wish I had been old enough to have recorded in some way Bailey's passion as he talked about his cherished homewater on the Yellowstone, about the Paradise Valley and the thousands of trout, game birds, and mammals that would perish if the Allenspur dam were built. (For more information about Dan's remarkable life, see Charley Waterman's book *Mist on the River: Remembrances of Dan Bailey*.)

The name Allenspur came from a discontinued railway stop located in the Paradise Valley between Livingston and Yellowstone National Park. The initial justification for the dam was to provide irrigation for dry landscapes downstream, but trout fishers like Bailey and Bud Lilly, among others, were able to show that the river also had great value as a recreational fishery. And while the latter prevailed in a significant victory for the river, the plan to impound the Yellowstone really never went away. In fact, it was just getting started, as we'll see later on.

The first Allenspur Dam debate underscored the need for better organization and public education if future battles were to be waged successfully against the powerful federal government and heavy industry. Money would be needed as well, along with a strong nucleus of leadership willing to stand up to the pro-development state legislature.

In the wake of the Allenspur battle, a group of fly-fishing enthusiasts met at Bud Lilly's Fly Shop in West Yellowstone. The conclave included some big names in Montana trout fishing and conservation, including outfitter Merton Parks, Pat Sample from Billings, Joe Halderman, Bud Morris, and John Peters. This group formed the first Montana Chapter of Trout Unlimited (TU), which today continues to defend Montana rivers. Dan Bailey's philosophies on conservation were in alignment with the important goals of TU, and he served as the organization's national director.

Dan Bailey never grew tired of fishing the Yellowstone, and he always marveled at the fact that it had remained the nation's longest undammed river. Wherever he went, Dan gathered friends and allies, warriors willing to step forward when needed. His band of brothers included people like Joe Brooks, Charles Waterman, John McDonald, and Lee Wulff, all willing to write feature stories about Montana in national magazines that could be read by millions of fly fishers across the nation—and many of these readers were willing to join in when a battle was brewing out West.

This groundwork would prove critical to the Yellowstone's future, because as we'll see later on, a much more difficult fight would occur on the river, again involving the proposed Allenspur dam site.

DAM IT ALL!

A growing sense of urgency over aquatic habitat loss reverberated from the pages of the Fish and Game Commission's biennial reports during the 1950s and '60s. But interest in big dam construction continued to swell. The Missouri River's Canyon Ferry Dam was finished in 1954, and Tiber Dam on the Marias River was under way. Tucked in the back pockets of both the Bureau of Land Reclamation and the Army Corps of Engineers was a stack of new plans to shackle more of the Missouri, Yellowstone, and Clark Fork watersheds. Projects on the table included Yellowtail Dam on the Bighorn River, Spruce Park Dam on the Middle Fork of the Flathead River, and Libby Dam on the Kootenai River. Unfortunately, nature would soon give these and other proposals a big boost.

Rumbling across the Rocky Mountains on June 8, 1964 came a colossal bank of steel-gray storm clouds, unleashing one of the worst rainstorms ever recorded in Montana history. In a single day, more than sixteen inches of rain fell on the still-heavy winter snowpack in the mountains. The mixture of relentless rain and melting snow caused many rivers to rise to levels never before seen. Already swollen with runoff, the Middle Fork of the Flathead rose from its normal spring level of 14,000 cubic feet per second (cfs) to more than 140,000 cfs in a single night. The tempest submerged the entire valley below, killing livestock and ripping mature trees from the ground.

Rivers and streams on both sides of the Continental Divide raged, including the Marias, Sun, Dearborn, Two Medicine, and Cut Bank Creek. Many were scoured to bedrock by the uncontrollable floods. High water on the Blackfoot, Swan, Thompson, Clark Fork, and Kootenai altered riverine ecosystems that had been in place for centuries. The spring flood also took the lives of thirty-four peo-ple, tallied more than sixty million dollars in property damage, and left rivers, streams, and creeks vulnerable to additional habitat loss due to the decimation of established stream channels. Many towns were threatened with destruction, includ-ing the agricultural center of Great Falls.

The political fallout from the flooding would last for many years, with each new dam proposal carrying the ominous tagline of "flood prevention."

LOOKING TO THE FUTURE

Meanwhile, by the end of the 1950s, scientists and sportsmen alike were expressing serious concerns over the future health of many Montana trout streams. Siltation from unchecked logging operations, road construction, and huge irrigation systems was wreaking havoc on trout eggs and insect emergence. And water pollution caused by mine wastes, pesticides, overgrazing, logging, and increased irrigation plagued the state legislature and the Fish and Game Commission. Pending high-way construction in the multimillion-dollar bracket loomed like a new tidal wave of prosperity over the state's immediate future.

Offered up as another economic boon, as well as a stimulant to a growing tourist trade, the new construction looked promising to many in Montana. More leisure time across the nation meant an increase in travel to remote places like Montana, and certainly more nonresident fishing licenses would be sold.

As the state turned its attention to developing tourism, it almost immediately became evident that the aesthetic and environmental integrity of Montana's natural resources—forests, mountains, streams, and rivers—would be important compo-nents in attracting big-spending visitors. Equally important would be a well-main-tained interstate highway system throughout the huge state, plus paved two-lane arteries to beautiful river valleys, mountain ranges, and blue-ribbon fisheries. Assessing the impacts of an interstate highway system that, for the most part, ran adjacent to already troubled rivers practically filled the radar screens of state biolog-ical planners. The serious environmental impacts of highway construction on wild waterways could have devastated Montana's rivers.

Luckily, by the time major highway construction really got under way, industri-ous biologists and conservationists had a wealth of studies on their desks and a few solid laws to help protect rivers and other natural settings from the onslaught of a proposed tangle of new highways.

One study, named after Bluewater Creek near Bridger, came on line in the late 1950s. It was designed to determine the effect agricultural pollution had on trout streams by looking at a number of factors, including siltation, decreased flows caused by irrigation draws, and steeply rising water temperatures. When the groundbreaking results began to come in, biologists could see clearly that the sections most heavily impacted by agricultural silt and high water temperatures were quickly reduced to rough fish habitat, while those not impacted by agriculture continued to maintain good trout numbers and had far fewer rough fish.

As the decade drew to a close, a new breed of warrior armed with a slide rule, sample jar, and a tattered book of scientific findings was joining the established conservation movement, bringing hard evidence of industry's environmental impact to the table. Through the hard work of many, there was reason to think the future might be bright—as long as lawmakers and others decision-makers could be compelled to consider emerging science and the word of experts, as opposed to industry lobbyists and promoters.

8
BIG INDUSTRY IS TOLD "NO"

}

Contemplating the lace-like fabric of streams outspread over the mountains, we are reminded that everything is flowing, going somewhere, animals and so-called lifeless rocks as well as water.... Rocks flow from volcanoes like water from springs, and animals flock together and flow in currents modified by stepping, leaping, gliding, flying, swimming, etc. While the stars go streaming through space pulsed on and on forever like blood globules in Nature's warm heart.

—JOHN MUIR, *My First Summer in the Sierra*

The natural beauty of western Montana's pastoral valleys, and the rivers that run through them, has always drawn humans like a magnet. As European-Americans began moving west, towns and industries large and small mushroomed along the rivers, directly dumping in raw sewage, industrial waste, and mine effluent in the form of dissolved toxins and heavy metals. As the decades flew by, new biological studies by the Department of Fish and Game began to reveal this pollution's impact on waterways—especially within the footprint of some of the most populated towns like Missoula, Butte, Great Falls, Billings, and Livingston.

One milestone study undertaken in the summer of 1960 on the Clark Fork River homed in on the Anaconda Mining Company's huge settling ponds near Warm Springs, which had been constructed as a stopgap for heavy-metal pollution originating in the Butte mines and the Anaconda smelter. The study results were startling, and would play a significant part in Montana's future. The thirty miles of water upstream from the ponds to the point source of the pollution was a biological wasteland, while the streambed stretching for some thirty miles below the settling ponds teetered on the brink of total collapse.

Adding to the Clark Fork's pollution problems, west of Deer Lodge the river historically was dewatered by private irrigators, especially during the peak growing season. The serious depletion of water resulted in sharp temperature increases and further compromised any aquatic life that might be surviving. Farther downstream, where the Clark Fork flows through Missoula, municipal sewage was flushed directly into the river, and had been since the timber town's inception. And just a few more miles downstream, Waldorf-Hoerner Pulp and Paper was discharging its own toxic wastes into the river, rounding out a network of contamination few rivers could tolerate. It was clear to scientists that the sad condition of the Clark Fork could become the fate of many Montana rivers unless aggressive steps were taken.

Healthy trout habitat in other parts of the state was being destroyed at an alarming rate as well. Along the Gallatin and Boulder Rivers, for example, the recurring problem with spruce budworms prompted the U.S. Forest Service to substantially increase their spraying of DDT on federally managed lands, without determining the effects it would have on local fisheries or entire ecosystems. The deadly pesticide drained directly into streams and rivers. Here was a federal agency responsible for protecting the forests, bumping headlong into a state agency tasked with protecting the state's valuable waterways. There seemed to be no common ground.

Again, when the chips were down, the Fish and Game Commission and the Department of Fish and Game joined forces with influential citizens groups and conservation organizations. This time, the Billings chapter of the Jaycees stepped forward. That powerful organization took sides with the commission and sponsored landmark legislation to protect Montana's rivers. Not long after, the Montana Wildlife Federation joined the coalition. Once again the state was poised for a bullish battle over natural resources.

Armed with strong grassroots support and a plethora of media contacts, the coalition lobbied legislators. As a result, in 1963 the legislature narrowly passed the Stream Protection Act.

This impressive legislation was the first of its kind in the nation, a sign of the increasing progressiveness of Montana's environmental movement. The new law mandated that federal and state agencies allow state biologists to review plans for any projects that could have an impact on state waterways. It was designed to expire in two years—plenty of time for the opposition to attempt to defeat it.

But in a replay of previous successes, state agencies and conservation groups generated a broad program of public education in support of the act. Again leading the effort was the state's conservation magazine, *Montana Wildlife*. The collaborative groups created an outstanding education campaign, and the law was renewed in 1965 by a large margin. The Stream Protection Act remains an important tool for protecting public waterways today.

With the new stream protection law tucked in their war chest, environmentalists once again turned their attention to the drone of diesel-powered earthmovers, which announced a flood of new highway construction throughout the state, many proposed along prized waterways. Fortunately, the law now required that federal and state agencies overseeing the heavy construction submit their design plans for approval. That advance biological review averted many stream channel alterations, rebanking, and vegetation removal, among other activities that would have had a detrimental impact on riverine environs.

The reviews were absolutely necessary. Well before the Stream Protection Act went into effect, state fisheries biologists had performed a study on a single section of road under construction in the Flint Creek drainage. The road's design called for removing a number of natural meanders along the creek, which greatly altered streamside vegetation and strata. Within the studied area, a staggering 95 percent trout mortality took place as a result of the construction—an ecological tragedy that might have been duplicated hundreds of times as the massive interstate highway project bulldozed through Montana.

Unfortunately, it would take another ten years before lawmakers required similar protective restrictions on work conducted in and around state waters by private landowners. But it finally happened, again following the concentrated, rigorous efforts of a dedicated sporting public, a growing conservation movement, and leaders in the Montana state legislature, such as Representative Hal Harper (D–Helena). The Natural Streambed and Land Preservation Act, known as the "310 Law," mandated biological review of all projects, even on private property, that might impact a public waterway. The review process fell under the jurisdiction of local soil and water conservation districts, with representatives from the Fish and Game as advisors.

As Montanans were settling some of the issues surrounding the health of our wild rivers and streams, the rest of the nation succeeded in finally getting the federal government to take a look at the valuable places from which many of the great rivers originated—the wildernesses in the Rocky Mountains.

A century earlier, Henry David Thoreau, lamenting the swift loss of untouched places, wrote in his journals, "I am the citizen whom I pity." His words expressed the all-too-real fact that we lose a critical part of our identity as Americans if untamed wilderness and silent places are annihilated.

In 1964, Congress passed the Wilderness Preservation Act, one of Montana's best allies. It is remarkable just how many of our admired streams and rivers originate in now-protected wilderness or national parks. In Montana, this includes the headwaters of the Madison, Big Hole, Yellowstone, Missouri, Flathead, Red Rock, and Boulder; the Belly, Bitterroot, St. Mary, Blackfoot, Swan, Sun, and Marias; and smaller waterways such as Rock Creek, Rattlesnake, La Marsh, Spotted Bear, and hundreds of other trout-rich streams and spawning tributaries.

This legislation was a crucial foundation for the long-term protection of Montana trout streams, as well as for our present efforts to restore valuable habitat for native cutthroat and bull trout.

PUT TO THE TEST ABOVE THE BLACKFOOT

Scientific data accumulated throughout the 1960s, continuing to inform decisions made by the Fish and Game Commission and the state legislature. But like two bighorn rams trying to establish dominance, the state agency and the factions of industry were positioned for a head-on collision.

Federal funds supported the systematic studies conducted by a team of young, outspoken biologists, who were, in turn, backed by the visionary management and proactive nature of the commission. The wildlife team held wide support from the general public, whose voter-activists further developed the growing conservation community in Montana. The strength of this partnership would be put to the test when it was catapulted into one of the darkest corners of the state's political arena—that smoke-filled space owned for almost a century by The Company (the

Anaconda Mining Company). It would prove to be the fight of the decade, staged on the headwaters of the Blackfoot River.

I am amazed when I look back on those rocky years, particularly because I can remember the very first time I saw the contentious words "Heddleston Mining District." They were written in blue ink on some of the small manila envelopes I worked with at the time.

I was attending the Montana College of Mineral Science and Technology in Butte, but to make ends meet I worked nights as a lab technician in the Anaconda Company's Geological Research Lab.

My job was to weigh and prepare for assay the thousands of samples that came to the lab from prospect properties scattered throughout Montana. I'd open each envelope and watch the drill sample's fine gray sand spill like dust from a shaman's pouch onto the brass scale in front of me. At the time, the names of the various prospect properties meant little to me. It would take me years to realize the ecological importance of many of those places—and the potential for destruction that lay inside those sample envelopes. In the case of the Heddleston Mining District, however, local newspaper articles about the happenings on the headwaters of the Blackfoot River significantly shortened my learning curve.

As early as 1866, the U.S. Congress had declared the West open for the precious metal exploration. Any rules regulating the eventual treatment of the land were left entirely up to each state.

During Montana's infancy, there simply were no rules. As a result, large sections of land and streambeds were severely scarred, in some places beyond repair. In an effort to establish some minimum guidelines—not environmental in nature, but aimed more at how individual miners worked with one another—President Ulysses S. Grant signed into law the General Mining Law of 1872. And this archaic law is still in effect today.

As a result of serious deficiencies in the mining law, as many as 557,000 abandoned, unclaimed mining sites are now spread throughout the West, the source of mine waste and water pollution of truly monstrous proportions. Montana contains more than twenty thousand abandoned mine sites, and may have a good many more. The Heddleston District holds the ominous distinction of being one of the worst in the entire Rocky Mountain West. Sadly, it still hovers today like a waiting executioner above the headwaters of the Blackfoot, a river made famous in Norman Maclean's book, *A River Runs Through It.*

The Heddleston District was made up of several old mining claims, which included shafts, adits, drifts, and tunnels already bored into the side of the Continental Divide in the area of Rogers Pass, southeast of Lincoln. It was first mined in 1898 when prospector Joseph Hartmiller stumbled off the Great Divide and wandered into the Beartrap Creek drainage. According to legend, Hartmiller was preparing breakfast over an open fire one September morning when a bear passed above his camp, causing his horses to "pitch a fit." In the commotion, one of the startled steeds kicked up a large chunk of quartz, which, in the eyes of a seasoned prospector, meant a potential booty.

Hartmiller named his claim the Mike Horse Mine, after the horse that had kicked up the first chunk of quartz. He burrowed several tunnels in the area, but never found a motherlode—the story of so many properties in Montana. After Hartmiller gave up on the mine, other owners took possession. Over the years, each new prospector poured money into searching for that elusive motherlode, and more tunnels went into the innards of the Divide. Significant groundwater halted some of the burrowing, but it was only a minor deterrent to most of the activity, because the water merely exited the tunnels and departed through the stream channels en route to the Blackfoot River.

The future cast of characters in the Heddleston District ranged from prospecting consortiums made up of private investors to large mining companies like American Smelting and Refining Company (ASARCO). Each new gambler tried its luck in the district and each left its own set of deep scars in the watershed.

For years biologists had been gravely concerned about the health and well-being of the Blackfoot River. Research revealed that groundwater coming from the old adits (nearly horizontal passages from the surface) was draining freely into the surrounding streams, carrying lethal levels of dissolved metals garnished from exposure to iron pyrite deep within the mines. This deadly soup, known as acid mine drainage, had been seeping into the river during the entire life of the mining district.

Additionally, the surrounding hillsides had been stripped of timber to support mining construction and feed the fires of steam-driven stamp mills and boilers.

The denuded hillsides caused an uncontrollable siltation problem in the river below, severely impacting cutthroat and bull trout. Road construction added to the silt and pollution, as did entire ravines filled to the brim with old mill tailings. On top of this amazing array of degradations, raw sewage from heavily populated mining camps in the area had been discharged directly into the headwaters of the Blackfoot. This destruction continued for a century.

Then, early one spring, the ominous hum of drill rigs filled the air, dispatched by the Anaconda Mining Company to explore the district. Their geologists smelled a deep copper deposit that had gone unnoticed by previous owners.

The Company drilled more than three hundred sites along the mountainsides, and shipped the results to their research lab for weighing, preparation, and assay. The crudely cut roadways and drill pads scraped in place to support the exploration were left as is.

When the results came back, the mining giant doled out another $1.2 million to purchase, lease, and otherwise control almost twenty-five square miles of adjacent property, nearly enough to develop an immense open pit mine on the headwaters of the Blackfoot River. The streets of the nearby logging town of Lincoln were abuzz with talk of good times and prosperity ahead: plenty of new jobs, a new hospital and school, and a new start at life.

The Anaconda Company had the technology and experience to unearth what geologists speculated were deep reserves of copper and molybdenum. It was, of course, a gamble, but the immense Berkeley Pit in Butte had taught The Company about excavating deep deposits and overburden disposal—and the historic weaknesses within mining law.

In 1966, The Company's preliminary Heddleston mining plan was considered complete. The state's permitting process, as sketchy as it was, had always been considered "a given" by the powerful mining company. As the final stages of planning swung into action, it looked very much like the Blackfoot's headwaters would soon languish amid settling ponds, tailings piles, diesel fumes, concentrators, and ore trucks.

But the very next year fate dealt the Blackfoot River a reprieve when the longest labor strike ever experienced in the Butte mines began. Plans for the Heddleston project ground to a halt, as did further geological analysis.

The industry-wide labor strike lingered for eight and a half months. Many copper mines, smelters, and refineries across the nation closed down, causing producers to curtail all expenditures not deemed essential to general maintenance. The long strike was very tough on the many mining families in Butte.

When work finally resumed, The Anaconda Company looked anxiously for any project that might turn a quick profit. They needed to bank some successes in order to keep nervous stockholders enthusiastic about the long-term gamble of metals mining in Montana. Heddleston wasn't a sure thing, but it was one of The Company's best options.

As winter snow began to accumulate on the banks of the Blackfoot River, word of the strike's settlement reached Lincoln. Once more, many residents talked excitedly of another boom.

In Butte, as miners returned to work and geologists and engineers shook the dust from the Heddleston plans, people realized they were operating in a totally different financial environment. So much had been lost during the long work stoppage that a new sense of urgency swept through The Company's halls. Decision-makers began to look at another project, this one located in the Stillwater Complex on the eastern flanks of the Beartooth Mountains. Ironically, it too involved a proposal to sink yet another mine into the headwaters of yet another major trout stream.

Eventually company profits started to stabilize, but then truly unsettling rumors surfaced. Years before, The Company had invested heavily in Chilean copper mining, speculating on its cheap labor and controllable costs. But politics were changing fast in Chile, and the building unrest could suddenly force The Company's holdings to be nationalized by an emerging government. If they lost their Chilean properties, the huge U.S. mining company would go on the ropes in a big way. Their only hope was to invest in new domestic properties like Heddleston and the Stillwater; they needed them to "prove up" in case they suddenly lost Chile.

So Anaconda announced its intent to start the Heddleston project in 1969, and for the first time publicly unfolded its final mining plan. The extent of the proposed disruption on the headwaters of the Blackfoot River shocked the public. Numerous water problems plagued the plan, entire gulches would eventually be clogged with waste dumps, and dangerous mill tailings were to be stored behind gigantic earthen dams of unproven strength or durability.

Quite a few "glitches" also lurked deeper in the plan, concerning estimated tonnage, grade, and mine life expectancy. One critical element, not even perceived as a possible problem by The Company, focused around a 680-acre piece of land then owned by the state of Montana. They needed an easement to use the land in order to proceed, but based on its past experience, getting an easement was nothing more than a bureaucratic formality. After all, there were hundreds of jobs at stake, with new taxes and new livelihoods for the residents of Lincoln. All it would take was a simple approval by the State Board of Land Commissioners.

Like a strict schoolmaster with ruler in hand, the Anaconda Company had always held a tight fist over most of state government. But they had not yet dealt with the new staff of state biologists, and did not anticipate the dramatic showdown that awaited them on the banks of the Blackfoot.

Almost as blind to the showdown ahead were the members of the Board of Land Commissioners, then under the direction of Ted Schwinden. The core mandate of the Land Board was that the best use of Montana's land, both then and into perpetuity, must be the determining factor for their decisions.

Strong river advocates opposed to the mining operation came together from all walks of Montana life, including the League of Women Voters, the National Wildlife Federation, Trout Unlimited, and the Sierra Club.

The Company controlled thousands of Montana jobs across the western half of the state and a formidable stable of supporting politicians who wielded strong influence over the appointed state boards. Tensions grew steadily until even the national media joined the frenzy. CBS News showed up when the Land Board held a public meeting to discuss the mine proposal. The media learned quickly that there was no better news story than a good western shootout centering around the life of a river.

The Montana Water Resources Board already had approved The Company's plan. This could have allowed the mine to proceed had it not been for the easement issue and the loud public outcry on behalf of the Blackfoot. The chief onus fell directly on the Land Board, and the pressure was tremendous. The board knew that the ruling would make front-page news across the West, probably accompanied by a face shot of Ted Schwinden, who had designs on the governorship of Montana.

They voted to allow the easement, but in an unprecedented move they mandated a number of special requirements designed to appease the negative public sentiment that had welled up against the project. One provision sent the mine planners into a tailspin. It required the miners to reclaim the land to fit its best beneficial use into the future—a nice way for the Land Commission to recognize its prime mandate under law.

This was a pivotal moment. A requirement to reclaim mined lands had never surfaced in Montana law, and the mining interests clearly recognized the important precedent it would set. The Company argued that the stipulation was unfair and added prohibitive costs to the project. Inflammatory editorials, pro and con, jammed state newspapers.

In the end, The Company was forced to back down, merely saying that senior geologists had taken a second look at the proposed plan and determined that their original tonnage estimates were way off the mark, and with the proposed reclamation costs the project simply was not feasible. Political upheaval continued to unfold in Chile, and less than five years after the end of the Heddleston debate, the Anaconda Mining Company showed up in "for sale" ads in Wall Street newspapers.

Astonishingly, in 1976 the dice switched hands and another gambler took a place at the table. The oil giant Atlantic Richfield Company (ARCO) made the Anaconda Mining Company a wholly owned subsidiary. Many of Montana's most complicated and costly pollution problems suddenly shifted into the files of the oil giant. This was one of the world's most costly wagers, one ARCO eventually would lose.

Metal mining in the mountains of the West always has been risky. The deep scars on our landscape remind us of past gambles taken. Thousands of abandoned mine sites, prospect tunnels, and adits now discharge acid mine drainage into once-pristine streams and rivers at alarming rates, marking some of the state's most serious environmental threats.

If the Heddleston plan had been approved in 1969, today we would have the remains of another abandoned open pit mine situated on the headwaters of another major trout stream, just like the one left behind on the headwaters of the Clark Fork River, now part of our nation's most expensive Superfund site.

A NEW POLITICAL MANDATE

Not only was the management of Montana fisheries evolving in a significant way through the 1970s, but dramatic change also was afoot in the political arena. By

1969 Congress had passed the National Environmental Policy Act (NEPA); Montana followed in 1971 with the Montana Environmental Policy Act, which protected the right of each resident to review and make comment on proposed resource management decisions, another big step forward for an already threatened environment.

On the heels of quickly rising public awareness about environmental issues statewide, Montana's electorate called for a complete review of the state's outdated constitution, written back in 1889.

Governor Forrest Anderson outlined the goals in frank terms when he addressed the Constitutional Convention's new delegates: "Each of you will leave a mark forever on the history of Montana. But more importantly, you have an opportunity to initiate a new history—a history of dynamic and responsive state government. Those who came before us changed a wilderness into a state. We have fought to lift this State up from its colonial status in the National economy. We are working to preserve our unequaled environment. We have undertaken many programs to improve our state and local governments. We are now beginning the task of revising our State Constitution.... I wish you well."

For the delegates to the 1972 Montana Constitutional Convention, the expectations of a waiting public rang loud and clear. Those who had made a profitable business from abusing Montana's natural environment were highly alarmed. By the time the forward-thinking, progressive new constitution was on the ballot for a final vote, it was clear that Montanans indeed were ready to answer Governor Anderson's challenge.

Not content to leave things at a minimum, the framers made another precedent-setting move when they actually recognized within the new constitution the right of Montana's citizens to live in a clean and healthful environment. The state was setting the pace nationally in terms of conservation.

The constitution handed a new set of tools to the people—important tools that were needed to reclaim a damaged environment. The list of legislative actions that followed the convention demonstrated a firm commitment by Montanans to support a new paradigm of environmental protection. It was a giant step on the road to changing a long legacy of industrial control over state government.

9

KING COAL WANTS THE YELLOWSTONE

First, the modern mind assumes an absolute separation between mind and nature, fact and value; second, nature therefore cannot in its own right be a locus of value, for humankind (mind) assigns all value.... Alternatively, Lord Man is extinct, since humankind (Human Finite) cannot live without even such elementary phenomena as sunlight and photosynthesis. In short, the human species is thermodynamically and biologically, and therefore inescapably, bound with natural process.

—MAX OELSCHLAEGER, *The Idea of Wilderness*

THE TIMES THEY ARE A-CHANGING

Montana has long been looked upon by the rest of the country as a treasure trove of natural resources. Even its moniker, the Treasure State, refers to the succession of natural riches that have been taken out: beaver pelts, gold, cattle, young soldiers for a couple of World Wars, hydroelectric power, copper, and silver.

One of the notions that defined the times was the misguided assertion of "use it or lose it," that Montana's water must be used to the fullest or be lost to down-stream consumers. No one really knew where this idea came from, but utility companies and agricultural interests looking to keep more water behind dams for power generation and irrigation and other natural resource developers, like coal companies at work in the Yellowstone River Basin, certainly stood to benefit from it. And they moved forward to take full advantage.

This new mantra swept across the West, and those who understood its true ramifications for Montana and her fish and wildlife began to speak out against it, including Montana's incumbent Director of Fish and Game, Frank Dunkle: "Most of the people passing the saying along don't have the vaguest idea what it means or what started it; it just sounds right. Somewhere in the back of their minds is a picture of millions of suntanned Arizonans and Californians with a thirsty gleam in their eyes, figuring out schemes to steal our water, every last drop of it.... With that kind of thinking, or lack of thinking, the vested interest groups have a pretty fertile atmosphere to foster their own plans—provided these plans look like they will 'keep Montana water in Montana.'

"There is no disputing the fact that the water-short parts of the country look with envy on the water-a-plenty places. The people that use this threat (use it or lose it) to their own vested advantage are doing Montana grave harm. The general public, if it gets duped into short-sighted solutions or, worse yet, if it does nothing, is guilty of worse harm.... The responsibility of Montana citizens is to find out what tune is being played by the band before they jump onto the wagon and also who is the conductor."

As concern rattled around the halls of state government, lawmakers looked at ways to further protect water resources. The Fish and Game Commission soon created a Water Resource Development Section within its agency. The move was designed to keep tabs on who would next try to lay claim to Montana's water.

The group had oversight of new projects proposed anywhere near a Montana waterway. From out of the ranks of middle management, fisheries biologist Jim Posewitz stepped forward to head the new section. Like other dedicated conservationists before him, he set a firm grip on the reins of leadership and held on for the ride of his life.

Right out of the chute the new Water Resource Development Section rammed headlong into proposed dams. Big dam projects meant thousands of short-term construction jobs for rural communities and new tax revenues for small, nearly broke, towns. During the 1930s, for example, an entire nation watched the world's largest earthen dam, Fort Peck, rise from the dust along the Missouri River, creating one of the West's most celebrated—albeit short-lived—booms.

More than thirty years later, dozens of rural communities down on their luck because of declining agriculture, logging, and backwoods mining turned their attention to the possibility of a new boom brought by constructing dams. The Army Corps of Engineers, U.S. Bureau of Reclamation, and private utilities moved in like a pack of carnival barkers and offered to impound local rivers and build new economies in dying one-horse towns.

At the same time that county commissioners and state representatives grew giddy over possible economic prosperity at the expense of free-flowing rivers, Posewitz and other biologists in Fish and Game continued to push the need for good strategic planning. They wanted plans for massive projects laid on the table long before anyone promised construction and the flow of federal money began to gush from the procurement spigot. However, some people grew a little edgy when talk of intervention by a group of fur-and-fish-hugging biologists started to circulate in their town.

The tone of the day is graphically represented in this 1965 article, "The Mighty Missouri: River That Was Finally Tamed," published in *U.S. News & World Report:* "Irrigation is counted on to bring stability to the region's agriculture, which has been subject to boom and bust because of the vagaries of the weather. Experience has shown that, wherever irrigation has been introduced, population stabilizes and new jobs are created in businesses serving farmers…. Up to now only 10 to 15 percent of the irrigation potential in the upper basin has been developed, according to officials of the Bureau of Reclamation…. Key Congressmen have felt that more revenue had to be derived from power generated at dams before irrigation projects could move ahead. A large part of the cost of irrigation works is paid for from power revenues…. Our economy is based almost 100 per cent on agriculture and 70 per cent is livestock…. With irrigation, we can raise the corn and other grain needed to fatten livestock…"

The new Water Resource Development Section had the authority to require engineers to build into their plans adequate protection for both aquatic habitat and fish populations, something most engineers and elected county officials viewed as simple interference.

The Corps of Engineers was so intent on getting its proposed projects approved by small-town elected officials and business owners that it worked "under the covers." The agency flew, at taxpayer expense, select rural community leaders on aerial tours of proposed construction sites. But at every tip of the wing, federal engineers bumped into the unrelenting questions pressed on them by the Water Resource Development Section team—questions requiring real data and biological studies.

On the drawing boards were huge projects like the High Cow Creek Dam proposed to cross the wild and scenic Missouri, and the Reichle Dam proposed on the Big Hole River. It became the passion of Jim Posewitz and his Water Resources Development Section team to get answers and protect Montana rivers.

Frank Dunkle penned an article in *Montana Outdoors* in 1967 that outlined the problems he foresaw: "Montana's use of water has always been considered in regard to agricultural benefits, or the water has been thought of as something to control for power or to prevent floods. Let's not forget the impact water can have on recreational development. A free-flowing stream in Montana in a few years may be as important to the state as any other given resource we can now consider."

In this article the director fairly accurately forecast the role our wild rivers would play in Montana's advancing tourist economy. However, he did some political tiptoeing as well. His comments continued, "When a water discussion arises, you should look at both sides and give serious consideration to the impacts of any so-called development or lack of development as well as what it can mean to us in Montana, before you make up your mind."

In a constant struggle to preserve precious riverine habitat, the Montana Fish and Game Commission approved plans for the State Recreational Waterway System. The 1965 proposal is clearly outlined in the commission's records and includes the concept that the system could eventually be employed to protect entire rivers, if authorized to do so by future legislation. The system's objectives included:

- Maintenance and improvement of Montana's prime streams, as free-flowing productive waters;

- Improvement of potentially important streams to prime condition so that they could eventually be considered for this system;

- To encourage and obtain multiple recreational uses through development and maintenance of the recreational features of waterways in the system. High quality fishing and outstanding scenic, historic, and scientific values are features to be especially considered in this regard.

A growing paradigm of preservation emerged with the passage of this legislation, a standard that mirrored what was happening elsewhere with the passage of the federal Wilderness Act. It appeared that the day might come when large sections of rivers could be set aside with at least a modicum of protection from dam development. The protected sections initially included parcels on the Flathead River above Flathead Lake and along the North and South Forks above Hungry Horse Reservoir. Also included was a significant stretch on the Yellowstone running from Yellowstone National Park downstream to Pompey's Pillar. Finally, it protected the Missouri River from Fort Benton eastward to the sluggish waters of Fort Peck Reservoir, a distance of 180 miles.

As Montana plowed forward into river issues, a monumental effort was afoot nationally, one first stimulated by Montana rivers and the premise of statutory protection. The idea of protecting rivers in their "wild" state was introduced by John and Frank Craighead, when the pioneering conservationist brothers were engaged in the struggle to stop the Spruce Park Dam proposed by the Army Corps of Engineers for the Middle Fork of the Flathead. The idea first was reported in a 1957 article by one of the Craigheads in *Montana Wildlife,* where the river advocate wrote of wild rivers like the Flathead as a "…species now close to extinction."

It took the Craigheads and a small army of others ten years to see the National Wild & Scenic Rivers Act passed in 1968. As the concept matured over the next fourteen years, the act was amended to state "…that certain rivers of the nation which, with their immediate environments, possess outstandingly remarkable scenic, recreation, geologic, fish and wildlife, historic, cultural or other similar values shall be preserved in free-flowing condition and that they and their immediate environments shall be protected for the benefit and enjoyment of present and future generations."

In the eyes of citizens spread from one corner of Montana to the other, indeed the times were a-changing. A new generation of environmental leaders had stepped forward, ready to continue the hard work done on behalf of the state's magnificent rivers. Unbeknownst to them, ahead waited perhaps one of Montana's greatest environmental challenges, led by the tycoons of large multinational corporations bent on having their way at any cost.

DAVID VERSUS GOLIATH

Buried under Montana's eastern plains, a large percentage of the nation's coal reserves remain untapped. These reserves create a serious challenge for the wild

Yellowstone River, though, simply because in order to convert hard coal to usable energy, water is needed—tremendous amounts of water. Some say more water would be needed than actually flows in the Yellowstone.

In 1969, Peabody Coal Company loaded its first shipment of Montana coal aboard a Northern Pacific train bound for a Minnesota-based utility. As the train rumbled through eastern Montana, the prospect of yet another boom era aroused the economic passions of the state.

Not long after, hundred-car-unit trains hauling tremendous loads of ten thousand tons or more rumbled daily through Montana, following the iron tracks anywhere a market for coal was found. They clacked and rattled alongside the Clark Fork, Missouri, and Yellowstone Rivers, passing fisheries biologists doing trout studies and collecting insect samples on the water below.

The lengthy trains and mechanical coal shovels—some the size of country churches—droned relentlessly. Even so, Montanans really didn't take seriously the likelihood of large-scale coal development. Sure, there was an oil crunch at the time, but few consumers linked oil with coal. That would not happen until the U.S. Bureau of Land Reclamation stepped forward with a plan to end all plans.

Before 1971, the federal agency had been talking with a number of large energy-producing businesses that had long before linked declining oil reserves to the vast coal reserves of Montana. Jointly, the Bureau of Reclamation and thirty-five private and public electrical power suppliers based in fourteen different states had prepared the North Central Power Study. Here were two thick volumes that would temporarily replace the *Holy Bible* as the selected reading in most small towns across eastern Montana. The proposal included the lengthy fine print familiar to big industry, plus all the bureaucratic muscle at the disposal of the federal government.

The magnitude of the development scheme was a bolt from the blue to the Montana populace. The new consortium proposed massive exploitation of coal and water resources across an astounding quarter of a million acres in adjacent regions of Montana, Wyoming, North Dakota, and South Dakota. The plan was conceived to ensure that fast-growing cities located hundreds of miles away would have a reliable power supply far into the future.

Forty-two mammoth coal-burning power plants were slated for construction.

Forty-two! Half of the giants would be built in Montana, and the rest nearby in the four-state area. Even more astonishing, energy experts calculated that power demand would double every ten years over the foreseeable future.

The proposed coal-burning complex would dwarf similar facilities already operating in the Southwest's Four Corners region, considered the world's leading cause of stationary pollution. An extensive web of transmission lines would leave each facility, head across the high plains, and climb over the Rocky Mountains before finally energizing bubbling hot tubs, street lights, and steel mills as far away as southern California.

Water is the critical lifeblood of conversion plants that are designed to turn coal into electrical power. In this case, that meant Yellowstone River water.

The North Central Power Study was unveiled the same year Governor Forrest Anderson chose to announce his Executive Reorganization Act of 1971. This legislation called for a substantial reduction in state government and, very interesting, much of the emphasis targeted the Montana Fish and Game Commission and the Department of Fish and Game. The realignment of power got under way with the removal of commission oversight of the department's operating budgets. Then they stripped the citizen group of the right to hire the department director, a responsibility the commission had held since its inception three-quarters of a century earlier. Just as things started to heat to a boil in eastern Montana, for the first time in the history of the state the director would become a political appointee, and the hunting and fishing license fees paid by Montana citizens would fall under his thumb.

Some who were close to the situation back then believe the shift in power came because of the growing authority of the Fish and Game and its staff of biologists, who had been influential in the denial of the Anaconda Company's Heddleston mining proposal. But all we'll ever know for sure is that the timing of the Executive Reorganization Act was highly suspicious.

Montanans were still trying to comprehend the North Central Power Study when a surprising second wave spilled off the federal planning boards. The 1972 Montana/Wyoming Aqueduct Proposal was an adjunct to the earlier power study. The proposal demonstrated how water from the Yellowstone River would be diverted for use in the planned conversion facilities. Dams, ditches, aqueducts, reservoirs, and cooling ponds the size of small lakes would be required to store and transport this water. An estimated 2.6 million acre-feet of the Yellowstone's water—one third of its annual flow—would have to be diverted or stored to meet the needs of the massive power complex. The entire water-transport system would originate at a new dam, to be built at the previously controversial Allenspur site near Livingston, its reservoir flooding the Paradise Valley. In addition, the black slush in a proposed new coal slurry pipeline would be carried by the once-clear waters of the Yellowstone River—the same water that had recently flowed from pristine headwaters in and around Yellowstone National Park.

The diverted water would be used for many purposes, such as turning mammoth steam turbines, cooling gasification plants, and trapping fly ash, all directly linked to producing the energy that was designed to leave Montana.

A CALL TO ACTION

After Montanans realized the scope of the proposed industrial development, discussions about water rights began to heat up across the state. What came out of the first wave of debate was probably an admission that most folks didn't know much about water law or, for that matter, the fine print contained in both the power study and the aqueduct proposal.

One of the more confusing topics in established water law was "beneficial use." As the debate continued over strip mining the eastern coalfields and draining the Yellowstone River, this nebulous term and its many inferences would become almost as commonly heard as the song of meadowlarks in summer.

One of the only requirements in the law stated that the water used had to be actually withdrawn from its source and, if possible, returned. The quality or quantity didn't matter much just as long as something grew from it or drank from it. Water law, similar to mining law, originated more than a century earlier in Montana, and it most often had to do with helping residents get along with one another while they exploited a resource. Back then, natural resources were viewed as infinite. Little consideration was given to protection or conservation. Any notion of maintaining "in-stream flow" to protect aquatic life, fish, and other wildlife would not come into play until decades later.

The industry's anticipated withdrawal of millions of acre-feet of water from the Yellowstone River focused the public's attention on the meaning of beneficial use.

For the first time in state history, front-page articles in newspapers and between the covers of national magazines dealt with the growing saga of majestic rivers, water rights, and energy sources.

Arnold Miller, president of the United Mine Workers of America, submitted one such article to *The Center* magazine, a publication of the Center for the Study of Democratic Institutions. Entitled "The Energy Crisis as a Coal Miner Sees It," it predicted a dire future for eastern Montana. Miller began his treatise on modern coal mining by quoting John Muir: "When we try to pick out anything by itself, we find it hitched to everything else in the universe." What the author found hitched to the exploitation of eastern Montana's coalfields was a batch of coal companies tightly tethered to giant oil companies.

Miller maintained that oil prices were allowed to increase only when the big companies wanted them to. Once the supply of oil dwindled, cost-efficient alternative sources of energy, such as coal, were made available to take the place of oil. The same companies owned both oil and coal, and could bounce the consuming public on a tight string while earning enormous profits from both sides of the loop. The process was simple to understand: Oil is hitched to gas, and both are hitched to coal. All were controlled by a very few companies, a cartel, of sorts.

The growing controversy also had to factor in the lives of eastern Montana ranchers. On this wind-blown prairie existed an entire way of life forged from living in harsh conditions and cultivated by generations who stayed on when others gave up. Unexpectedly, that ranching life was up for grabs and billions of tons of strippable coal could go to the highest bidder.

Most of Montana's coal rested under private land, so hand-to-mouth ranching families now had to contend with the massive multinational corporations. The major oil and coal companies bought, leased, or otherwise acquired much of the available land for a song, compared to the colossal profits that awaited the shovel. The representatives worked through subsidiaries and the off-shoots of subsidiaries, using whatever worked to talk a struggling rancher out of his family's land.

By the early 1970s the ownership of the countryside started to resemble a who's who in the oil and gas industry: Peabody, Shell Oil, Getty Oil, Exxon, Mobil Oil, Tenneco, Sun Oil, Chevron, Continental Oil, Westmoreland Coal, Consolidation Coal, and Gulf Mineral.

Of the approximately forty-eight billion tons of strippable coal pressed beneath the sedimentary layers of the Fort Union Formation, a massive chunk of it quickly appeared on the asset sheets of some of America's most powerful corporations—1.2 billion tons for one, 2.6 billion tons for another, and a whopping 8.7 billion tons for a third.

With all the grand plans for coal gasification, conversion, liquefying, dredging, piping, and pumping, the Yellowstone River would pay the heaviest price. To be expected, the Fish and Game Commission and their trained scientists were drawn into the debate. Biologist Jim Posewitz was perhaps the first to sum up the situation in lay terms, as quoted in *Business Week:* "He who controls the water controls the destiny of a place…"

Realizing the magnitude of the proposal, the state legislature enacted a three-year moratorium on major industrial water rights claims for withdrawals from the Yellowstone River. The moratorium temporarily stifled further development, allowing state regulatory agencies the time to catch up to the curve being dictated by industry and the federal government.

In addition to the new State Constitution, legislation like the Montana Utility Siting Act, the Montana Strip Mining Act and Reclamation Act, Strip Mined Coal Conservation Act, and the all-important Water Use Act also came from this era.

In a 1992 issue of the *Montana Farmer-Stockman,* Susan Higgins looked back on some of the details behind the creation of the important Water Use Act, and how the finished law balanced on a single idea. When energy companies filed to pull large quantities of water from the Yellowstone River and its tributaries in 1972, Gary Wicks, head of the Department of Natural Resources, appointed a five-member Water Advisory Council to review the status of water law and make a final report to the legislature. The Council recommended that a water-use permit system become law, similar to laws already adopted in other western states.

But as this didn't specifically address the large water-use filings by energy companies in the Yellowstone Basin, Wicks asked Ted Doney, Chief Legal Counsel and later Director of the Department of Natural Resources and Conservation, to draft a bill allowing individuals to acquire permits for in-stream flows. But the Council turned down this unconventional concept.

Doney then offered a revised bill that contained a provision for in-stream flow "water reservations" by public entities, which had originally been part of a failed bill from the late 1950s. This was critical because it allowed state agencies, conservation districts, and municipalities—and not individuals—the right to in-stream and consumptive-use reservations.

Had this work not been done, the Yellowstone River we enjoy today might have been lost forever. As it turned out, the 1973 Montana state legislature agreed with the foresight of Wicks and Doney and passed into law the Montana Water Use Act, which included the provision that allowed state agencies to apply for in-stream reservations on Montana rivers, expanding the definition of "beneficial use."

The law was enacted in the nick of time, as the Arab oil embargo gave the energy industry additional momentum. But standing in their way was the three-year Yellowstone moratorium, a united Montana populace and a squadron of protective lawmakers. For the first time since the enactment of the Murphy Rights, which allowed the state to file limited in-stream rights on certain sections of blue-ribbon streams, the new law meant that the needs of fish, wildlife, and aquatic life would be considered a beneficial use of the state's water.

Then another consideration surfaced: Montana didn't own all the water in the Yellowstone River. As a matter of fact, it owned less than half of the river's flow, according to a preexisting agreement ratified by Congress in 1951. The Yellowstone Compact focused on the notion that, because the headwaters of the Yellowstone River originate in Yellowstone National Park, Wyoming was entitled to 51 percent of the river's water. Montana owned 48 percent, and the remaining 1 percent went to North Dakota. Back when the compact was first signed, the subject of importance was, of course, irrigation for agriculture, and the states agreed to appropriate the Yellowstone River's water, by varying percent, at the mouth of each of its major tributaries: the Clarks Fork, Bighorn, Tongue, and Powder Rivers. As part of the compact, the signatory states agreed to honor preexisting water rights filed before 1950, but prohibited additional diversions from the basin without the approval of each signatory state's legislature.

As the Bureau of Reclamation proceeded with its plans to develop coal, it bumped into the Yellowstone Compact and the entirely different approaches taken by each state. Early in the debate, Wyoming campaigned for development, but the citizens of Montana were ready to fight over the loss of homeland and heritage. Montana lawmakers sought first to quantify the state's volume, then compare it to the historic flows of the Yellowstone.

The big river drains 68,000 square miles of rugged territory along its journey through Montana. That's better than one-third of the state. Using a sixty-six-year average, as reported commonly by most agencies in cubic feet per second (cfs), the river's average flow has been set at 3,717 cfs. (Its lowest flow was set in 1989 at a mere 540 cfs, compared to a high flow in 1974 of 36,300 cfs.)

Another measure of water is the acre-foot, the volume of water it would take to cover one acre a foot deep, which is about 325,853 gallons. In a normal year, the Yellowstone might carry 8.8 million acre-feet at Sidney (near the Montana/North Dakota state line), a U.S. Geological Survey figure generally relied on when folks talk about the true bounty of the Yellowstone. Its low flow could be as little as 4.2 million acre-feet, a figure long ago imprinted on the minds of water users across the basin during years of drought.

Impatient, Wyoming surged ahead by declaring that their share of the river constituted at least 2.4 million acre-feet, which accounted for about 27 percent of the "average" annual flow of 8.8 million acre-feet.

The part of the discussion that most bothered Montana biologists, conservationists, farmers, ranchers, and lawmakers was that the U.S. Geological Survey had estimated the Yellowstone's lowest annual flow to be only 4.2 million acre-feet. This figure was, no doubt, recorded during a drought, which comes and goes in Montana with dogged regularity. It became fairly obvious to anyone who had an eye on Montana's share of the Yellowstone River that a withdrawal of 2.6 million acre-feet, for the coal industry or for any reason, would leave only a trickle to be divided among historic users already on record in county courthouses throughout the basin.

The handwriting was on the wall. If Montana let the energy companies have their way, it could kiss its water supply on the Yellowstone goodbye, along with the fish, aquatic life, and wildlife that relied on the river for survival.

Weighing in on one side was the mounting energy alliance. On the other was everyone who loved the Yellowstone River and rural life in Montana. At the head of that pack stood Jim Posewitz, whose new business cards verified that he had just been promoted to the new position of Director of Environment and Information for the Montana Department of Fish and Game.

Today Jim Posewitz lives and works in downtown Helena within shouting distance of the offices of some of Montana's most respected and senior environmental organizations. He likes it that way. Because over his long career he has learned that when the chips are down, the more friends that you can gather behind you, the better your odds for survival.

One afternoon while sitting at his kitchen table, I asked Pos how it felt to go up against the world's most powerful energy companies. In his matter-of-fact style he answered, "I wasn't alone—if I had been, it would have scared me, but I looked around and saw many others willing to chip in, put their careers on the line. That made me feel as strong as a bull and I knew we just couldn't lose."

That first morning when Pos walked into his office and was told he had been promoted to the new Environment and Information Division, he had a good understanding of the "Environment" side of his new title, but he didn't yet know how powerful the "Information" would prove to be. The intense battle over the Yellowstone River would ultimately be waged in ink and pressed between the colorful layers of movie film.

"He who controls the water controls the destiny of a place" became the marching song of river advocates. If they couldn't gain control of it, the Yellowstone River's water would be taken elsewhere. It was just that simple. If they worked quickly, the three-year moratorium would provide the team of biologists enough time to inventory the natural assets of the Yellowstone and tell the public about the trout that would perish, the insect life that would be decimated, and the wildlife that would disappear once the water was gone. They needed to tell the story of migrating geese that returned to the islands in the river year after year to raise their broods, the saga of the beavers just returning from the brink of extinction brought on by trappers a hundred years before, and the rare sightings of the brilliant ivory plumage of trumpeter swans. The American white pelicans needed to be counted, along with the lime-green plants that would be lost if the river's water went to industrial ponds and pipelines of slurry.

But preparing an ecological profile of the Yellowstone and getting the word out was only a part of the equation. They also had to convince the rest of America that they were right about the river and somehow get people to stand up and take notice.

MAKING THE CASE FOR THE YELLOWSTONE

If I can say anything about Bill Schneider over the many years I have known him as a journalist, author, and publicist, it is that he has never been unwilling to speak his mind. Begging his indulgence, I would go as far as to say that he seems to get a sort of Machiavellian pleasure out of the frankness and power of his words, a style that would win for him a sizable and dedicated audience. Luckily for Posewitz and the biologists, Schneider occupied an office just down the hall. It was he and his staff who made up the "Information" arm of Jim's new division.

Schneider was the editor of the Fish and Game's magazine *Montana Outdoors.* And right off the bat he broke an important rule of journalism. He got very, very close to his subject, and wrote about proposed strip mining in eastern Montana as if he intended to expose the devil himself. It was he who first coined the title "King Coal," and he had the guts to stick with it in article after article even while a political debate boiled over all around him. Reading his articles back in the 1970s, I couldn't help but think he wrote like a man who had already lined up his next job and was a little anxious to move on. His frank style of reporting the changing events in Montana attracted repeat readers and, more important, other outdoor writers.

Drawn by the fortitude of Posewitz and Schneider, more strong activists surfaced. Filmmaker Craig Sharpe created *A Yellowstone Concerto,* a striking film celebrating the natural wonders of the Yellowstone River, its wildlife, scenic splendor, and abundant and healthy trout.

And suddenly the year was 1976 and the three-year Yellowstone moratorium was about to run out. Empowered by the Montana Water Use Act, biologists hurriedly finished their work, compiled data, and drafted an impressive document. One November morning, Fish and Game's water specialist, Liter Spence, donned his coat and departed his office, carrying under his arm the three-hundred-page instream Yellowstone reservation application. During his short walk between buildings, Spence carried with him a lynchpin of Montana's outdoor legacy. Win, lose, or draw, the Fish and Game employees had given it their best shot. He hand-delivered it to the Montana Board of Natural Resources and Conservation, whose job it was to allocate the water.

Fisheries managers requested 8.2 million acre-feet of flow on the Yellowstone. When asked about the considerable request, especially considering the whole Yellowstone recorded only 8.8 million acre-feet on an average year, Jim told me that he and his staff had simply acted on behalf of the fish, wildlife, and aquatic life on the river that could not speak for themselves. He felt certain they had to ask for 8.2 million acre-feet, just barely enough to ensure the river a bountiful future.

To gain some perspective on the issue, it helps to know that so many interests applied for so much water in those years that the Yellowstone River would have gone dry many times over had they all been granted.

The work facing the Montana Board of Natural Resources and Conservation was without question overwhelming, and the review process used to arrive at its important decisions would prove to be one of the most closely watched in the state's long history. They had to balance a seemingly tremendous economic opportunity with the life and future of the Yellowstone River.

Now that the applications had been received, the "word battle" over the river could begin, and many of the heaviest blows would be delivered from the pen of Bill Schneider. *Montana Outdoors* published a special edition stressing the value of the river and its surrounding ecosystem, designed to inspire statewide support for the agency's application while the Board of Natural Resources and Conservation was soliciting public comment.

At first, the word war was confined to Montana turf, but it wasn't long before national outdoor and environmental writers picked up on what Schneider was saying and the message started to reach a wider audience. One after another, Schneider's articles began showing up in national publications.

With the biologists defending their studies, Schneider at work behind his keyboard, and Posewitz making speeches to any group who would have him, the Board continued to gather public comment as the months went by and a decision loomed.

Just when the whole crew of embattled activists needed it most, a helping hand came from a surprising place. The call came one morning as Jim Posewitz sat behind his desk amid the clutter of spiral-bound reports and coffee-stained news articles. He answered the phone on what might have been the last ring, and heard the husky voice of a whiskey peddler, an executive representing a Louisville, Kentucky, outfit named Glenmore Distilleries. For the first few minutes of the conversation, Pos asked himself what possible interest the distiller of Kentucky spirits could have in Montana Fish and Game. He gathered that the call had come at the urging of Tom Pero of Trout Unlimited, who was out in the big world gathering support for the cause.

As it turned out, Glenmore Distilleries owned a subsidiary called Yellowstone Distillery, which had been engaged in making whisky for over a hundred years. The company's founder just happened to have been present the day Yellowstone National Park was dedicated. He was so taken by the raw beauty of the landscape that he had named his distillery after the place. Now the fellow on the other end of the line announced to Pos that his company was about introduce to an important new product, Yellowstone Mellow Mash, and they wanted to tie its introduction to the conservation effort taking place on the Yellowstone River.

With just a hint of reservation, Posewitz agreed to partner with a private enterprise that no one in state government could control. His only stipulation was that the company not exploit the situation on the river and, to ensure they didn't, he wanted to review the content of all material connected to the campaign. The agreement made, Pos hung up the phone and sat in amazement. A new savior had come to the aid of the river, planning to spend a whopping fifty thousand dollars to tie a nice tight bow around the ad campaigns. As an adjunct to their Yellowstone Mellow Mash marketing plans, the creative staff at Glenmore also intended to mount a national fundraising campaign to help in the fight.

John Bailey, son of famed Yellowstone defender Dan Bailey, happened to be in charge of a memorial fund created in the name of fishing great Joe Brooks. Here was the privately managed fund that could handle outside donations in the fundraising effort. In the first leg of the campaign more than ten thousand dollars flowed in, along with name support from river advocates from around the country.

Glenmore already had a well-designed ad strategy on the drawing board, created by Madison Avenue marketing wizards Rand Public Relations. Posewitz, Schneider, and a staff of sun-weathered biologists were suddenly backed by the world of big-time mass media.

Pos realized what Rand Public Relations could do for the battle over the river, but he also knew how such a move would sit with others in state government, especially those who liked to stay in control of things.

Posewitz's famous line "He who controls the water controls the place..." is just half of the full quotation. It continues, "...and that is not a role people are used to Fish and Game having." The Fish and Game Commission had been significantly throttled back by the 1971 Executive Reorganization Act, and its new politically appointed director was just a little uneasy with the momentum created by his own agency's partnership with the whiskey industry. Jim Posewitz understood that just as soon as he nodded his head to the distillery and its high-powered public relations firm, a much different political debate would take place. He and his staff were prepared to watch the sparks fly—and they knew they might get singed in the process.

In January, the marketing campaign for Yellowstone Mellow Mash came roaring out of the gate. Flyers picturing the threatened Yellowstone River were handed out by the thousands in liquor stores across the country, asking whiskey drinkers one and all to support the effort in Montana. The public relations firm next bought thirty copies of *A Yellowstone Concerto* and distributed them to key contacts; before long the beautiful Yellowstone River was flowing across American television screens.

The horse was out of the corral and on the loose, and not much could be done about it in Montana political circles. Rand then pulled yet another trick out of the bag when they invited a whole herd of nationally syndicated writers and photographers to the Yellowstone River, including *National Geographic Magazine, The New York Times,* and even *Penthouse* magazine. The journalists were taken on an aerial tour of the proposed "boiler room" and were then whisked off for a day of fishing. To fortify themselves, the guests were invited to enjoy a lavish breakfast at Chico Hot Springs, located in the heart of the Paradise Valley. Posewitz was an early presenter to the group that morning and spoke of the natural wonders of the river, its biological heritage, and all the work that had been done in an effort to save it. He was dressed in blue jeans like any seasoned trout fisher, and his piercing blue eyes reached deep into the audience as he told his story of Montanans working to preserve this natural treasure for future generations.

Waiting in the wings was the morning's keynote speaker, a familiar fellow who in the worst way wanted to be Montana's next governor, Ted Schwinden. The Fish and Game's huge water reservation application had Montana ranchers and farmers on edge, which had put their political representatives on edge, and they had long-time politicians like Lieutenant Governor Ted Schwinden soundly on point. Amid the symphony of clicking knives and forks, Schwinden delivered the only message he could that morning. He urged the visiting writers to look deeply into "all" the details of Montana energy development; "Seek out the other side" of the story, he pleaded. He also asked his listeners to remember that many interested parties had applied for water reservations and, as of that moment, none had been granted. He predicted that when the reservations were acted on, "probably nobody will come out happy."

Even before Schwinden's carefully chosen words about getting "the full story" had completely settled on the ears of his listeners, Jim Posewitz, Bill Schneider, and others passed out a list of the river's primary opponents. It read like the "ten most wanted" list stapled to the walls of environmental groups across America.

With Schwinden off to his next scheduled speech, Schneider and his colleagues hit the river with the national reporters and photographers. The high catch of the day was a respectable twenty fish, and newsstands coast to coast soon carried the dramatic story of the Yellowstone River, accompanied by full-color photos of its glory.

Not long after, the Montana Board of Natural Resources and Conservation announced the water reservations. Agriculture and ranching were granted their share, and 5.5 million acre-feet of in-stream flow went to the fish and wildlife of Montana. Left in the dust were the energy conglomerates.

Without the water to make it happen, their massive plans would never come to fruition. Jim Posewitz, Bill Schneider, John Bailey, Ted Doney, Gary Wicks, and many others involved in the Yellowstone battle had accomplished more than saving a river, they had etched a victory in the hearts of fellow Montanans.

THE FALLOUT

Ted Schwinden was only partially right when he predicted nobody would come out happy. The least happy of all just happened to be the Montana Chamber of Commerce, the city of Billings, and the Montana Power Company—some of the power brokers who would finally get Schwinden elected governor in 1981.

Posewitz's phone rang again one morning. But this time it was an invitation to visit the new governor.

Even though Pos left that meeting after hearing a promise he would be given other "meaningful work at a policy level," the Environment and Information Division was soon after broken up and its employees spread like a handful of goose down thrown to a strong wind. Jim went to one end of the bus and Bill Schneider to another, while everyone else who had had a hand in things ducked for cover.

But Jim's future was to be even brighter than his past. For the next ten years he refused to not make a difference when it came to his beloved Montana, and at one point he served as U.S. Co-Chair of the International Joint Commission Study Team to address a proposed coal mine on the North Fork of the Flathead River. The team did its work and the mine was never built. In 1993, Jim retired and took with him a wagon full of memories, mostly good.

When asked today what motivates him to continue working, both as the founder and executive director of Orion, the Hunter's Institute, and executive director of the Cinnabar Foundation, he answers in typical Pos style: "I just want to hit the end of my chain running, that's all."

10

WHAT THE HELL DO YOU MEAN YOU'RE NOT STOCKING TROUT ANYMORE?

We have got it backwards. Life has the power to destroy us, and to do so with our connivance, using our own misaligned means and purposes. A few degrees of climate change, a few more inches of topsoil lost, and our descendants may read the record for themselves.... Is it destined to be law with us, an iron and withering rule, that anything that cannot be tamed, dominated and put to use, shall die?

—JOHN HAINES, *"Shadows and Vistas"*

When we look through the rearview mirror and consider all the profit-driven schemes that have been promoted in Montana over the years, it is amazing that we've sidestepped so many. Montanans have managed to save their resources from proposals to start mining operations on the headwaters of the Flathead River, the Blackfoot River, the Stillwater, and Rock Creek; killed plans to mine any more gold using cyanide; deflected proposed dams on the Swan River, at Kootenai River Falls, and on other important rivers; and thwarted King Coal's efforts to dewater the Yellowstone River. Yet throughout the 1970s, other environmental issues continued to sprout up throughout the state. There were interstate highways to be built, railroads to satisfy, farmers and ranchers to please, tourists to entice, jobs to create, dams being proposed, and a new economy to build.

Meanwhile, a new type of drama was playing out on another of Montana's premier rivers.

As early as the 1950s, various fisheries biologists had toyed with the concept that continuing to plant hatchery trout in our rivers and streams actually did more harm than good. But they had never possessed the technology or data to back it up.

Every river has a limited of amount of energy it can produce in the form of food for aquatic life. Pollution, siltation, increased water temperature, and dewatering by irrigation or drought all play significant roles as trout species compete with one another for available food. In lay terms, the equation is: More competition requires more expenditure of physical energy, leading to less growth. Older and larger trout, especially wild rainbows, browns, and cutthroats, simply cannot compete as effectively with younger, more aggressive feeders like stocked trout.

This idea plagued biologists for years, but they could not prove it right or wrong. A more basic question might have been whether our rivers were healthy enough to sustain a population of wild trout. Or was Montana simply another western state firmly tied to the chum-line of "put and take" trout fisheries? It was time to find out.

Many trout fishers of the day felt that we really didn't need to understand the complex cycle that occurred when trout were planted, as long as we had fish to catch. After all, the stocking process had been the backbone of good trout fishing for three-quarters of a century.

When electro-shocking technology became usable on larger rivers, the means suddenly existed to test the lingering hypothesis that introducing hatchery trout increased competition among all species within ecosystems already subject to a finite food system.

The issue actually had as much to do with the declining presence of trophy trout as it did with sheer numbers. As more anglers proved their skills on Montana rivers, the general observation was that there were fewer large trout of any species, with native cutthroat all but absent. The "good old days" when Charlie Cook landed his eleven-and-a-quarter pounder on the Big Hole seemed to have slipped into the past.

I was twenty-five years old when I first heard the scuttlebutt about stocking and fisheries studies, and I have to admit that I was sold on the easy take already available on my favorite waterways, like the Red Rock, Big Hole, and Boulder rivers and Rock Creek. Of course, I had not lived through the glory days of wild trophy fish about which fly fisher George Grant and others talked.

While the fisheries biologists entertained each other with visions of beefy, slab-sided rainbow and brown trout coexisting with a thriving population of trophy-size natives, Art Whitney sat behind the manager's desk in the state Fisheries Division. One morning in the early 1970s, Whitney reviewed his appointment list for the day and saw the name of an enthusiastic research biologist, Dick Vincent, who wanted to talk about planted trout on the Madison River, one of Montana's finest and most popular fisheries.

Vincent arrived at the appointed hour and proposed a study on the Madison to test the stocking theory once and for all. As he outlined his research plans for studying two independent sections on the river—one stocked and one not—thoughts of anglers old and young working to perfect a hangman's noose wound through Whitney's head. He had been around longer than Dick; he knew that well over half of Montana's anglers were satisfied with the way things were. The decision to actually test the ramifications of stocking would be a courageous one. Generations had watched hatchery trucks back up to rivers, followed by anglers reeling in seven-inch trout, one after another. Adding further weight was the fact that Montana was beginning to attract thousands of nonresident anglers; a whole industry was fast building around fishing on the state's rivers.

Why upset the applecart? As Whitney contemplated the proposal, Vincent recited reasons why the Madison population study should be funded. When he came to the argument that "it makes perfect biological sense," Art Whitney, a biologist himself, nodded in agreement.

Talk of the pending study oozed through the town of Ennis like a plague. It didn't take long before rumors spread to the Bighorn, Yellowstone, Flathead, and Big Hole. On one side were those who felt our rivers already provided the type of trout that pleased the general public. On the other side were those who felt our fisheries could become healthier and more bountiful and, in the end, produce wild trout—trout that had a chance to grow to maximum size and age.

As time went on, indignant talk of the renegade study on the Madison died down. Through a couple of hot, dry summers on the river, the biologists stunned trout and compared the sections of river. On the water-soaked pages of log books, they quietly scribbled their notes day after day, and handed in numbers and observations for compilation and analysis.

Despite some initial resistance to even considering the idea of not stocking fish, the lure of possible trophy-sized trout had seeped into the minds of most locals. If some biologist with an armful of papers could make that happen, perhaps he might be worth listening to. Trout numbers had remained high on the Madison, but practically everyone who owned a drift boat or had staked claim on a certain acre of the Madison agreed that fewer big trout were taken every year.

When all the results were in and analyzed, Dick Vincent set up another meeting with Art Whitney: he had irrefutable scientific proof that stocking trout on the Madison caused too much competition.

I imagine that Whitney's final question to the young biologist was about who would make the inflammatory announcement to anglers in Ennis. It turned out to be Dick Vincent.

"What the hell do you guys mean you're not going to stock trout on the Madison anymore?" was pretty much the gist of the question-and-answer session after Vincent finished his first presentation. Some folks wanted more assurance that what he was saying was correct and a few others believed him outright, but the vast majority called for his immediate and orderly administrative lynching. It would be weeks, even months, before tempers cooled.

The simple fact revealed by the multiyear research project was that increasing the trout population with planted fish meant increased competition. It was particularly clear that increasing the population during summer, the peak feeding season, achieved nothing more than to divide an already-limited food source among too many mouths.

It all made perfect sense from a biological perspective. From an infuriated put-and-take trout fisher's point of view, however, it would take years of convincing.

Around the same time Vincent appeared in Ennis, Art Whitney showed up for the scheduled Fish and Game Commission meeting. There he made the same announcement: He and his staff of biologists had determined that stocking trout on Montana rivers was a problem.

The commissioners, many fly fishers themselves, greeted his words with much the same reaction that Vincent got in Ennis. Whitney handed out the data, and a charged debate began. In a taped interview a few years before his death, Whitney recalled that commission meeting, describing one commissioner in particular who was particularly outraged. But Whitney stood firmly behind the science of the

Madison River study, and his momentous decision to stop stocking trout on all Montana rivers that had the natural capacity to generate and sustain wild trout.

The questioning commissioner said frankly that if it turned out Whitney was wrong, it could mean his job. Whitney responded that if it was a bad decision, he would quit his job—and he meant what he said.

It took only a couple of years before the "big ones" started coming back. Fish numbers also continued to grow until, at last, they stabilized. Wild trout once more ruled the rivers of Montana. As a bonus, the stock of native cutthroats steadily improved on some rivers, as the frenzy of competition among more aggressive species diminished.

In 1974, when the state stopped planting fish in streams and rivers able to sustain populations of wild trout, the hatchery program simply shifted in another direction and began stocking trout in remote mountain lakes, ponds, and recreational reservoirs. The hatcheries remained busy and fishing steadily improved in many places never before stocked.

More than thirty years have passed since Dick Vincent bravely spoke at that meeting in Ennis. He and Art Whitney had predicted that fishing not only would get better, it would become more challenging and more sporting, and eventually bigger trout would come back—and they were right on all counts. Today, Montana's wild trout continue to hold their own, even against the menacing effects of drought familiar to semi-arid regions like Montana.

II

THE FIGHT GOES ON

}

Ability to see the cultural value in wilderness boils down, in the last analysis, to a question of intellectual humility. The shallow-minded modern who has lost his rootage in the land assumes that he has already discovered what is important; it is such who prate of empires, political or economic, that will last a thousand years.

—ALDO LEOPOLD, *A Sand County Almanac*

HEADWATERS THREATENED AGAIN

In the early 1980s, coal development again reared its head. This time, however, the challenge came from across Montana's northern border. Plans for an open pit coal mine on the North Fork of the Flathead River in British Columbia ultimately prompted an intense biological study. The wastewater coming from the proposed mining operation would have a tremendous impact on the North Fork and could ultimately end up in Flathead Lake.

The North Fork of the Flathead is one of Montana's most fragile riverine ecosystems, the result of receiving low-nutrient water from tributaries that emanate from extremely mountainous terrain in Glacier National Park. Throughout its history, the North Fork has been known as a vulnerable system, albeit an extremely important spawning tributary for several species, including westslope cutthroat trout and bull trout.

The baseline environmental study was funded by the U.S. Environmental Protection Agency and completed in 1983. The work was designed to define the impacts of mining, logging, and oil and gas development on the North Fork, and to identify what effects these activities would bring to the river's native species.

With the study results in hand, Montana fisheries biologists determined that 10 percent of the spawning bull trout on the North Fork would be directly impacted by the mine alone, a revelation that brought an unusually positive reaction from across the border.

In 1984, the government of British Columbia did indeed grant tentative approval for the mine. In response to concerns raised by U.S. biologists and supported by a pack of Montana citizens, however, the Canadian government requested that the developer prepare and submit additional information to support its claim that the mine would have little, if any, impact on the fragile river below.

The government's challenge was unusual for Canada, and the coal venture was tentatively tabled because the mining company never responded. But relentlessly over the next two decades, various Canadian mining companies have renewed proposals to mine right across the border. Today, the purity of the North Fork of the Flathead still hangs by a thread.

Fortunately for the river, this situation remains on the radar screen of Montana's U.S. Senator Max Baucus who has, over the years, led his share of citizen groups to the international border to argue against mining, drilling, and development on the Flathead.

BALANCING DROUGHT AND IRRIGATION

Following one of nature's most reliable cycles, the 1980s witnessed the harsh effects of drought. Each new wave of hot weather, remaining for years at a time, took a devastating toll on rivers, fish, and aquatic life. Several times over the decade, smaller Montana rivers went utterly dry, and larger ones were dewatered to a trickle.

As has always been the case on the settled plains, the longstanding tug-of-war for water escalated. Irrigators facing crop loss dried up entire impoundments like the Ruby Reservoir and, as a result, twice during the decade caused destructive purges of silt to invade the Ruby River. Trout, insects, waterfowl, and streamside vegetation suffered immense damage. Hay crops barely hung on in adjacent fields.

Trout streams like the Big Hole, Jefferson, and Beaverhead were reduced to their lowest levels as the age-old disputes between water users, biologists, and sportsmen flared to new heights. In the years 1985 and 1987, significant fish kills occurred in Montana. Even though the 1969 legislature had granted Fish and Game in-stream water rights through "Murphy Rights" on certain sections of the state's blue-ribbon trout streams, fish on unprotected sections throughout the state continued to suffer enormously as dewatering for agriculture continued unchecked. (The Murphy Rights, named after the bill's principal sponsor, James Murphy of Kalispell, carried the stipulation that the water rights were to be respected until a district court determined that the protected water was needed for a "more" beneficial use.)

Meanwhile, thousands of trout continued to perish in irrigation ditches statewide for lack of the simple barriers that had been advocated for decades by Fish, Wildlife & Parks.

In 1988 the Montana Department of Natural Resources and Conservation continued to work through its Drought Advisory Committee in an effort to make sense out of the demand for water during times of drought. They eventually produced a Drought Contingency Plan that outlined the department's strategic and management role during dry years. It was a much needed step in tackling this endlessly divisive issue.

In the future, if we are to nurture both agriculture and trout fishing as important engines for our state's economy, we must work out serious compromises. The 1980s saw some of the first legitimate steps taken in that direction.

RESTORING NATIVE SPECIES
Grayling

From the late 1970s through the 1980s, Montanans started to pay more attention to threatened and endangered species indigenous to the state. The ecology and habitat of Arctic grayling and bull trout were immediately drawn into sharper focus.

Historically, grayling were plentiful in many of our rivers. They were at one time considered to be a subspecies, called Montana grayling. As biological science inched forward, genetic assessment determined that the grayling occupying rivers under the Big Sky were actually an identical match to those found in similar environs as far north as the Arctic; hence, today's name Arctic grayling.

The ancient migration of early grayling from their original home in the north to the dancing rivers of Montana is a remarkable story. Experts believe these beautiful fish, each adorned with a sail-like dorsal fin, originally arrived in Montana as eggs encased in Ice Age glaciers.

Grayling require a special type of habitat and ecological purity in order to survive. They did quite well in many Montana rivers until industrialization and development brought pollution. Sadly, today the last indigenous native stock hangs on only in the waters of the Big Hole—a river itself threatened each year by irrigation dewatering, as well as by years of streambed alterations.

In the early 1980s, the grayling's imminent survival was not jeopardized by lack of water in the Big Hole. Ironically, the real problem started over *too much* water. The spring of 1984 was extremely wet, and runoff swept in torrents down the Big Hole River. The huge flush initially stressed the river's ecosystem, and the long, dry summer that followed played havoc with the grayling and other species. Fisheries biologists organized the Fluvial Arctic Grayling Workgroup, including representatives from Trout Unlimited, The Nature Conservancy, U.S. Fish and Wildlife Service, Bureau of Land Management, U.S. Forest Service, and the renamed Montana Department of Fish, Wildlife & Parks.

The group recognized the significant problem on the Big Hole. They also looked to other rivers that might have appropriate habitat to help rebuild the threatened grayling population. By planting new trial populations in other rivers the group felt it was conceivable that the primary focus for survival could be taken off the Big Hole.

As a result, they developed a recovery plan and identified funding to help the Arctic grayling recover across its native range in Montana. A primary piece of the puzzle was the formation of the Arctic Grayling Recovery Program, a grassroots, nonprofit, fundraising group dedicated to restoring this wonderful part of Montana's wild heritage.

As the 1990s got under way, so did a grassroots drive to collect names on petitions to list the Arctic grayling as Endangered under the Endangered Species Act. This organized effort caught the attention of ranchers on the Big Hole River. If listed, the remaining grayling could have brought an entirely new set of management regulations to the valley, particularly when drought gripped the river.

By 1994, locals formed the Big Hole Watershed Committee in an attempt to protect minimum flows. The committee created a new paradigm for working together, including drilling wells to water stock instead of removing river water. And they participated in grant-funded watershed studies designed to explore new irrigation alternatives. The proposed listing of the Arctic grayling pushed the agricultural community against the wall and their response was admirable. In the end, their tactics perpetuated increased stability for grayling populations.

Bull Trout

For decades, the native bull trout had been considered a nuisance to anglers in Montana. "It is especially desirable that the Dolly Varden trout (called also 'bull trout,' 'salmon trout' and 'char'), should be taken at any time and by any means because it is a cannibal fish, and eats all varieties of other fish, and is very destructive to fish life…" noted the Game and Fish Commission's biennial report of 1912. When caught, the predatory giant was generally thrown in the bushes, treated much the same as today's native mountain whitefish. And fisheries managers actively suppressed bull trout in many Montana streams, rivers, and lakes. The trout's bad reputation probably came from its proclivity for feeding on trout species favored by human fish-eaters, including the smorgasbord of planted hatchery trout.

The plight of the bull trout has been made even dicier by the reality that the pristine cold-water habitat needed for its survival is incessantly impacted by logging, mining, and backcountry road development. These intrusions are increasingly common in mountainous areas where spawning tributaries are located. Migratory habitat loss is not exclusive to upper watersheds or smaller spawning tributaries. The vital connection between the bull trout's remote spawning grounds and its downstream rearing grounds, generally located in larger rivers, is crucial for the survival of the species. Unless the trout has access to clear mountain creeks that are unsilted and unblocked by human development, as well as unspoiled habitat in larger rivers, its future in Montana remains in serious jeopardy.

Open access is hard to achieve in mountainous regions marred by man-made obstructions. On many waterways, dams or diversions still block the upstream migration routes so vital to native trout. In a 2006 article entitled "Logging-for-Watershed-Restoration Paradigm Disingenuous, Ineffective," the Montana-based environmental watchdog Wild West Institute reported, "The watershed restoration needs here in the Northern Rockies are immense, with Forest Service estimates indicating that nearly 85% of the fish-passage culverts in our region are currently impassible to fish coupled with a road maintenance backlog of over $1.3 billion on 67,000 miles of roads that crisscross our forests and watersheds."

In 1986, Montana Fish, Wildlife & Parks listed the bull trout as a "Species of Special Concern," which led to a bull trout recovery plan some years later.

By 1992, steadily rising concerns over the declining bull trout population prompted closure of all Montana streams to harvest of the struggling trout. A year later, Governor Marc Racicot convened a roundtable to devise a plan to protect existing populations and study the immediate and long-term prospects for bull trout. The governor's conclave eventually formed a Restoration Team that studied twelve major drainages in which the threatened species had once existed in western Montana. At the end of the day, however, after all the studies were in place, the exchange of information complete, and support was on the rise for listing bull trout on the Endangered Species List, the same governor who had convened the round-table refused to support the listing.

Despite such confusing signals from shortsighted leaders, in 1998 the bull trout finally was listed as Threatened throughout the Columbia River Basin, which led to special efforts to protect it from further ruin. Only time will tell if these meas-ures will be enough to bring populations of this native species back to healthy levels.

CONSTANT VIGILANCE

As the final years of the 1990s melted away, some good things were happening on Montana rivers at the grassroots level. The increased activity showed up as better trout fishing, cleaner water, and increased attention to the needs of threatened species like the native cutthroat. Hydroelectric mitigation funds started to trickle into the state, and watershed projects and biological studies began to come to fruition. New watershed groups and committees organizing on rivers throughout the state began to deal with local problems such as the loss of streamside vegeta-tion, tributary decimation, and loss of spawning habitat. "Restoration" became the watchword of trout fishers and conservationists throughout Montana.

Yet there was still much to do to ensure the long-term health of our fisheries.

Continuing gridlock remained between important groups such as sportsmen and ranchers. It continued to reveal itself in one of Montana's longest-running wildlife disputes: the mass killing of fish in unscreened irrigation ditches.

Even as we moved toward the twenty-first century, despite all the fine advances in biology and fisheries management, and despite having passed complex laws to protect river resources and initiate restoration programs, thousands of wild trout were still being trapped and suffocated each year in privately owned irrigation ditches. And it seemed that nothing could change this thoughtless practice.

Juxtaposed dramatically against this sad loss of trout at the hands of agriculture was the willingness of the 1989 Montana legislature to pass the River Restoration Act, which allowed fifty cents to be set aside from the purchase of each resident fishing license and twice that amount from nonresident licenses to stimulate streamside restoration. Montana's Future Fisheries Program was created and monies were earmarked for habitat restoration projects on the state's watersheds. Not only did the Act recognize quickly changing riverine habitats, it conceded that well-managed trout waters and trout fishing were key components of a fast-changing Montana economy.

In the first year the fund grew to more than one hundred thousand dollars, and the projects began. By the start of the twenty-first century, 191 habitat projects had been completed for a total expenditure of $3.8 million.

An excited citizen's advisory group worked hand in hand with the Future Fisheries Program, doling out funds for new restoration projects that would help save and improve threatened habitat. Again the "yin and yang" of Montana politics acted out its seemingly eternal drama. On one hand, we continued to allow trout to be lost in poorly managed irrigation systems, while on the other, resident and nonresident license holders were asked to pony up to save precious riparian habitat. Despite all the advances over the years of hard conservation work, some things in Montana never change.

As the new century began, conservation groups like Trout Unlimited worked to address the serious issue of in-stream flow and dewatering on Montana rivers and streams; more and more water leases were signed to offset the injurious effects of drought. Local groups also flexed their muscles in the arena of conservation politics, much as the old rod and gun clubs had during the early part of the previous century. People who had never before been active in politics stepped forward as important river issues surfaced. Special regulations and a new catch-and-release ethic kept millions of trout in the rivers each year.

We had come full circle in Montana, from Lewis & Clark's record of remarkable abundance to an era when trout were scarce in our rivers to a time of superb fishing. We got here via meaningful management, protective regulations, public involvement, and powerful laws. The fingerprints of Montana's most noteworthy conservationists are evident in all of this. Some made their stand in the spotlight; many more remained in the background, unnamed but certainly not unfelt. Tens of thousands were content to share in the victory merely by being here, loving Montana, and savoring her rivers.

12

SONG OF TWO RIVERS

Environmentalism, like Romanticism, constitutes a defence of value. I am now asserting an even more fundamental role, the defence of meaning. We call people environmentalists because what they are finally moved to defend is what we call environment. But, at bottom, their action is a defence of cosmos, not scenery. Ironically, the very entity they defend—environment—is itself an offspring of the nihilistic behemoth they challenge. It is the manifestation of the way we view [and speak of] the world.

—NEIL EVERNDEN, *The Natural Alien: Humankind and Environment*

A massive table-shaped ridge rises at the far southeastern tip of Yellowstone National Park, rightfully named "Two Ocean Plateau" by early explorers. The secluded rim is surrounded by a special sense of solitude, for here is a setting as primitive and wild as any remaining in the West. To take a trip to this sacred place of beginning requires planning, and an equal helping of backwoods savvy.

Runoff from the west side of the plateau collects in puddles and rock-lined tarns before it begins the long journey to the Pacific Ocean via the Snake River and then the Columbia. Snowmelt tumbling off the east side joins a labyrinthine tangle of ever-growing rivulets, brooks, creeks, and streams that eventually become the headwaters of the Yellowstone River, ultimately draining into the Atlantic Ocean.

Not only is the Yellowstone headwaters region rugged and remote and pristine, it is the ancestral home of two of the West's most seriously threatened species. The smaller of the two is the Yellowstone cutthroat trout (*Oncorhynchus clarki bouvieri*), a fish with prehistoric qualities. The other is the often feared grizzly bear (*Ursus arctos*). Both of these animals serve as indicator species, telling us much about the fragile health of isolated regions. They also tell us about our willingness to act as stewards of our planet.

After flowing through its twisting headwaters maze, the Yellowstone River leaves the backcountry to mix with the massive waters of Yellowstone Lake. Here, the pure stock of native cutthroat trout, so prolific in the upper tributaries, are thrown into a hodgepodge of nonnative trout descended from stock that was planted by hatchery workers driving horse-drawn wagons. In the early days, trout were looked upon as a food source so plentiful their supply would simply never run out. When the fish, inevitably, did diminish throughout the park, the federal hatchery in Bozeman answered the call with nonnative species like rainbow and lake trout.

Immediately below the lake, the Yellowstone River ambles along gently like a huge spring creek. Its glassy surface is smooth and still, oftentimes topped by a cloud of insect hatches: mayflies, stoneflies, and caddis, along with a variety of terrestrials. Here the Yellowstone is not only a piece of fly-fishing heaven, it nourishes and provides the breeding and nesting habitat for river otters, mink, beavers, pine martens, elk, deer, black bears, and thankfully, grizzlies. Daily the slow-moving water comes alive with cackling geese followed by their broods, ducks brightly painted with gaudy plumage, predatory blue herons, and the distinctive trumpeter swans.

Framing the banks of the upper Yellowstone River, willows, aspens, and cottonwoods play host to the clatter of yellow warblers, western tanagers, pine grosbeaks, and clay-colored sparrows. In spring and summer, elk calves, deer fawns, and bear cubs hide in the thigh-deep grass.

The river gains volume as it drops from the mountains, picking up tributaries that splash from magical places like Elephant Back Mountain and the Hayden Valley. It continues to push northward, all the time building girth until, in what seems a purposeful act of euphoria, it plummets over two of the world's most amazing waterfalls. The first free dive covers 108 feet. Minutes later, the river plunges another 308 feet, far more than the renowned Niagara Falls. These two falls set the stage for the spectacular Grand Canyon of the Yellowstone below.

This canyon and its waterfalls were featured in the landscape paintings of early artist-explorer Thomas Moran. His portrayal of the canyon's magnificent beauty helped lawmakers decide to set the area aside as the nation's first national park.

Below the whitewater gorge, the river relaxes and is joined by the graceful cascade of Tower Falls, a more feathery drop than the mighty falls upriver, and then the Lamar River flows in from the high mountain valley where, in 1995, wolves first were reintroduced back to the wilds of Yellowstone.

Beyond the park's boundary, the river enters a dramatically different environment. From Gardiner north to Livingston, the river is closely paralleled by US 89 for a good part of its route. The river carves Yankee Jim Canyon and then pushes out into the Paradise Valley, a broad open vale caught between the steep, soaring Absaroka Mountains and the smooth, rolling foothills of the Gallatin Range. Here the river is bestowed the prestigious status of "blue-ribbon" trout water as it flows across an ancient floodplain adorned by tall stands of cottonwoods.

The Paradise Valley is home to a remarkable number of wildlife species, ranging from sandhill cranes stopping over during their migration north to resident waterfowl and indigenous birds of prey like golden eagles, great horned owls, red-tailed hawks, and American kestrels. In addition, upland birds such as sharp-tailed and blue grouse and Hungarian partridge live in the meadows among mammals like elk, deer, moose, pronghorn antelope, and bighorn sheep.

The valley is also home to families who have ranched here for three, four, and five generations. Several of those families have nurtured and protected the world-renowned spring creeks that originate in the rolling foothills and soft ridges edging the riverbottom. By some accounts, this water has been collecting in underground aquifers for hundreds of years.

The old railroad town of Livingston is situated where the Yellowstone swings in a rounded arc and heads east toward the high plains. Below that bend, the Yellowstone becomes a prairie river guarded by sandstone bluffs and sage-scented, deeply fluted coulees. It is soon joined by the Shields River, which courses through an agrarian bottomland shadowed by the Crazy Mountains.

The river here still teems with wild trout—rainbow, brown, and some Yellowstone cutthroats—sided by a population of mountain whitefish that outnumbers trout in some places by ten or more to one. Some years ago the Yellowstone cutthroat was considered a rarity on the river's middle section, but after decades of conservation and close management, the trout are more plentiful today.

As it continues to meander eastward, the river slows and its temperature gradually rises. After carving a deep furrow through layer after layer of the sedimentary strata that covers the badlands and plains of eastern Montana, our nation's longest free-flowing river finally reaches its confluence with the Missouri River just across the state line in North Dakota.

～⌒～

Another Montana river, similar to the Yellowstone in physical girth and geographic origin, has not been so lucky. The Clark Fork of the Columbia's headwaters begin as a trickle on the flanks of the Continental Divide, just outside the so-called "richest hill on earth." The valley surrounding Silver Bow Creek, a key tributary of the Clark Fork, has been a mining center since the 1880s. And this mining continues today, as huge trucks further penetrate the skin of the earth in search of copper and molybdenum.

During the latter part of the 1950s, while conservationists were preparing to shoot down the proposed Allenspur Dam on the Yellowstone, the copper magnates on the headwaters of the Clark Fork in Butte were finishing plans for one of the world's largest open pit mines: the Berkeley Pit. Today, that abandoned pit looms as an immense scar on the face of the Continental Divide. It carries enough toxic mine water to fully destroy what remains of the Clark Fork River, and this tainted water daily works its way into the groundwater under the city of Butte.

Ironically, in 1872—the same year the mining law was enacted that helped fuel the early destruction on the Clark Fork—Two Oceans Plateau was protected within the nation's first national park, Yellowstone. Juxtaposed against the awesome beauty that reigns over the headwaters of the Yellowstone River are the smoke-killed ridges from which the Clark Fork flows. One river is our nation's last long free-flowing river while the other is our nation's largest and most expensive Environmental Superfund Site, a designation that will cost the past owners of the Butte mining operations over a billion dollars in cleanup costs when the river is finally brought back to health. Remarkably, that price tag doesn't include the Berkley Pit, which even today has the EPA, Montana Department of Environmental Quality, and the American public scratching their heads over what to do with it.

During the energy crises, oil embargos, proposed coal development, and fast-developing mining technology of the 1970s, the Yellowstone came close to sharing the same diminished fate as the Clark Fork. Instead, it got all the breaks because it had a consortium of determined dreamers looking out for it. The other river got more abuse than nearly any other river in the country. Its visionaries saw only profits coming from the depths of the earth and from the surrounding hillsides, creeks, and ravines.

As a youngster, I worked my way through the ranks of the Anaconda Mining Company, eventually becoming a midlevel manager in its communications department.

One day my supervisor came into my office and handed me a feature article to help write. It had to do with a national silver medal the Butte operations had just been awarded for its cleanup of the headwaters of the Clark Fork River.

I interviewed the company's director of environmental research, John Spindler, to get the details. John showed me all the right things: the new water recirculation system, the floating barge on the storage pond, and the impressive company laboratory where daily water samples were run and recorded. I would find out later that John previously had worked for the state of Montana as the very first Pollution Control Biologist, a position created in 1957. There he was responsible for handling pollution violations, with enforcement carried out by the Montana Board of Health. So he was certainly qualified to talk about the pollution problems coming from the Butte operations of the Anaconda Company.

The silver medal article was one of the last I worked on for the Anaconda Company. The evening I conducted my final interview I drove by the old course of Silver Bow Creek. In my youth I had known clean mountain streams and healthy trout. Now I saw the headwaters of the Clark Fork River still running with the same bright orange cast, and I could recognize the vast difference, silver medal award or not.

～✂～

Here then are two rivers in Montana, both born atop the Continental Divide. The one was fought for and protected, and today remains relatively healthy and free. The other was put under the yoke of the mining industry, and it has taken years of legal battles costing millions of dollars to get it moving in the right direction again. I wonder if Montana will ever learn that it is far less costly to avoid environmental mistakes than to repair the damages from short-term thinking.

PROFILES IN ADVOCACY

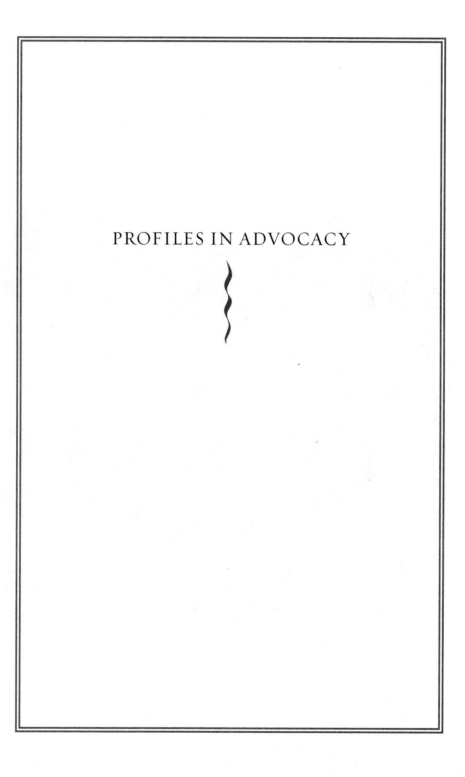

13
FREESTONER AND TAILWATER

The heart of a place is the home, and the heart of the home is the firepit, the hearth. All tentative explorations go outward from there, and it is back to the fireside that elders return.

—GARY SNYDER, *"The Place, the Region, and the Commons"*

For every river there seems to be a special advocate who stands guard, ready to go to the mat when threats arise. So no treatise on the Montana river conservation movement would be complete without the stories of some of these brave souls who show up each and every day to protect that domain we trout fishers call homewater, our primal sense of place, nestled within a riverine landscape where one's spirit is free to roam.

The day has long since passed when a fly fisher can simply take a homewater for granted. We must voice our opinions and seek workable solutions to the challenges facing our waters and the environment that nourishes them. We simply cannot put a problem aside, thinking someone else will address it. The anglers you'll read about below have turned their love for the places they fish into action. And there are lessons in their approach from which we can all benefit, no matter where our homewaters flow.

BLACKFOOT RIVER AND PAUL ROOS

My friend Paul Roos and I were sitting in his vehicle in the bright morning sun outside the Stray Bullet Café in Ovando. Paul is a veteran fly-fishing guide and a sage when it comes to conservation efforts waged on behalf of rivers. I had traveled here to interview Paul and, if time permitted, fish a few hours on the Blackfoot River. Just as Paul put his key in the ignition, a dust-coated truck pulled up next to us, and out stepped a field biologist from the U.S. Fish & Wildlife Service. The technical conversation they had through Paul's window proceeded like a couple of neighbors talking over the back fence. When the biologist left, Paul said, "Now there's a fellow who knows what he's talking about," his voice full of friendship and professional respect.

Minutes later we were traversing the gravel roads that zigzag to the Blackfoot River, talking of Paul's history in the valley, his boyhood, and how things had changed over the years. He pointed out familiar spots along the rolling landscape and shared memories while his Brittany paced anxiously in the back. We parked beneath a pair of towering trees dressed in full autumn regalia, and the dog ran around sniffing maroon-leafed bushes and clumps of nut-colored grass for lingering bird sign.

Watching a fly fisher like Paul work the Blackfoot is like eavesdropping on a solo cellist perched center stage in an empty, velvet-chaired concert hall. His easy movements had been rehearsed over a lifetime spent on the same river, and nothing around him seemed much involved. Paul cherishes the Blackfoot River. It is just that simple. The river is a part of him, more than just another great trout stream, it is his homewater.

That morning, Paul waded to the outside edge of a fast riffle. I wondered, as I watched him, how many times he had stood in that exact spot; how many trout had he taken from that riffle; how many dogs, over his lifetime, had waited patiently on the shore or waded in next to him.

Paul was born in Lincoln, Montana, in the Blackfoot Valley. He can bring you to the small tributary where, one morning while fishing with his father and grandfather, he hooked his first trout on a fly. Somewhere in the brush along the river, he can show you a spot under a cottonwood tree where he dreamed as a teenager about someday becoming a seasoned fly fisher, not knowing the course had already been set simply because he so loved that river.

He can also ferry you to the spot on the river's bank where, one day, he decided his river was terribly ill, almost dead, and he vowed to do something about it. Over the next thirty years, his efforts, and the efforts of others, resulted in an association of national acclaim entitled the Blackfoot Challenge. Paul Roos was one of the many residents of the Blackfoot Valley who had grave concerns about the river. Some of these individuals continue to play a fundamental role today.

When Paul decided to act on behalf of the river, he was employed as a school administrator who spent his summers guiding fly fishers. He worked only on the stream's middle and lower sections, because the upper portion was seriously compromised by acid mine drainage from abandoned mines.

It has to be a tragic day when finally you admit that your homewater, the lifeblood of the land, teeters on the brink of collapse. The question was, could anything be done about it? The activists were not all sportsmen and died-in-the-wool conservationists or fly fishers. Instead, most were ranchers, loggers, and business owners, folks who had grown up close to the river and knew in their hearts that major changes needed to come in their lifetimes. Joining the group were new arrivals to the Blackfoot Valley, some from places outside Montana where similar decimation had been allowed to happen. Statewide conservation groups also came to the table, followed by some federal and state employees.

According to Paul, the first few meetings held the key to whatever success the newly emerging movement might have in the future. The original organizers felt that if they could just get the diverse assembly talking they might coalesce into a group.

At the onset, the new group demonstrated remarkable internal leadership by putting into play a management tool that should be noted by all those who face huge issues. Instead of jumping into the many complex, contentious problems that faced the river, they chose a few smaller issues, things the whole group could get behind. As a result, trust steadily grew among the members; they got to know one another in a personal way before more controversial topics were discussed.

"Nothing like this happens at the behest of a single person," he said emphatically. "The idea that one man ever stands up and singlehandedly saves a river is, in my opinion, a myth. Sure, there are some strong leaders who step up when necessary, but I believe they are able to accomplish what they can only because other like-minded individuals join with them.

"We have succeeded here in the Blackfoot Valley merely because we all came to the table, put aside our differences, and sought common ground. Some of the strongest leadership for what has been accomplished in the valley has come from those whose lives are given to the agricultural industry, second- and third-generation families who I believe truly love the land, raise families on it, and want as much as anyone else to see it returned to health.

"The key to the coalition that came about here on the Blackfoot happened only because we all came to the conclusion that we were a part of the problem. We all, even us in the trout fishing industry, were polluters, and if we were going to make good things happen on the Blackfoot we needed to start there."

More individuals and groups were attracted to the Challenge, more chairs added to the table. Before long all those who wanted to play a role in renewing the river had an equal voice. The key was that no single voice dominated the discussion, no economic driver took the lead, no lawyer filibustered, and no interest group stormed out in disgust. State and federal agencies fully participated but shared the same level of importance as all others.

As the Blackfoot Challenge identified ecological problems faced by the river, each of the partners had a chance to debate the issues. In the end, workable strategies flowed into place. All those impacted by the health of the river gave of themselves by bending strong positions that had sometimes been fostered over generations of divisiveness.

Sadly, one group did not step forward to participate in the good work of the Challenge, a polluter of long standing: the mining industry. "In this valley they are not playing an important role," Paul said. "They are just sort of out of the picture and have not chosen to be a part of the process."

A significant part of the trouble faced by the Blackfoot River comes from decades of mining on the river's headwaters. The wastewater impoundment of the old Mike Horse Mine is a particular problem. The earthen dam had already burst in the 1970s, sending heavy metals, floury silt, and toxic waste downstream, resulting in a fish kill approaching 85 percent on the headwaters' upper section. Although the dam was rebuilt by the Anaconda Company, it has never been right. Recently the U.S. Forest Service—the same agency that oversaw the dam's reconstruction after its failure in 1974—has condemned it as being unsafe, along with noting significant leakage into the Blackfoot.

The Anaconda Company was bought by Atlantic Richfield Company

(ARCO), which in turn was bought by oil giant British Petroleum (BP). Regardless of the corporate juggling, it appears that today the responsibility falls on BP.

Another potential responsible party for the headwaters pollution could be American Smelting and Refining Company (ASARCO), a mining company that has chosen the path of bankruptcy, leaving the state of Montana and others holding the bag for billions of dollars of cleanup costs while appealing to the court system and the U.S. Department of Justice to lessen their responsibility for an unfathomable mess left behind in once-wild places.

Over the years, the Blackfoot Challenge has managed to invest more than ten million dollars in various restoration projects throughout the valley. Many of these involve revitalizing secondary tributaries, controlling weeds, recovering wetlands, and repairing damaged riparian habitat. Work parties made up of local ranchers, fly fishers, loggers, state and federal biologists, and business leaders are a common sight in the Blackfoot Valley.

"What has made the Blackfoot Challenge a success over the years is simple," said Paul Roos. "We have simply placed the emphasis on what we can do as opposed to what we cannot do. That elementary paradigm has kept negative energy to a minimum and helped us focus on achievable goals."

The progress of the Blackfoot Challenge is something we all should watch closely in the years to come. This novel approach to problem-solving will remain a shining example of how well we river lovers can work together if we are only willing to participate in a new approach and not spend energy assigning blame. But it still comes down to individuals willing to take the challenge and do the hard work of change.

BIGHORN RIVER AND PHIL GONZALEZ

Bighorn Canyon slices deeply into Montana's southeastern sagebrush-steppe country. And the murky river a thousand feet below the rim of the canyon wanders like an immense snake sidewinding through ancient beds of sedimentary sand and gravel. You need to watch closely to appreciate the inexorable power of water moving over this landscape, as the seemingly lethargic river continues to dig deeper and deeper into the very heart of the prairie. At some point, you realize that water owns the right to select its own course through a place.

As a youngster, before Yellowtail Dam went in, with no more than a few weeks of fly fishing under my belt, I once traveled to the Bighorn River with an uncle. I remember standing on the bank beneath a pair of colossal cottonwood trees, wondering how so much mud could possibly be suspended in a moving river. Gazing into the river was like trying to look through a cup of hot chocolate. I wondered where the silt came from, and how a fish could possibly live in such a murky froth.

The Bighorn originates on the eastern slopes of Wyoming's Continental Divide, where hundreds of rivulets, creeks, and streams converge into Boysen Reservoir. From the northern end of the reservoir, the river pushes northward for approximately one hundred miles before entering Wyoming's portion of Bighorn Canyon. Here the river is pressed tightly between the vertical canyon walls before it slips into Montana and makes up the principal attraction of the wild Bighorn Canyon National Recreation Area.

Some seventy miles later, the river splashes headlong into the 525-foot-high concrete face of Yellowtail Dam. Here the river completely changes its character. The massive dam and reservoir, occupying a narrow finger of land on the historic Crow Indian Reservation, was constructed following almost a decade of controversy over environmental impacts, disruption of indigenous life, the invasion of ancestral Indian lands, and loss of important artifacts. The impoundment was completed in 1966.

As if by some act of wizardry, a totally new river had appeared below the dam. The dark silt that had been carried down for millennia now was trapped behind the dam above, where it settled out in the still water. Not only was the water clear below the dam, but a flourishing ecosystem had been created—complete with clouds of mayflies, caddisflies, leafy aquatic plants, and trout—unbelievable in both number and size. Understandably, there also were fly fishers; the word had gotten out about the miracle on the Bighorn River.

One afternoon, when Phil Gonzalez was a kid growing up at the Huntley Project northeast of Billings, he discovered his first trout rod—locked in the trunk of a wrecked Buick sedan that had been hauled to the edge of the Yellowstone River to serve as rip-rap on an eroding curve in the river. The rod, a treasure to Phil, was a metal telescoping model, complete with attached reel and fly line. After a few years of fishing with the metal rod, Phil finally stored it and upgraded to a signature fiberglass wand, a featured headliner in the newest edition of the Sears and Roebuck catalog.

The moment the new rod arrived, Phil and a buddy embarked on a fly-fishing trip to Yellowstone National Park, the trip of a lifetime. En route, they stopped at several likely looking places along the Yellowstone River to try their luck. At a bend in the river just outside Livingston, Phil's buddy slammed the car door—on the new signature rod.

Phil had heard stories about a master angler running a fly shop in the Livingston area, so the pair decided to visit, if only to drool over the new rods on display before turning back to Huntley. An hour or so later, they walked through the front door of Dan Bailey's shop in downtown Livingston.

"Can I help you lads?" The questioner was Dan Bailey himself, and the pair of young fly fishers stood mesmerized as Bailey walked around the counter. Somewhere in the ensuing conversation the subject of the broken fly rod came up, and Dan asked Phil to fetch it and let him have a look. Maybe it was reparable. Phil returned with the rod, and Bailey declared it a goner. "Go ahead and take one of those rods off the rack, go on to the park," Bailey ordered. "Just return the rod when you're done."

Phil's eyes still light up when he tells the story today. "I was so appreciative, I dug into my dusty pockets and came up with enough to buy two flies from Dan Bailey. I knew it wasn't much, but it was all I had and somehow I think Dan realized it, so it took on a different meaning," Phil said. "I have never forgotten the generosity and trust Dan Bailey showed that day. He was a hell of a guy."

That encounter with Dan Bailey has a lot to do with the way Phil Gonzalez views the sport of fly fishing today and what he believes it means over the long haul.

Phil started to fish the Bighorn River shortly after Yellowtail Dam was completed. He watched the river gradually change from the color of cocoa to the transparency of glass. Not long after, the legendary legal controversy over Crow Indian lands and access to the river flared. It was the mid-1970s, and tensions between Native Americans and non-Indians were on the rise across the entire nation. In consideration of the Crow's legal position, founded on the assumption that their reservation included ownership of the Bighorn River, fishing was closed during the long years of tenuous litigation. As court arguments raged, the trout on the river continued to gain weight. In 1981, the Ninth Circuit Court of Appeals finally disagreed with the Crow's argument and the river was reopened.

Tempted by the possibility of truly great trout fishing, Gonzalez and his young family moved to the area and opened their fly-fishing service.

"It did not take long for the river to clear up after the dam was finished," said Phil. "But what a remarkable gift Mother Nature provided once everything stabilized. Before the dam was finished, you couldn't find a trout on the Bighorn without a lot of effort, but after, it was amazing to watch nature stock the new environment. We were left with one of the world's most productive trout fisheries serviced by a quickly flourishing ecosystem—one that seems to always hang on even through years of drought that seem to mount up in Montana.

"Each year, some gigantic browns in the area of twenty-three to twenty-five inches are taken from the Bighorn," remarked Gonzalez. "Incredibly, browns have never been stocked on the main river, they came from the feeder streams and simply took to the Bighorn and thrived over the years, a sign of the species' keen ability to self-adapt to changing conditions."

During the same period that the brown trout moved to the river, state biologists, responding to the public's interest in catching feisty rainbows, introduced a number of different strains. At last, one took hold. This strain became the foundation for those bulky rainbows common to the fishery today. By the 1980s stocking was discontinued, which had little effect on the river's already-established trout population. "Any trip down the Bighorn today," said Gonzalez, "is likely to produce an equal catch of brown trout and rainbow, and possibly a few stretching the tape to twenty-four inches."

So rich is the Bighorn's ecology that brown and rainbow trout prospered and grew at a rate uncommon to many other Montana rivers. For example, a seven-inch trout in the Bighorn back then could grow as much as eight inches a year. Trout, aquatic vegetation, and insect life thrived in the nutrient-rich, alkaline environment, a gift of dissolved nutrients from the canyon above—a direct result of millions of years of sedimentary buildup and erosion.

The growth rate on the Bighorn is enhanced by another factor: the river's consistently cold water temperature. Riverine environments with water temperatures ranging from 45 to 65 degrees Fahrenheit are especially suitable for growing trout. This optimum temperature range is maintained on most free-flowing Montana rivers for only three to four months each year, when the temperature is naturally maintained by snowmelt or the chill of autumn.

On the Bighorn, the optimum range is maintained for twice that long, the result of both the more temperate eastern Montana climate and the thermodynamic effects of Yellowtail Reservoir. Dam operators have the ability to draw water from a number of different depths within the reservoir, where it is naturally cooled. This selective ability now exists on many dams in Montana.

Gonzalez pointed out another important component leading to trout growth: "As you float the Bighorn, take a close look at its natural vitality. The diversity of aquatic vegetation, the streambed makeup, and bank cover are all great components to stimulate sometimes huge insect hatches. There is no doubt, when the Bighorn River came back from the damage originally caused by construction, it did so in a truly remarkable way. Back then, the stage was set for the development of one tremendous dry-fly trout fishery—but that was all destined to change as time went on."

During the early years, brown trout populations took off right away. And because of the abundant natural food supply, the stocked rainbows ballooned, creating a trout many locals knew as "swimming pigs." These rainbows featured small heads and robust bodies, reminiscent of a hardworking weightlifter on massive doses of steroids. Everything on the river, especially during the early years, seemed to overperform, probably because of the newness of the aquatic environment.

At one point around 1988, the trout population on the Bighorn River was estimated at an unbelievable ten thousand per river mile, with more than a few pushing trophy size. The number and size of trout attracted the attention of a flock of outdoor writers and, subsequently, a massive wave of anglers. A steady flow of traffic streamed along the single-lane highway between Hardin and Fort Smith as the word spread about trophy trout the size of footballs.

As so often happens when things in a natural system tilt out of wack, some great equalizer steps in. "You know Mother Nature has a way of working things out over the long haul. You know, just to make sure everything remains in balance," said Gonzalez.

In this case, the adjustment was done by weather. The drought years of 1988 and 1989 caused a sudden lack of water on many Montana rivers, including the Bighorn, and along with the lack of moisture came a significant rise in water temperatures. The drought's impacts on the Bighorn River resulted in mortality as high as 98 percent among some of the larger trout in the system. The overall decline among all sizes approached 50 percent.

"Mother Nature has made a gift of this magnificent river to us. She created what is here today, to repair the ecological damage caused by the dam," reflected Gonzalez. "Nature is very good at repairing the damage humans bring to the environment. In the case of the Bighorn, we ended up with a special trout fishery, one we need to trust nature to continue to protect as our generations move forward. We need to trust in nature's ability to heal her own wounds and, in some cases, we fisheries managers and sportsmen should stay out of it as much as possible—after all, it is not just about trout, fly fishing, personal recreation, or big fish and small fish, it's about the extended life of the entire ecosystem. In that, we can play only a minor role."

These are the words of a mindful steward of his own homewater. They are words we all should take to heart before we consider playing god on Montana's rivers.

Over the last several years, the Bighorn River ecology again has been heavily impacted by drought. In a 2004 trout survey, Montana Fish, Wildlife & Parks biologist Ken Fraser pointed to a lack of recruitment fish in the river's general population, which, at the time, tallied about 1,100 trout per mile. The trout that survived lower water levels, caused in part by continuous irrigation draws over the prior six years, were in good shape and strong, perhaps due only to a decrease in competition as the population declined. The bad news was the lack of replacement stock. Most of the big trout in the system were believed to be four and five years old, with species like rainbow rarely lasting over five years, and browns often less. Mortality is a natural response to a sustained lack of water and increased water temperature. It was the lack of recruitment stock, however, that had biologists most concerned.

Fortunately, something changed on the Bighorn River during the spring of 2005. People whose lives depend on the river, others in positions of management, and still others who just plain love it began to talk. Meetings among the various groups included farmers solely reliant on the irrigation, dam managers concerned about present and future water levels, and the steadily increasing population of fly fishers and outfitters like Phil Gonzalez. Despite strongly independent agendas, needs, and expectations, a compromise was reached—one that effectively put the health of the river above all else—a minimum flow of 2,400 cubic feet per second would be maintained.

"You wouldn't believe the difference sustained flow has on fish recovery. The numbers are not yet available, but I am very, very pleased," said Fraser.

One advantage of a reservoir is that it truly serves as a "heat sink," a situation that permits downstream temperature control. This management tool is available because the lower you go in the pool, the cooler the water. If managed right, operators can provide an almost perfect in-stream temperature even in times of drought, assuming adequate water level is maintained.

Talking about the benefits of a tailwater fishery, Phil Gonzalez pointed out, "Of course the dam also stores water for use during periods in which seasonal flow would have naturally declined, particularly during years of sustained drought. We trout fishers just need to be kept in the management loop, as do all the other water users that have a mixed bag of demands on rivers like the Bighorn."

Blessing or curse, the jury probably will always be out on the benefit of Montana dams. Only after sizing up the total picture, over generations, will we begin to understand the overall impact dams have on fisheries. However, some marvelous things can happen to a trout if a minimum flow is established and maintained over a number of years. This is a special consideration on rivers like the Kootenai, Flathead, Missouri, Beaverhead, Ruby, Marias, and Madison. Biologist Ken Fraser is right when he says, "You wouldn't believe the difference sustained flow has on fish recovery."

Minimum flow, what conservationists now call "in-stream flow," is perhaps the most overused phrase in the ecological debate presently taking place on Montana rivers. But in the case of rivers like the Bighorn, where irrigation and fly fishing can sometimes operate parallel to one another, maintaining in-stream flow through effective reservoir management is at least an option. In order for it to be a priority, the river must be looked at in a multifaceted way, not simply as a source of irrigation or hydroelectric production.

Bruce Farling, Executive Director of Montana Trout Unlimited, cites maintaining adequate in-stream flow as the most serious problem facing Montana rivers and streams today. Farling pointed out that only the willingness of different stakeholders to come to the table and create workable solutions will benefit rivers and aquatic life, as well as prolong our legacy of trout fishing. The discussion of in-stream flow pits two longstanding adversaries against each other, sportsman and irrigator.

While it might be true the Bighorn River is not what it used to be, it remains one of the West's most productive and challenging trout fisheries. The river is open all year and is used by hardy fly fishers even in the dead of winter. High runoff is seldom a problem because of the dam. During the peak of the fly-fishing season between July and September, when most of the larger hatches take place, fishing can border on the fantastic.

The present drop is further complicated by silt buildup in some of the river channels. Over the previous well-documented two decades, the Bighorn River had maintained a reputation as the quintessential dry-fly stream, with exceptional mayfly and caddis hatches. Today, that image is changing.

"So many fly fishers come to the Bighorn with a set of expectations; I guess the result of all the past publicity," noted Gonzalez. "They come to catch the trout of their lives on a dry fly, and I can't say I blame them. I have to admit, there is nothing more exciting than a trout of any size coming to the surface for a number twenty dry fly. But you know, rivers change from day to day and from season to season, especially following an extended drought."

Gonzalez continued, "When people decide to come to a river like the Bighorn, if they are going to be successful they have to be able to change technique, go from a dry fly to a nymph, for example, just because that is what the conditions call for.

"This year, more trout and bigger trout have been taken on nymphs, probably because of the way the river has changed. One thing that never changes on this river is the beautiful and historic setting through which it flows, so I tell fishermen who call and ask about the Bighorn that they have to come prepared to enjoy the whole experience around fly fishing. If the trout cooperate, the door of heaven will open, if not, the experience itself should account for something.

"There have been years when dry-fly fishing has been absolutely remarkable, and national articles tout the wonders of the Bighorn," Gonzalez remarked. "But there have also been years when dry-fly fishing is off and outdoor writers start asking questions like 'Is the Bighorn dying?' Lately the river fishes great but it fishes different than before because of the low water and drought. We are currently experiencing water levels at minimum flow, in which silt beds build up along some of the channels. Of course, the beds choke off the emergence of some surface insects, which greatly reduces the surface action, but you know, trout have to eat, they are adaptive and can change their menu much faster than many fly fishers can lessen their expectations. The trout on the Bighorn the last few years are gorging themselves on scuds and sow bugs under the surface and you can see why—it takes a lot of blue olives to make up even one scud, much less the huge burst of protein.

"Every once in a while, down the pike comes word of a big flush to remove the silt beds and return the river back to a dry-fly heaven. You have to look at this type of fisheries management carefully and ask yourself how much we should play around with nature just to meet the expectations of fly fishers. If we ever get to the point that we are managing the Bighorn, bringing about huge change just to bring back a certain type of trout fishing, I think we are managing for the wrong reason, regardless of what it might mean to the local or state economy. I think the biologists are good at this, but at the same time, there is a lot of pressure from within the industry and from trout fishers alike who want a certain experience on a certain river. We need to think about our priorities on Montana rivers and keep some things out of the equation."

In a parting comment, Phil Gonzalez summed up his vision of fly fishing, and a hint of his experience with Dan Bailey shows through: "The best thing I can leave to my granddaughter, Kaitlyn, is this river as it was when I arrived after the dam went in. Here she can build her own legacy and conjure her own feelings about nature and rivers. If we ball it up during our short life, we are robbing our offspring of a tradition that has been so important to us."

14
NORTHWEST RIVERS

⁂

Man has empathy towards rivers because, of all the inanimate elements of nature, they are the most personal. Rivers have a birth, a strengthening youth, a majestic maturity. They move. They speak. They have moods, laughing or angry, brooding or serene. Man, who yearns for immortality, observes the eternal life of rivers with admiring awe.

—JOHN M. KAUFFMANN

Geologists have chosen to call northwest Montana's ramparts "the Columbia Rockies," and not just because our rivers tend to flow in the direction of the Pacific Ocean by way of the Columbia River. The decision goes much deeper than that, starting with the physical layout and origins of the mountains. Here the ranges lie tight to one another, the valleys are steep, rocky, and twisting, and the rivers drop precipitately. I live deep inside these mountains, beneath the towering silhouette of the Cabinet Mountains, and call the Kootenai River, the state's second largest river, my own homewater.

The moist, temperate clime of the Yaak and other isolated regions in northwestern Montana allows abundant life to thrive in the dense stands of redcedars, hemlocks, firs, spruces, larches, birches, and alders. At the margins are cottonwoods, aspens, and more kinds of willow than can be counted on a single outing. The area is pleasant enough in winter to attract northern bird species, including hoary redpolls, sparrow-sized hermit thrushes, and black-and-white-headed Lapland longspurs, all Arctic-nesting birds that use Montana as a wintry refuge.

In a temperate rainforest the biological productivity emanates from a mixture of zones that exist from the forest canopy to the thick, soft layer of duff. Within this humus layer are thousands of different life forms. Wood ants, springtails, mites, burrowing beetles, and millipedes are joined by microscopic fungi and bacteria. Their vigorous activity eventually softens the forest humus and allows it to decay, adding life-giving nutrients to the newly created forest soils. It is an amazing truth that a huge conifer—a fallen larch for example—lying prostrate on the forest floor is actually more lively than it ever had been while standing upright.

Several species of lichen hang like clumps of coarse hair from the branches of conifers. Some gather nitrogen from floating dust particles. Others, in a mysterious form of alchemy, fix nitrogen from within. In both cases, the nitrogen is ultimately delivered to the forest floor, supplying up to half the nitrogen needed in a functioning forest.

Yet the bulk of the diverse biomass does not reside above the ground. Instead, the greatest accumulation exists in the subterranean layer located inches or feet below the forest floor. Here, billions of miles of fungal threads, or mycorrhizae, interweave like a net through the hardened duff and soil, stretching from one tree, plant, or bush to another, connecting the entire forest in an unbroken web of life.

Rain and melting snow carry a groundswell of these forest nutrients to the waiting rivers. As a result, aquatic life flourishes, and insects and trout further enhance the nutritious web of life.

KOOTENAI RIVER AND DAVE BLACKBURN

The headwaters of the Kootenai River drain from the west-facing slopes of the Canadian Rockies. The river flows southward through the mountains and crosses the international border just west of Eureka, Montana. By the time it arrives in the United States, its current already has been slowed to a crawl, impounded in the late 1960s behind Libby Dam in the backwaters of the huge Koocanusa Reservoir.

When full, Koocanusa is a formidable lake, but when low, the basin resembles a gigantic brown bathtub with unsightly rings. The latter are created by the thousands upon thousands of cubic tons of silt that have settled on the lake bottom.

The reservoir rests in a valley rimmed by the Purcell Mountains to the west and the dense Kootenai National Forest and Salish Mountains to the east. Just below, one of Montana's best tailwater fisheries stretches forty-eight miles from the face of Libby Dam to the Montana/Idaho state line. From there, the Kootenai swings north in a smooth arc and heads back to Canada and the Kooteney Lakes.

The silt-rich Fisher River joins the Kootenai a short distance below the dam. And a quarter mile below that point is the spot where, in 1980, fly-fishing outfitter Dave Blackburn first fished the Kootenai River.

Dave had grown up fishing tiny dry flies on Pennsylvania's famous limestone spring creeks, such as the Letort and Yellow Breeches, and earned a college degree in forestry. He originally came to Kootenai country not to fly fish, but to meet his future father-in-law and see his fiancée's home town. Interestingly, his future relative just happened to live near the river, so after the proper introductions were made, Blackburn gathered up his light tackle and slipped off for his first encounter with the river.

The soon-to-be bridegroom crept up on a pod of rising trout in a spot he now calls the "home pool." From the bank opposite, Dave made a couple of false casts to judge the distance, and let the third one land a tiny dry fly just upstream of the pod. The microscopic imposter drifted a few feet and was suddenly inhaled by Dave's first Kootenai River rainbow. There is still excitement in his voice when he recalls the event:

"The very first trout I hooked on the Kootenai River straightened the hook out like a needle. I had him on for only a few seconds, and with my light rod bent in a perfect C suddenly everything came loose. I really thought I had just hooked the biggest trout in the pod, but the next couple turned out to be a little larger and every bit as assertive, breaking tippets or bending hooks each time, recoiling my rod tip back like a rubber band.

"I was amazed, and went back to my rig, forgetting for a few hours my future family, took out my tying kit to beef things up a bit. It was clear the trout on the Kootenai were not going to give either me or my light gear a break. Returning to the river, I managed to lose a few more trout, again from the same spot, but I finally managed to bring one to the net.

"There was no doubt whatsoever after my first outing on the Kootenai that the wedding was on. I moved here shortly afterwards and committed to sinking deep roots in the valley, to learn the remarkable fishery and raise a family."

Dave not only staked his claim on the Kootenai River, he opened The Kootenai Angler, the first fly-fishing outfitting service in the valley. He is similar to so many others who fell in love with Montana like a teenager on a first date, but in this case that love affair remains as enduring as the surrounding mountains.

But Blackburn's connection with the river would not be all warm summer days on crystalline water with a growing group of new friends. Instead, much of his experience turned out to be a series of battles he and others waged just to keep the big river ecologically fit and under some degree of protection from misguided development.

Almost as soon as he landed in Lincoln County, Dave began to hear about additional dam projects proposed for the Kootenai River. Libby Dam had been built years before his arrival, and already had seriously compromised the river's ecology with gas supersaturation just below the spillway, loss of precious aquatic habitat, and unnatural flow regimes. The Kootenai was already in serious trouble, but there was still hope as long as additional hydroelectric projects did not compound the existing problems.

The issues were not simple. They rarely are. Construction of Libby Dam had created a boom of new jobs and industry in the area. New road construction on MT 37 between Libby and Eureka was under way, the timber industry was moving forward, and a vermiculite mine west of the river—which would later be revealed as the cause of hundreds of deaths from asbestos exposure—was in full operation. Men were at work, kids filled new high school classrooms, and wages were high. A good share of the runaway prosperity was associated with dam construction, but like most boom eras, the whole thing came to a sudden end when construction was complete. Working families moved on to another dam project, and local stores, businesses, schools—and the county tax base—slipped into decline. That was when the Corps of Engineers came up with the idea of pouring more concrete in the river for a reregulation impoundment situated between the original damsite and the town of Libby. Community leaders grew giddy at the prospect of the boom times returning.

Dave Blackburn and other conservation-minded residents of the Kootenai Basin, including writer Rick Bass, had a different idea, discerning that the real value of the Kootenai River lay in its future natural state. To throw away that future for another short-term gain was a real mistake, one that would surely rob the river of its life.

Some of the conflicted community's story is revealed by the bumper stickers that showed up on local vehicles: "Save the Kootenai" was almost instantly countered by "Pave the Kootenai," a good indication of how the arguments were going to shape up.

"There was a strong group of citizens in town who just didn't care about the river, aquatic health, fly fishing, or anything short of making a few quick bucks," Dave recalled. "Right off the bat we got on their bad side, and that included almost everyone in power within the community. We couldn't go anywhere in town without running into the pro-dam side and their idea that if you oppose them it simply meant you were an extremist. They didn't care about the fishery that had almost been destroyed with the first dam, or the litany of broken promises made by the Corps of Engineers, the dead fish, or even the river's downstream importance to native white sturgeon or Pacific salmon or the Kootenai Indians. It was all about making fast money, increasing tax revenue, and bringing back the boom times."

The boarded-up plywood storefronts, the outlying saloons, the patchwork settlements of trailer courts that followed the last boom were not enough to demonstrate the false security brought by temporary economic upturns. New promises had already clouded the eyes of many civic leaders, and the daunting task of saving the Kootenai River was certain to be an uphill effort.

Blackburn and the rest of the Lincoln County residents who fought against the new dam were for a long while outcasts in their own community. In a town like Libby, where only a select few industries power the town's economy, stepping out of the pack means serious problems. But in the case of the proposed reregulation dam, all that short-term ostracism didn't seem to matter when weighed against the future of the entire river basin.

"The Kootenai River is like no other river in Montana," Blackburn stated. "Not just because the trout fishing can be great, but it is one of the Columbia Basin's primary tributaries…. Every season we have to deal with what is happening hundreds of miles downstream, as Fish & Wildlife fights to save species like the white sturgeon and Pacific salmon. The Columbia River is so screwed up with the effects of decades of development and misuse, that today it gathers almost all its primal strength from the Kootenai. It is Montanans who now get to make up for a century of mistakes all along the Columbia. Today, it is the Kootenai that pumps life back into the Columbia, its life diminished by massive dams, industrial and municipal development—all on a large scale."

Montana's Governor Brian Schweitzer agrees with Dave Blackburn's impression, stating publicly, "Montana is the motherlode of clean water for the entire nation."

Back when Libby Dam went in on the Kootenai, many Montana residents were concerned about the effects on fish and wildlife within the Kootenai basin. Nobody really knew what was going to happen.

The dam's objectives were twofold: first and perhaps foremost, to supply hydro-electric power to a consumer market well beyond Montana; second, to control flooding within the Kootenai basin. For the latter, engineers relied on historic records, including the maximum flow from 1916, which topped out at 121,000 cfs as it raged past the fledgling town of Libby.

Millennia ago the entire riverine ecology had adapted to the pattern of high spring runoffs and steadily lower levels the rest of the year. While it is true the new dam did control seasonal floods, it also leveled out high flows during spring runoff. The Bonneville Power Administration (BPA) was required to make available mitigation funds to study and repair the dam's environmental impact on the basin as well as replace or restore lost wildlife and aquatic habitat. In a 1975 *Montana Outdoors* article entitled "The Mitigation Myth," writer Bruce May commented, "The obvious lesson of the Libby project is that mitigation cannot replace destroyed natural resources with something of equal or comparable value.... Before impoundment, the Kootenai River produced a year-round quality fishery for westslope cutthroat, rainbow and Dolly Varden (bull trout) and mountain whitefish. The winter fishery for whitefish and trout was one of the best if not the best in Montana.... The reservoir drawdown (1) prevents establishment of aquatic insect and root aquatic plant populations in areas alternately flooded and desiccated, (2) concentrates fish, which increases competition for food and space between game fish and rough fish, (3) results in fewer fish and fish food organisms in the reservoir, (4) eliminates the winter fishery and (5) severely limits access to the remaining pool for as long as five to six months."

Clearly, the BPA's wildlife mitigation funds initially did little to stop the decimation of trout and aquatic habitat, including the gas supersaturation that killed fish as well as aquatic insect species like the stonefly.

May went on to explain supersaturation and the brutal death it causes: "Air is entrapped in the form of bubbles in the water as the water falls over the spillway of the dam. The water then plunges to the bottom of a 60-foot stilling basin where the weight of the water forces the trapped air into saturation. In effect, the air is dissolved into the water. Fish tissues and blood soon become supersaturated with gas until the gas comes into equilibrium with the surrounding water. As long as the fish stays in the deep water, the gas stays in solution because of the heavy water pressure. However, when the fish rises to the surface or moves to shallow water, water pressure is reduced and gas bubbles form in the tissue and blood vessels. Under chronic exposure, these bubbles eventually block the circulatory system and causes death.

"Torrent sculpins, an important forage fish for trout, have almost disappeared from the first 10 miles below the dam apparently because of the gas bubble disease."

Hydroelectric dams are a huge business, with huge profits. Fish species and insects clinging to the bottom of a varial (stream edge) zone, habitat mitigation, are secondary to the bottom line. In 1968, when the dam was completed but the generators not yet operational, engineers released massive amounts of water that killed indigenous fish through the horrific effects of gas supersaturation.

Once the generators were activated and profitable hydroelectric power began to pour from the site, an ecologically dangerous management paradigm followed. In those days it was called "power peaking," today it is known as "load following." Whatever the nomenclature, it creates seriously compromised conditions for fish and aquatic life on the river, as huge fluctuations in flow repeatedly alter their environment.

Power peaking is by far the most profitable way to operate a dam; anything less costs the power industry money. The simple albeit harsh fact is that dams are managed for profit. For decades after its initial opening, Libby Dam operators would increase the flows on the river from 4,000 cfs to a whopping 20,000 cfs, sometimes in less than a few hours. Water levels on the Kootenai bounced around like a rubber ball, dictated by the electric demands of West Coast consumers. The BPA's answer to the serious destruction on the river was to propose the reregulation dam.

Conservationists viewed the rereg dam as more riparian habitat decimated and additional private property compromised or taken over by rising water. If the reregulation dam were to be built, the first ten miles of the river below Libby Dam would die, it was just that simple.

At every juncture of the debate, the well-funded Corps argued that there was no science that proved the negative effect.

"We got to calling the Army Corps of Engineers, the managers at the Libby Dam, 'the untouchables,' because everything we tried to get them to understand the awful effects their management was having on the river bounced off closed ears," Dave Blackburn recalled. "We demanded that the operators, through the initiation of wildlife mitigation funds, do a series of studies outlining the effect power peaking was having on the river, and like many other government agencies they dragged their feet.

"I think they already knew they were killing the resource, but to get them to own up to it we needed conclusive science by way of studies. That was my first introduction to the concept of government suppression of science. All we could do is be persistent and keep up the battle to save the Kootenai. The huge releases were killing insects and trout and everyone knew it except the Corps of Engineers.

"When we took issue with the new dam and all the past mismanagement of the original dam, we found ourselves up against our own political leadership, the Chamber of Commerce, and a whole herd of federal employees, all of whom wanted to see the second dam go into place as quickly as possible."

Amazingly, at the same time, Northern Lights, Inc. and a consortium of other rural electrical cooperatives proposed a third barrier, a "run of the river" dam (which means it operates with a much smaller reservoir pool). Their proposed dam would have stretched across the top of the marvelously beautiful Kootenai Falls, a sacred site for the native Kootenai Indians. Fortunately, the tribe filed an objection, and this proposal was stopped by a court action—one of the original handful of Native American sacred sites to be protected by the federal court system.

The Corps of Engineers forged ahead and started significant work on the rereg dam without a permit to do so. Amazing as it is in retrospect, the federal agency was openly violating the very laws it was entrusted to play a part in enforcing. A federal court injunction filed in Butte slowed the unauthorized construction of the reregulation project.

"Just about the time we thought we had lost the fight, we found out the Corps didn't even have a permit to do the work," Dave recounted. "Fate started to play a real hand on the Kootenai that ended in another real surprise that came down in our favor, one that stopped the whole process."

The ally was the Northwest Power Planning Council, an agency empowered by Congress to find a way to balance the need for hydroelectric power against the needs of salmonids throughout the Columbia River Basin.

For decades the government's approach to mitigating lost habitat, wildlife species, and aquatic life resulting from dam construction was to insist mitigation monies be in place and used to help restore impacted environs. The funds to date had served merely to restock rivers with hatchery fish, build fish ladders, and fund biological studies needed to better define ecological problems.

Suddenly, Congress felt it was time to do something about the havoc dams were causing within the Columbia River Basin. They had already consumed up to 30 percent of the steelhead and salmon habitat in the huge Columbia Basin, as well as decreasing annual salmon runs from over 7 million fish to a pitiful 2.5 million. Pushed by legislators, the eight-member Northwest Power Council reacted admirably by establishing what they called the "Protected Areas Program," which effectively identified forty-five thousand miles of certain streams in Oregon, Washington, Idaho, and Montana as off-limits for hydroelectric development. The newly protected areas represented 15 percent of the total stream miles in the Columbia Basin. There were more than three hundred applications like the Kootenai rereg project on file at that time. With the council's announcement of the protected areas, 241 of those projects were immediately shut down.

The news came hard to many in Libby, and their hopes for another boom faded. On the river, however, a short celebration took place among Dave Blackburn and his friends. Despite the victory laid at their door by the Northwest Power Planning Council, they knew they still desperately needed a reliable insect study in order to scientifically demonstrate their concerns over the changing environment, particularly to document the extensive damage caused by fluctuating flows.

A baseline insect study performed in 1979 had established the population and number of aquatic species, but during their daily experiences, fly fishers were noticing a serious decline in insect emergence. They linked the problem to the wildly fluctuating flows created by power peaking, but needed the money in the mitigation funds to prove it. Unfortunately, the Bonneville Power Administration had different plans for the fund.

Persistence in holding public meetings and writing magazine articles finally paid off for the group of river advocates in the 1990s, though, when the Flathead Lake Biological Station of the University of Montana mounted an aquatic insect study entitled "Long Term Influence of Libby Dam Operation on the Ecology of Macrozoobenthos of the Kootenai River, Montana and Idaho."

The trout fishers waited. In 1997 university investigators released their findings that compared the population of insects found on the river in 1979 to the same sections in the present day. In underlined text, the study stated: "That portion of the river channel that is wetted by the river continuously for several weeks is colonized by benthic (bottom dwelling) organisms.

"If the discharge in the river is reduced in rapidity sufficiently to expose portions of the channel wetted perimeter, a significant portion of the benthos occupying the varial zone (river channel) is stranded and dies. The ecologically sound solution to this can be achieved through slow rather than rapid reduction in dam discharge. Current dam operations permit rapid fluctuation in dam discharge that frequently results in daily fluctuation in river discharge between 4,000 and 20,000 cfs. However, an analysis of the rate of decline in river discharge prior to dam construction reveals a typical rate of fall on the hydrograph from 20,000 to 10,000 cfs to occur over a 15–30 day time period, depending on the water year."

The study went on to identify particular aquatic species that had been adversely impacted by the capricious flows, a list that included mayflies and caddis. But particularly alarming was the finding that the entire inventory of stoneflies had all but disappeared on the river. "The river downstream of the dam has an expansive varial zone that is essentially devoid of zoobenthos whenever the dam is operated with dramatic flow fluctuation. Dominant species present are those that emerge as adults off the surface of the water column (e.g., *Trichoptera*, *Diptera* [caddisflies, midges]), rather than crawling out on the lateral margins of the river (e.g., *Plecoptera* [stoneflies]), where they must deal with the vagaries of the varial zone as a consequence of Libby dam operations...we believe that the low stonefly density and diversity with continued loss of species in the Kootenai River below the dam is because of 1) rapid and frequent flow fluctuations and 2) change in substratum character that results from elimination of stream power associated with high flow events."

Leaving the world of insects for a few paragraphs, the scientists turned their attention to the fish: "Fish behavior may also be significantly affected by frequent flow fluctuation. Juvenile fish, particularly young-of-the-year, must remain near shore where generally more cover, less predation, and slower current velocities (occur). However, under a frequently changing discharge regime juvenile fish not only must move long distances to remain near the shore, but during high discharge are forced to reside in a portion of the river without benthic organisms (i.e., food). Likewise, adult fish behavior may be directly affected by the recurring change in discharge as dominant individuals attempt to occupy ever shifting microhabitat spatial structure."

At last there was scientific proof that the dam management had, in fact, caused the significant loss of insect life on the Kootenai.

One might think it all ended there, but it did not. Meetings and exchanges continue even today, and regardless of the perceived progress, each year seems to present a different set of management problems, as evidenced by the postscript below.

BIG WATER GETS BIGGER

Most quiet spring mornings a heavy veil of mist swirls above the dense forests along the Kootenai River. On one particular morning in 2006, though, a new sound filled the air, a consistent swish that was hard to ignore. It was the big river raging through the valley at a remarkable rate as high as 72,000 cfs. The Kootenai is normally no small river—even in the doldrums of summer it shows a certain strength while others in Montana are drying up. Typical summer flows range between 9,000 and 13,000 cfs, and they are a little over twice that during spring runoff. But the spring of 2006 was very unusual, and mostly the doing of the U.S. Army Corps of Engineers and the Bonneville Power Administration.

That spring, they "miscalculated" the massive snowmelt coming from the river's headwaters on the west-facing slopes of the Canadian Rockies. As I watched the big, buff-colored Kootenai thunder under the bridge on the main street of town, I wondered how the river ecosystem would fare, what the effects would be on its population of trout that had been building over the last four years since the last big spill, that one a test conducted by the Corps at the urging of the U.S. Fish & Wildlife Service.

For anyone not used to numbers like 72,000 cfs, that amount of water is more than nineteen times higher than the mean flow of the Big Hole River and almost four times larger than any flow ever recorded on the Yellowstone River. The miscalculation went on for weeks, the violent outpouring running the color of butterscotch pudding as dam managers released water to avoid overfilling the reservoir.

As the runoff raged through the valley and shot in astonishing torrents over Kootenai Falls, local fly fishers by the dozens showed up in Libby-area churches, lighting candles for the river and its trout.

We'll never know exactly how much living matter was washed downstream, but we do know that in the aftermath of the mighty torrent, huge banks of silt that had been building on the river's bottom for time unknown were now located somewhere in Idaho and possibly even on into Canada. Sediments that had plugged the small pores between alluvial gravel and cemented the basement boulders—those, huge flat slabs of indigenous rock for which the Kootenai River is renowned—were suddenly diminished.

After the great torrent had passed, a completely different Kootenai River awaited the season's fly fishers. So much silt had been removed that the stark outlines of the river slabs were now completely exposed. Places I had thought only five feet deep turned out to be over ten. The river's bottom had been literally vacuumed by the runoff, and the only thing that needed accounting was last year's trout population.

"Just as soon as the flush died down we got out on the river. Amazingly, we started to catch fish, but in unusual places, different than we had grown used to over the years," said Dave Blackburn.

What the big flush meant to the river ecology and what part it would play over the next few seasons remained a question. Nutrients that had built up for years in the reservoir above the tailwater had been redistributed. Lush green weed beds heaved and swayed in the current in places where even old-timers could not recall them ever having existed. The aquatic vegetation grew well into the autumn, and the troublesome algae blooms that had moved into the river a few years earlier were suddenly gone.

The most amazing part of it all centered on the trout. Many of the fifteen- to twenty-inch fish were either gone or so flood-shocked that they refused to show themselves, but dry-fly fishing remained fantastic for the more average ten- to fifteen-inchers. Not a single spark of energy had been lost by the Kootenai trout that can, pound for pound, outfight any trout in Montana. Unfortunately, the protected bull trout didn't fare so well, though. During the season that followed their numbers really dropped off.

It is impossible to go through such an event without gaining a tremendous amount of respect for the resiliency of the rainbow stock in the river. How any trout could survive such an ordeal has to be one of nature's great mysteries.

YAAK RIVER AND TIM LINEHAN

Rivers that flow through densely forested landscapes absorb a part of the land into themselves, sharing in the health and biodiversity of a region. A perfect example of this is the Yaak River, which is one of the final western tributaries of the Kootenai before it spills out of Montana and into Idaho. From start to finish, the Yaak is an archetypal example of a Pacific Northwest stream forged by the unique opulence of a temperate rainforest. The woodlands of the northwest corner of Montana are classified as rainforest simply due to their placement in the humid Columbia Rockies, those distinctive ranges west of the Rocky Mountains. Warm, moist Pacific air currents settle in and stay a while, especially in regions like the Yaak.

The rainforest of the Yaak is special, in part because it still boasts large sections of unspoiled land. It is an ecosystem graced by old-growth cedar, larch, and other timber tucked well inside roadless areas. As might be expected, this unusual environment also contains one of our nation's rarest native trout species, the redband rainbow, Montana's only indigenous rainbow trout species.

Taxonomists believe we will one day find the origin of the Kootenai strain of redband rainbow as far back as the Pleistocene epoch. Redbands are a nonanadromous (not migrating to salt water) trout uniquely adapted to harsh, isolated, mountainous environments, where natural fish barriers such as waterfalls segregate them from other more aggressive and competitive species. Thus, this notable trout demonstrates some of the purest genetic qualities to be found in the natural world of fish.

Several centuries ago the Kootenai redband rainbow probably thrived in many of the northern tributaries of the Columbia Basin. Because of its long isolation in headwaters streams emanating from undeveloped forests, the redband rainbow is particularly vulnerable to habitat degradation from human intrusion into places like gallery forests, roadless areas, and wilderness places like the Yaak.

Montana biologists tell us the redband rainbow previously inhabited many of the Kootenai's eastern tributaries above Kootenai Falls, but decades of forest alteration, road construction, mining, and dam development took a toll. As a result, the redband simply disappeared before we took meaningful notice of its presence or its eventual scarcity. We also may have robbed the redband of its native habitat in the early part of the twentieth century by our well-intentioned stocking, dumping large numbers of nonnative species like brook trout throughout the surrounding mountains.

Regardless of the tragic mistakes of our past, a pure strain of redband rainbows, in very limited numbers, still exists in a few remote tributaries of the Yaak River. Despite years of determined advocacy by organizations like the Yaak Valley Forest Council and Yaak residents Rick Bass, Tim and Joanne Linehan, and a small army of others, permanent protection in the form of designated wilderness for this special region has thus far been denied by the U.S. Forest Service.

We need places like the Yaak Valley; its unspoiled remoteness shows us what the land must have been like before our arrival. We must preserve and cherish settings like this to counterbalance our ongoing madness to develop wild places around us. Here, unroaded ancient forests hold on and rare trout somehow still survive. Sadly, rarity and remoteness are two words that also keep showing up in contemporary real-estate ads that offer unusual sites for building second homes or retirement villas.

The Yaak River gathers its uncommon strength from the surrounding temperate rainforest. Its east fork originates on the south-facing slopes of Mount Robinson, then meanders between Robinson and Mount Henry before arcing to the south to pick up the waters of its north fork, which originates in Canada. Spilling from the high, well-watered forests surrounding the river, hundreds of smaller creeks, brooks, and tributaries eventually help the Yaak River gain girth before it plunges over the horizontal slabs of Yaak Falls, midway through the narrow valley.

Below the falls, the river rumbles around midstream boulders, some the size of doghouses, and eventually rushes mightily through a narrow gorge filled with deep holes and excellent pocket water. The Yaak joins the Kootenai River near the end of that river's forty-eight-mile tailwater run through northwestern Montana.

Geologists tell us ancient landscapes reveal their age by their smoothness of contour, a gentle roundedness like the slope of a shoulder. Such is not the case in the Yaak, where the terrain is chiseled in the rough edges of youth, with craggy rock outcrops, dislodged boulders shoving the river this way and that, and abrupt mountain slopes.

A fly fisher finds big trout in the river only during certain times of the year, most likely spawning rainbows from the Kootenai River below the falls, en route to and from their natal redds. For most of the season, fly fishing on the Yaak brings pan-sized brook trout or juvenile rainbows, which circle like moving clouds through deep, rock-lined holes.

"Something unusual is beginning to happen in the world of fly fishing," said Tim Linehan, who runs Linehan Outfitting with his wife, Joanne. "In the same way birdwatchers concerned about the longevity of rare birds keep life lists verifying species encountered, fly fishers are now doing the same with rare trout. Every year we get a few bookings completely dedicated to the experience of catching a Kootenai redband rainbow. These fishers seem to be the John James Audubon of trout fishing. They are well-versed in the ancient story of the redband rainbow and its importance to our world of trout fishing. I believe these trout watchers are interested in making a clear statement about native trout and unsullied places like the Yaak."

Tim told me about the fishing life list one winter morning over the telephone, just before I left to fish midges in a fast riffle of the Kootenai River. All day I thought of fly fishers traveling hundreds, maybe thousands, of miles to experience a trout no longer than a child's hand. The idea was incredible to me. That afternoon, as I returned a nice fourteen-inch rainbow to the chilly waters of the Kootenai, I wondered if any of the wildness of the redband rainbow still makes its way to the big river. Certainly somewhere along the line the genetics were passed along, perhaps under a plunging waterfall or overflowing pool during a particularly wet spring—or maybe I would just like to believe that is the case.

Regardless, as my trout finned back to its riffle, I realized why river people like Tim and Joanne fight so hard for old-growth forest and pristine places. Even without the rarity of its redband stock, the Yaak River still calls out to fly fishers like me. What it lacks in trout size, it more than makes up for in a surplus of solitude. Drop into its steep-walled canyon, and all that surrounds you is the noisy rush of river muscling through an unsettled landscape where wild grizzlies still roam.

The Linehans came to the valley decades ago to build a fly-fishing business capable of servicing a number of great rivers, from the nearby Kootenai and Clark Fork to Big Spring Creek in north-central Montana. But the Yaak Valley owns their hearts, because every morning they awaken to the natural melody of its song. They can tell you when the elk move down from the high country, where blue grouse take shelter, or the number of bald eagles that ride the air currents above the river during a season. They know secret waterfalls in backwoods places and certain plunge pools where the redband rainbow still clings to life.

A river like the Yaak is truly their "firepit," the central place from which their fly fishing experience extends.

A few times each season, Tim and Joanne steal a day from their busy outfitting schedule and hike back into the humid rainforest, to one of those magic little tributaries where they know special trout swim. For as long as it takes, they stare into the swirling water, watching, waiting for a diminutive, shadowy form to appear, a sign that all remains right in their homewater. With each sighting, the two advocates reaffirm that all their efforts working on behalf of trout, rivers, and wilderness is worth it.

SWAN RIVER AND ERIC BJORGE

On a warm autumn morning, under a canopy of blue skies and pillowy clouds, Eric Bjorge backed his trailer to the edge of the upper Swan River. Chris McCreedy and I slid a small rubber raft into the swift current and held tight, waiting for Eric to park. Nearby, an oversized sign put up by the Department of Fish, Wildlife & Parks outlined a list of hazards on the twisting, logjammed section below, a caution not to be taken lightly on this energetic little river.

A colorful mosaic of rounded cobbles shone like stained glass through the clear water, the low-angle light enhancing the grays, maroons, greens, and tans. Tree swallows performed aerial acrobatics above the river while gobbling caddisflies emerged off the riffles. On the opposite bank a pair of ravens strutted like old-time church deacons, scolding us for intruding on their private place on the river.

For weeks I had been eagerly awaiting this trip, one of the last of the season. When we first talked about a day on the Swan River, Eric, who owns Two Rivers Outfitters in Big Fork, informed me he guides on the section only sparingly, a commitment not due solely to the area's remoteness or difficulty. Instead, he is concerned that in the future it may receive more angling pressure than it could stand, and he worries about the ecological changes that might result.

Over my life as a fly fisher, I have invaded many small, unheralded fisheries like the Swan. They represent the true essence of fly fishing: a day to be alone in nature, in solitude and silence. Sadly, that unique character and fragile beauty now needs to be aggressively protected from the growing popularity of fly fishing.

So often we get caught up in the exuberance of larger rivers, swept away by their strength, challenge, and reward. We forget that within the gigantic 147,138-square-mile footprint of Montana there flow some nine thousand streams and rivers. Tucked into this maze of water are thousands of smaller fisheries that never find their way onto the pages of national publications.

That morning on the Swan River, we strung 5X tippet and tied to it whatever dry fly made sense. As we rounded the first sweeping corner, we rammed headlong into the first of several dangerous logjams. The buttress was equipped with raft-sinking points of broken branches and half-submerged cottonwood logs, around which a canoe could wrap itself. Once beyond the first barrier, an unusual silence fell between the three of us as we acclimated to the river, the loud chirping of yellow warblers, the rustling of autumn leaves, and the constant gurgle of the flow winding through the mountain valley.

The silence broke as Eric, from the front of the raft, brought the first trout of the day to the surface. It charged from beneath a length of submerged gray cottonwood that probably had plunged into the river decades earlier. The fourteen-inch westslope cutthroat raced back and forth beside the boat as if it actually possessed enough strength to pull Eric overboard, if only the right leverage could be found. When the struggle waned, the outfitter leaned forward and gripped the fly's barbless hook, gave it a sharp twist, and the trout was released without ever being touched by a human hand. Eric's second trout was a nice rainbow, his third another cutthroat.

He lost the fourth fish and I relaxed a little at not having connected yet, when from the dense shadow of an overhanging bank a nice speckled brook trout came and took my dry fly. So round was the trout's arc that he was headed back to cover before he realized he'd been fooled.

After releasing the trout, I took out my camera and wide-angle lens to photograph the spectacular scenery that surrounded us—autumn trees so brightly colorful they challenged the eyes, shrubs of red, orange, and maroon along the bank that cast long reflections in the flowing water.

A mile downstream Eric announced it was time to stop fishing. He tucked his rod on the side of the raft as Chris pulled us into a slow cove.

"There's a bunch," Chris whispered, pointing at the shade-dappled water near the opposite bank. "There, right there, at ten o'clock." I squinted hard into the pool and finally caught the outline of a white-edged fin moving through the current, a fin attached to a bull trout eighteen, maybe twenty inches long. It swam just above the brightly colored bottom. My eyes eventually adjusted to the shaded waters and I could pick out more shimmering bull trout, all swimming upstream to a narrow tributary that flowed through a tunnel of golden cottonwoods before joining the river.

Each autumn on mountain rivers like the Swan, when the leaves drop and collect in back eddies, bull trout buck the river's current and reach for their natal stream, where they can once more perpetuate their troubled species. Exactly what lures these travelers through the maze of waters on their journey back to the particular tributary from which they came remains unknown. Some experts believe the draw is the result of a minuscule difference in the physical composition and makeup of the water, maybe a trace of phosphorus, selenium, or some other mineral found in one tributary but not another. They believe trout, through their olfactory senses, can recognize the subtle differences between tributaries and are drawn home by what they remember, a recollection buried in their imprinted genetic code.

For a long time that late afternoon, we watched dozens of big trout glide past the boat in the shadows of immense cottonwoods, as though it was our sole reason for being there. They swam determinedly, sometimes in pairs or three abreast, tirelessly pushing against the hard current.

The remarkable display of strength we watched unfold has, over the last half century, grown uncommon on many rivers in Montana because many natural migration routes have been blocked by human "progress." Migrating trout cannot overcome man-made obstacles that block a certain tributary—a diversion dam or a culvert or a landslide of silt sliding from the side of a new gravel driveway leading to a mountain retreat.

When we eventually rejoined the river's flow, I took more notice of where the trout came from, those hidden places under willow branches, tangled logjams, deep sweeping pools, and cavernous undercut banks. The river and the landscape had become my focus of attention.

I can't recall how many fish came to net that day, or even how many hours the float took or the number of dry flies I left hanging on cottonwood logs. I can't even remember where we ate lunch or dinner—maybe there isn't enough room in my memory for mundane details, displaced by the awesome parade of bull trout swimming to their spawning grounds.

Eric is right to worry about the Swan River and other places like it, simply because so much hangs in delicate balance: the trout, the chirp of the western tanager, the flash of a black-chinned hummingbird as it darts between trees, the beaver that surfaces with the flip of a tail, the dank smell of the forest beside the river. We Montanans are blessed to still have places of mystery, places of unique diversity, and special meaning. Perhaps the only way to protect them is to leave them untrod. But then what would rekindle our own wild spirits?

FLATHEAD RIVER AND JUSTIN LAWRENCE

For Montanans who judge the authentic value of our homeland by the wildness it retains, the remarkable 1.5-million-acre wilderness complex of the Bob Marshall, Scapegoat, and Great Bear is sacred. The farthest distance across the vast complex is an impressive 140 miles, between Rogers Pass on the southern edge and Glacier National Park to the north. Even though a modern traveler can circle the region on state highways, not a single roadway is permitted to cross the wilderness expanse.

The area's geology is displayed on a stage of massive limestone walls and ridgelines pushed upright and tilted eastward by a tremendous thrusting within the earth. Within this broken country are some of Montana's most precious trout streams: the headwaters of the Dearborn, Sun, Teton, and Blackfoot, along with hundreds of tributary streams. Two of Montana's most valued blue-ribbon trout streams also originate in the wilderness complex, the Flathead River's South Fork and Middle Fork.

From a single glacial buttress skirting the Continental Divide flow the South Fork Flathead's highest tributaries: Danaher Creek, Youngs Creek, Hahn Creek, and a dozen smaller creeks. The first mention of the South Fork of the Flathead River on a modern map comes when Danaher Creek is joined by Youngs Creek at the high end of the Danaher Basin.

Coursing through the middle of that basin, Danaher Creek builds strength as it tumbles from the mountains and picks up water from smaller creeks, grinding tender meadowland to bedrock on its way to becoming the South Fork of the Flathead River. The South Fork is truly a wild river for its entire length, flexing and brawling around massive logjams and undercut banks. And its clean water harbors a profusion of native trout.

On its own journey to join the South Fork Flathead, the amazing but unheralded White River parallels the magnificent Chinese Wall, a prominent cliff accentuating the Continental Divide. The White's two branches splash over huge boulders and drop into plunge pools holding native trout any dry-fly fisher would trade a new rod just to have a go at.

More than a few Montanans believe the Flathead's South Fork is the best native fishery in the state, and not solely on the merits of the wild setting through which it tumbles. The river is furnished native cutthroats and bull trout from a wild nursery below, the Hungry Horse Reservoir. The South Fork is one of those dreamed-about havens for serious enthusiasts willing to hike or horsepack into the wilderness.

The Middle Fork Flathead River also originates in the Bob Marshall Wilderness, beneath the high walls of the Continental Divide at the confluence of Strawberry and Bowl Creeks. Tributary creeks, springs, and seeps add to the steadily growing waters until at last it is called by some "Montana's Wildest River."

The Middle Fork proceeds from "the Bob" through the Great Bear Wilderness before finally carving a westerly course through a steep-walled canyon paralleling US 2, where it delineates the southern border of Glacier National Park. The river crashes and spins over huge boulders and rams headlong into sheer rock walls, a perfect playground for whitewater rafters. Here is perhaps one of state's best examples of a quickly maturing multiple-use waterway, a place where trout fishing is but one of the many recreational uses.

Many tributaries in the wilderness, as well as those flowing from Glacier National Park, serve as spawning grounds for native cutthroat and bull trout. Both the Middle Fork and South Fork are managed by Montana's Department of Fish, Wildlife & Parks as native fisheries, a designation that in the past has meant removing nonnative species, particularly rainbow trout.

The final big branch of the Flathead, the North Fork, begins on the west-facing slopes of the Canadian Rockies in the vicinity of Crowsnest Pass. Above the international border, the North Fork is continually threatened by mining interests, oil and gas exploration, and logging. Once in the United States, even though it makes up the western border of Glacier National Park, it is still not free from serious environmental challenges in the form of urbanization, road-building, and poor logging practices in adjacent national forest lands.

The North Fork covers about 58 miles in Montana, pressed between the Flathead National Forest and beautiful Glacier National Park, America's "Crown of the Continent." Along its upper reaches, the river receives glacial and seasonal runoff from highland lakes of the type geologists call "sinks," each scraped to bedrock thousands of years ago by massive Ice Age glaciers. The significance of these drainages rests in their supply of remarkably pure water, water containing only sparse levels of nutrients due to the proliferation of bedrock strata through which the tributary streams flow. Complicating the situation are the sinks themselves, because they trap any nutrients originating from seasonal freshet above the lakes.

Compared to some of the Montana's southern rivers, like the Bighorn, Madison, or Yellowstone, where water courses through sedimentary strata offering tremendous nutrient loads to fisheries, the North Fork of the Flathead might be considered sterile in comparison. This leads many fly fishers to believe that the river to be less of a trout fishery than it actually is. One individual who has worked to understand what happens on the entire Flathead River system happens to be one of my fishing buddies, fly-fishing guide Justin Lawrence.

"I came to Montana from Colorado, where I had worked as a fly-fishing guide,"

Justin said. "When I left Colorado, I was in search of an area that offered diversity as a trout fishery, so I dragged out the Montana map and began the search. As soon as I saw the network of blue lines smeared across northwest Montana and the Flathead Valley, I realized that was the place for me.

"I moved to Montana, and the first time I laid eyes on the Flathead system, I have to admit I was a little intimated, blown away by the amount of water. I had never seen so much beautiful trout water during my career as a fly fisher.... We live and play in heaven up here. If you're willing to adapt your fishing style, the trout fishing can be awesome, second to none, especially for native fish. Both my wife and I thought the Flathead Valley had to be the perfect place to dig roots, start guiding, and raise our family in the outdoors."

Justin Lawrence elaborated on what it means to adapt to a region. "I have to admit, after perusing the Flathead drainage a little, I was stunned. So at first, I took a couple of years and just fished the different forks. After I got my bearings and learned the migratory habits of the trout, I hung out a shingle and went to work as a fly-fishing guide.

"What most people don't understand about the Flathead River is that it is truly a migratory fishery. It gets a large share of its game fish from the big lake below, and if you haven't got the migration scheme of things figured out, you can get left in the cold. I mean you can fish a spot one week and make a good catch, return with clients the next and find nothing, simply because the trout have moved on."

In the past, water coming from Hungry Horse Dam significantly decreased the water temperature below the dam and, as a result, downstream on the river's main stem. Trout do best in water temperatures between 45 and 65 degrees Fahrenheit. In the years after completion of Hungry Horse, water released into the lower South Fork was taken from the lower portion of the reservoir, simply because of the dam's outdated design. Discharges of 39 degrees were common, a condition unfavorable to maximum trout growth or reproduction. Not only did the chilly water impact trout growth, it had a negative effect on aquatic vegetation and insect emergence, both necessary elements of a healthy fishery. The adverse condition prevailed for decades, until in 1996 the dam was finally retrofitted with draw gates that allowed operators to select water from various levels in the pool. In the eyes of everyone who knew the Flathead, the retrofit was a major improvement, a wonderful benefit to downstream ecology. Fishery biologists even went on record as saying that finally the Flathead's main stem might have a chance to regain an ecological foothold similar to that enjoyed prior to the dam.

None of the biologists would hazard a guess as to how long the regrowth process might take, or how long it might take to mitigate the damage already done by decades of poor water management. What sketchy projections were made supported the notion that resident trout populations on the river would increase appreciably as long as water managers remained sensitive to the biological and ecological needs of the river.

Looking at the three forks of the Flathead and their present role as game fisheries, it is important to consider two factors. First, the resource is managed as a native trout fishery. Second, on their best day the drainages are primarily migratory fisheries almost completely reliant on Flathead Lake or Hungry Horse Reservoir. Notably, some trout travel as far as 130 miles through the Flathead system during their spawning ritual.

Flathead Lake serves as an enormous nursery for a variety of game fish that eventually find their way into the branches of the river, most specifically trout and Lake Superior whitefish. Early in the season, around April, sometimes earlier, lake-raised cutthroat suddenly feel the primal urge to spawn. They leave the still water and begin an ancient journey upstream, first through the Flathead's main stem and eventually to the Middle Fork or the North Fork and on to their natal streams. The trout travel in schools, always on the move. Only the best river guides can anticipate their impatient movements.

Each season the cutthroats are followed by the larger bull trout, compelled in the direction of the gravelly redds upon which they started as eggs. They will not stop their upstream migration until that exact spot is reached, that is, unless their natal tributary has been blocked, or their spawning habitat clogged by silt overload from logging, road development, mining, and housing development.

Their migration journey finished, the cutthroats are thought to return to Flathead Lake much more quickly than they ascended, sometimes in less than twenty-four hours. Again, on their downstream journey, they are accessible to fly fishers, many of whom have stories of particular days spent on a certain section of river alive with waves of moving trout.

Unlike the no-nonsense, up-and-back cutthroats, bull trout hang around the mouths of their smaller tributary streams most of the summer, waiting for their genetic alarm to kick off. When autumn cools the air, the heavyweights—some as large as twenty pounds—start up the smaller tributaries, in many cases traveling through water barely deep enough to cover their backs. With their act of procreation complete, the bull trout head back downstream, bound for the deep waters of Flathead Lake.

"There are some trout fishers in Montana who believe the Flathead is a real bust, and there are those who even say the river is sterile," said Lawrence. "I hear it all the time when I guide clients on different rivers like the Missouri or the Clark Fork, but I just pass the comments off, realizing these poor devils just have never had a great day on the Flathead."

To top off the Flathead's fishing, each year as the cottonwood leaves begin to drop from branches overhanging the river, the dark shadows cast by hundreds of big fish appear along the bottom. These are not native trout but big Lake Superior whitefish, planted decades ago in Flathead Lake. These fish are the quarry of hordes of fishers who line the river's banks in autumn. The whitefish ascend only as far as the confluence of the Middle Fork and the North Fork, then turn around and head back to Flathead Lake.

This part of northern Montana also once boasted one of the West's most outstanding runs of kokanee salmon, a run that today is a tragic memory.

Hundreds of thousands of kokanee migrated from Flathead Lake to spawning tributaries, including McDonald Creek in Glacier National Park. The autumn spawning was a celebration of ecological wonder, one that attracted a huge congregation of bald eagles. Thousands of Montanans joined the ritual by traveling to the park and lining the bridge on the upper end of Lake McDonald in Glacier Park, just to stand in the company of eagles and grizzly bears seeking a meal of kokanee salmon. I always ran into people not seen for years, respected park employees and other professionals out to participate in our natural heritage.

Then in mid-sixties came the call to stock more lake trout in Flathead Lake so boat fishers might increase their take. Lake trout numbers quickly grew by enormous proportions as these predators decimated the kokanee salmon. The dramatic effects of its poor foresight had just started to sink in when, in 1968, Fish,

Wildlife & Parks decided to add a stock of Mysis shrimp to the same ecosystem in an effort to help the kokanee. The introduction was a total failure, and in short order the kokanee salmon population was all but wiped out. Within just a couple of years the bridge over McDonald Creek was empty; there were no fish left to make the run.

We humans far too often make tragic mistakes when we manipulate the delicate balance of nature. Hundreds of examples are all around us—the coyote, wolf, golden eagle, bull trout, passenger pigeon, Florida panther, black-footed ferret, and on and on. Perhaps fishery managers need to stay away from our waters, let them function naturally and, if possible, regenerate under their own primal power.

Justin Lawrence has thought a lot about the Flathead system. "I think today the most serious problem facing the Flathead drainage as a whole comes from the unhealthy condition of the lake," he said. "It holds the very lifeline of the river, and if the lake is managed poorly, the river suffers. Once the kokanee disappeared as a food source in Flathead Lake, the huge lake trout predators, some as large as thirty pounds and over, turned on the growing cutthroat population as a new food source.

"Montana Fish, Wildlife & Parks wants to manage the Flathead drainage as a native fishery and is even willing to go as far as to remove rainbows from the system by blocking off spawning routes. But in the lake that supplies almost all the native species to the river, the managers can't seem to do anything about the proliferation of lake trout, a voracious species that devours our native fish.

"Something aggressive has to be done if the Fish, Wildlife & Parks plans for a native fishery on the river are ever to come to fruition. The real problem facing the managers is the popularity of the lake trout fishery among boat and property owners on the lake. To kill off the lake trout or even allow a commercial fishery to develop and lessen the number would not go over very well from that segment of our angling public.... In my opinion, we are caught between two types of anglers. I just can't see how we are going to balance the two in the future. If the Flathead River is ever going to be a true native fishery, it has to be managed like a native fishery and something definitely has to happen to the nonnative lake trout or the whole thing is just smoke and mirrors."

BLACKFEET INDIAN RESERVATION AND JOE KIPP

In Montana these days we hear a lot about crowded rivers, fishing pressure, and the possibility of coming regulations designed to control the overuse of some of our more popular fisheries. When I hear about twenty boats per hour passing a certain spot on a river, wade fishers pushed aside by boaters, anger on rivers, or the shortage of parking space at certain put-in sites, I always think about my friend Joe Kipp on the Blackfeet Indian Reservation.

Located in northern Montana adjacent to Glacier National Park, the Blackfeet Reservation represents one of the state's finest trout fishing resources. Perhaps best known are the beefy rainbows taken from Duck, Mitten, and Mission Lakes. Not as well known is the spectacular stream fishing, available as long as you are in the company of a Native guide.

Of all the memorable experiences I've had fishing trout waters in Montana, time spent with Joe Kipp ranks high on my list of favorites. There are, of course, the wonderful lakes where trout can run as long as a tall man's leg and are as healthy and robust as any to be found in the West, but my mind invariably returns to small streams, those precious gems coursing through the mountains where great fishing memories are made and remade each season by only a very few anglers. It just doesn't get better.

Purchasing a reservation fishing permit is only the start, because Joe will complete the transaction by telling trout fishers a remarkable story about what trout and fishing mean to his people, and he will end by asking you to respect those ancestral traditions. For trout and land alike he will ask reverence, something all fly fishers should offer to all places.

Down through history, the Blackfeet were considered the fiercest of all Northern Plains warriors. They protected their lands and hunting grounds with the passion of a grizzly sow protecting her cubs, and that longstanding sense of stewardship still remains strong. We trout fishers are lucky their land is open to those of us who seek something different in the way of sport.

One late summer day, my lifelong friend, Joe Cerise, and I joined Kipp on the reservation, to fish isolated spots. That evening, while traveling back from Cut Bank Creek, the dusky light stretched long shadows across the sagebrush plains and Glacier's mountains slipped gracefully into darkness. For the longest time we were silent in the truck, drinking in the scene unfolding in front of us.

Suddenly, Kipp broke the mood by asking, "Hey, are either of you afraid of grizzlies?"

Joe is not the kind of guide who would ask such a question without cause, so Cerise and I waited for a few minutes, exchanging glances while Kipp's eyes stayed glued to the horizon. Cerise finally broke the lingering silence with, "Well, I guess anyone who has been there has to admit being intimidated by grizzlies, and anyone who doesn't just hasn't been there or is either full of it or looking for a shortened life."

"Well, I just wondered," said Kipp, "because I know a spot west of here, over by the mountains, that is hardly ever fished. It's on tribal ground and definitely on the wild side. I mean, there are grizzlies in there, and I'll admit we've had some trouble with them in the past, but the cutthroat fishing is out of this world."

"What do you call trouble?" I asked.

"We can't make it on this trip," he continued, as if I had not spoken, "but if you give me some notice we could make the trip in a week or two, if you don't mind sharing the stream with a few grizzlies."

The inside of the pickup truck was as silent as the confessional in an old country church.

Once again my friend spoke up: "I don't know about Gordon, but it sounds great to me."

"What about you?" Kipp asked, facing me.

"Sure, I'm game as long as I can pack a can of bear spray along, assuming it's legal for a nonnative to carry bear spray on the reservation."

"Bear spray, what's with bear spray?" Kipp quipped. "I was thinking about carrying a sawed-off shotgun myself. As for you packing, we Indians stopped trusting white men bearing arms a long time ago."

Laughter replaced apprehension, and for the next half hour I was harassed by both Joes about my ability to use bear spray if challenged, whether I could point it in the right direction, and even about the possibility that I would end up shooting myself.

Two weeks later, I sat across from Joe Kipp in the same black pickup, rolling across the same Northern Plains. This time the prairie was blushed by the first light of morning, the frosted mountains shining in the distance as bright as mercury. After an hour's drive we pulled off the pavement, went through a locked gate, and started in the direction of the high mountains. We crept through dense groves of aspen trees the color of mustard with the windows rolled down, the rattle and swish of windblown vegetation filling the truck. We stopped on a high ridge rimming a steep-sided, timbered valley. Below us tumbled a small stream, a brilliant silver ribbon unraveling between the rugged glacier-carved mountains. Short runs of a few hundred feet or more stretched between deep pools where the creek swirled slowly, then quieted for a while before starting the next whitewater run. The stream looked as perfect as any I had ever seen.

We each took a pinch of cut tobacco and placed it on rocks high above the valley, our way of thanking whatever god we felt might be listening.

After stringing up a rod and tying up wading boots, we started down the steep slope. Joe carried a shortened shotgun and, out of character, talked loudly as we slid down toward the creek, his way of announcing our presence to anything napping that morning on the brushy hillside.

We arrived on the downstream end of a glass-clear pool. With a hand motion, Joe pointed to the narrow riffle entering the pool and nodded his head. Mutely, I acknowledged what he wanted me to do. When trout fishers arrive on the edge of promising pool, we invariably speak to one another in sign language, despite the fact that we know how unlikely it is that fish huddled deep underwater can hear a human voice on the bank above. I wonder sometimes if the silence we observe is not meant more for us than for the trout we seek.

I had a fresh October caddis tied to a 5X tippet. With a short cast, the fly landed next to the riffle and began to drift. Kipp watched it like a good bird dog on point. The fly drifted through the pool untouched, and he mimed for me to make another try. For the second time the fly touched down next to the riffle. It had covered only a few inches before it was consumed amid a spray of water and taken to the very bottom of the pool. Fueled by two weeks of anticipation, I set the hook hard, and when I looked up I saw Joe's grimace. "Take it easy. Give him a break," he barked in a tone loud enough to carry across the stream and halfway up the aspen-banked hillside.

In that instant, I learned a lot about being a good trout fisher and gained a great deal of admiration for Joe Kipp. He is a man who has managed to keep the sport of fly fishing in honest perspective, honoring the quarry he seeks.

I do not believe I have ever waded among a purer strain of cutthroats—wild, willing, and un-shy. We encountered no grizzlies that day, and I cast flies until my arm ached. A few miles upstream I held the shotgun while Joe fished the deep pools beneath a sacred mountain. While he stood, bent slightly forward, waiting for a trout, I put the gun aside and photographed him fishing, standing there on his native land with porcelain-white clouds drifting across the sky above.

I could spend the rest of my fishing life trying to learn a stream like the one we fished that day and never come close to what Joe Kipp already knows about it. As I sat on the bank and watched the image of my friend captured inside the viewfinder of my camera, I realized Joe doesn't just see the natural world around him, he blends into it. He is part of a land, a stream, and a valley, a landscape for which his ancestors once died. He hears the voice of the ancient animals that once provided life for his people, and he hears their whispers on the wind. Joe is a traditional leader among the Blackfeet people, he cherishes the old ways, and he listens to the old voices. He knows he has to listen each day if that ancient ancestry is to remain alive in a modern world.

15

MISSOURI RIVER AND ITS TRIBUTARIES

Such a being is man, who has flowed down through other forms of being and absorbed and assimilated portions of them into himself, thus becoming a microcosm most richly Divine because most richly terrestrial, just as a river becomes rich by flowing on and on through varied climes and rocks, through many mountains and vales, constantly appropriating portions to itself, rising higher in scale of rivers as it grows rich in the absorption of the soils and smaller streams.

—John Muir

Spend enough time in Montana and you will eventually hear talk about our waters being better in the "good old days." Looking back, it is easy to think that things were better forty or fifty years ago, that more trout came to the net, rivers ran clearer, and special places remained hidden. But was that really the case? Perhaps it is our memories that have somehow morphed and grown, just like the story of that first trout we each caught on a fly.

One morning I was on the Yellowstone with Skip Gibson and John Bailey, and during a break in the action I asked Bailey how he thought today's river stacked up against the early days when his father, Dan, taught him to pitch a fly.

"The Yellowstone is in far better shape right now than it was five or six decades ago," he declared. "In years past, our community used to dump municipal sewage in the river, as did Yellowstone National Park and every little burg in between.

"In the past, mine waste has been discharged in the river, as well as toxic material from rail yards. The list goes on. We just didn't take water pollution seriously, but over the years we have learned that without clean water we all stand to lose a great deal—especially fly fishers on the prowl for native trout.

"Since the old days, because of public concern and outcry inspired by a lot of environmental education, we have imposed much stiffer laws and are willing as a state to enforce them. There is no question our water quality has improved and with it the quality of our trout fishing. Sure, we still have a long ways to go, but we should give ourselves credit, a solid pat on the back, for what has already been accomplished by a strong network of advocacy."

Montana Governor Brian Schweitzer expressed a similar opinion: "In those go-go years of digging...the early coal mines were dug right alongside our rivers and people of the day really didn't care if a bunch of dirt and coal was shoved down in the river. The folks mined copper, gold, and silver in the early days, and when they got done and walked away and a little trickle of acid water ran out into the stream it didn't bother them a bit because those rivers were so big and there is so much territory—how could we be hurting this environment...

"Those days are gone," Schweitzer noted. "Those people weren't bad people, by the way. They were our grandparents. They did their level best, they thought they were doing right by the folks and the land, and they made mistakes. We dug holes in places where we should not have, we cut trees in places we should not have, we put roads into places that were not well thought out, and we built roads in the wrong way. We ended up with a lot of siltation, we ended up with acid water, we cut trees where we decreased our watersheds and wildlife habitat; those were mistakes."

Schweitzer concluded by saying, "As we move forward we will continue to be in the natural resource industry, but I think we now have the technology to be more responsive to the impact we have on the landscape."

John cautioned me that Montana's battle for clean water was far from over, but at least today we have a network of advocates able to recognize the causes and speak out. A good example of that "take charge" attitude is apparent in a recent Montana River Action news alert, which reads in part: "A lawsuit was filed by five Montana environmental groups against the U.S. Environmental Protection Agency (EPA) for tolerating the failure of Montana's Department of Environmental Quality (DEQ) to comply with the U.S. Clean Water Act, the Act passed by Congress in 1972. Thirty years later, the goals of the Act are yet to become a reality. Protections that the public used to take for granted are unraveled by the policies of national administrations and the program to address impaired waters through the 'Total Maximum Daily Load' (TMDL) program has yet to be seriously implemented in Montana.

"The lawsuit forced the EPA to insist that Montana DEQ establish TMDLs for polluted streams and establish cleanup plans for the state's impaired waters." (In short, this means determining the amount of pollution allowable on a water system during a given day, and the requirement that Montana set and enforce those levels.)

The news alert went on to list some troubling statistics from a draft of a new federally required state report: 47 percent of 9,858 miles of Montana's rivers and streams and 81 percent (489,582 acres) of lakes are still contaminated, and on many more waterways there isn't even sufficient data to determine the status. This report is intended to measure water conditions as part of a program to protect and improve the quality of rivers and lakes—something state and federal agencies were supposed to be doing already.

When we think about the vital connection between our state's water quality and the enjoyment of fly fishing, it is imperative to realize the hazards we still face. Imagine, five privately funded environmental groups had to sue the Environmental Protection Agency—the very agency we taxpayers believe is protecting our environment—just to do its job, while the members of our own state government for thirty years basically ignored mandates established under federal law.

In his book *John Muir and His Legacy: The American Conservation Movement*, author Stephen Fox comes to the startling conclusion that, historically, amateur warriors have carried the torch when it comes to protecting the environment, and generally their strongest enemy has not been the vampires of industry but the federal and state agencies we have entrusted to protect our rights. It is a valuable lesson for all of us in the fight to protect Montana's waterways.

MISSOURI RIVER AND PETE CARDINAL

More than two hundred years ago the Corps of Discovery arrived at the three headwater forks on the Missouri River, their schedule getting a little tight as autumn approached. The left fork headed east while the right fork veered due west and the middle headed south. Their choice was between the soon-to-be-named Gallatin, the Madison, and the Jefferson Rivers, and if they had been trout fishers, any one would have been the right decision. But the explorers needed to find a way across the western mountains and onward to the Columbia River Basin, so it was the Jefferson they followed.

From that very point on the Montana map, where the three rivers merge, the Missouri River is born. It has as complete a human history as any river in Montana, primarily because of the explorations of Lewis & Clark. However, sometimes overlooked is the river's ancient history, which might stretch the imagination because at one time the Missouri River flowed to the Arctic Ocean instead of the Gulf of Mexico. Not until the continental ice sheet was carried southward some fifteen thousand years ago did glacial debris shift the river's course to the east.

Today, the Missouri River flows due north from the junction of the three forks, pressed between the Elkhorn Mountains to the west and the Big Belts to the east. Here is an open landscape dotted with cattle ranches, huge grainfields, and a few small towns. The river is first pinched off by a dam just outside the town of Toston, then twice more outside Helena. North of Helena the river snakes through the towering cliffs of the Gates of the Mountains. The huge white Madison Limestone buttresses edging this feature were entirely cut by the mighty force of water and show the tremendous effects erosion can have on even a solid rock landscape.

Beyond the Gates of the Mountains, the river is again blocked, this time by Holter Dam.

After backing up behind four dams, you would think the Missouri would have forgotten how to be a real river, but the stretch of water immediately below Holter Dam, between Wolf Creek and Ulm, offers some of the state's best tailwater trout fishing.

Beginning at the face of the dam, the river swings in an easterly arc and flows through an area littered by the remains of a massive volcano, believed by experts to have been active about fifty million years ago toward the end of the era in which the Rocky Mountains rose above the high plains. The remnants of past volcanic activity can be seen in several areas from Wolf Creek Canyon to Cascade, particularly in the six-mile stretch between Mountain Palace and Pelican Point. Dark basalt dikes rise above the river in this area, marking the point at which the Missouri tailwater transforms into a truly prairie river. It remains that way until it meets more dams at Great Falls, where it suddenly relinquishes its identity as a coldwater fishery.

There is probably no river in the state whose face has been changed more by the combined actions of man and nature than the Missouri. But through its blue-ribbon tailwater section, the river is everything a trout fisher like Pete Cardinal could want.

Cardinal earned a degree in fisheries biology from Michigan State University, and then a master's from Montana State University in 1980, after which he took a job with the Montana Department of Fish, Wildlife & Parks. To his good fortune, Pete's first assignment was on the Missouri River, a fishery he learned to cherish as he worked to understand its unique dynamics. After spending just a year on the Missouri, he was transferred to the Stillwater River, where his employment lasted only a few months before he and the agency parted ways. According to Pete, "We just didn't see eye to eye on several important issues regarding the state's rivers and trout management."

I am constantly surprised at how many dedicated and knowledgeable people like Pete Cardinal spend years in college preparing for important professional field assignments, only to end up leaving federal and state agencies to strike out on their own. Yet somehow they find the wherewithal to remain around the natural resources they love.

Satisfied he made the right decision but unmoved in his commitment to work on behalf of rivers and trout, Cardinal returned to the Missouri River, where he started Missouri River Angler, a fly-fishing service that thrives today on a strong base of return clientele.

Pete is not only one of the strongest advocates on the Missouri, he is one of the best fly fishers I know. His skill comes from his passion and in-depth knowledge of his homewater—plus, he has the patience of a glacier and the cleverness of a predator.

In his work as a river advocate and a fly-fishing outfitter, Pete is a self-professed perfectionist, a good caster unafraid to use artificial flies of microscopic dimensions. For Pete, there is no better fishery on which to practice than the Missouri between Holter Dam and Cascade, known for its blinding hatches, late-evening spinner falls, and remarkable nymph fishing. The river's gentle flows, soft glassy runs, and high trout numbers are perfect for the dry-fly enthusiast. While it is true that whirling disease has had an impact, the dread infestation seems diminished among the healthy trout, including a growing population of browns less prone to the effects of the disease.

The summer season on the Missouri begins in June, which coincides with the arrival of the most intense rain of the season. Normally, by July the weather has calmed and air temperatures rise steadily, reaching the nineties and occasionally higher.

The cycling climate and moisture influences the emergence of insect life on the river. Heavy *Tricorhythodes* begin to appear each morning as the warm days settle in. When things on the Missouri are in balance—water quality, healthy aquatic environment, well-oxygenated water—the ecosystem turns into a cornucopia of insect life. Caddisfly and mayfly hatches fill separate biological niches, subtly opening and closing, as July wanes. As the season progresses and hot, midsummer days become the norm, terrestrial insects like grasshoppers and ants join the menu. Hopper fishing can be tremendous, given the gentle breezes common to the high plains and the river's closeness to open meadows, pastures, and cultivated fields.

Anglers who patiently present hoppers right along the bank usually attract big trout, their size a sign of the present vitality of the system. Grasshoppers on any prairie river signal the vital link between surrounding geography, seasonal climate, and the overall health of riverine ecosystems. Trout in more mountainous, timbered areas exchange this menu item for terrestrials such as beetles and ants.

As in other Montana environs, heavy frost and snow can come to the high plains as early as September. At that point, terrestrial insects swiftly decline, followed by smaller flies like caddis. As if the ecosystem is fattening its watery inhabitants for the cold days of winter, large October caddis, those mahogany marvels, begin to appear. Here is a final feast for trout and whitefish before the water cools and winter sets in. The prairies and softly rounded hill country of north-central Montana, through which the Missouri flows, is famous for frigid arctic fronts. Winter temperatures can plummet to subzero, and hold. At the other end of the winter temperature cycle, however, strong chinook winds can arrive just as quickly and melt all the snow in a single day, while bouncing warm air off everything in their path.

As with most Montana tailwaters, the Missouri doesn't freeze over in winter for miles below the dam. Tiny dark midges by the billions make up whatever surface feeding occurs. Beneath the surface, fish rely on scuds, sow bugs, minnows, and worms. Farther downstream, the river is likely to plug with ice.

For almost twenty-five years, Pete has been introducing fly fishers from all parts of the nation to the bounty of the Mighty Mo, and tossing in information about important issues that now face the river. He believes that the more people become aware of critical issues, the more friends a river will have when the need arises.

He knows this firsthand. For when Pete returned to the Missouri River in the first half of the 1980s, he almost immediately joined others seriously concerned about the tailwater. The Montana Power Company—the owner/operator of Canyon Ferry, Hauser, and Holter Dams—had decided to increase hydroelectric profits by using the habitat-damaging process of power peaking. The capricious increase and decrease in water levels resulting from that management system put at jeopardy the entire tailwater—seventy miles of fantastic trout water.

Right out of the chute, Pete and others locked horns with the power managers. Following years of meetings and unrelenting objections by concerned citizens, the huge power company agreed to at least try to manage the water so it didn't directly jeopardize the welfare of fish and aquatic species or compromise the safety of wade fishers.

Because of the early work of these advocates, today's flow regimes on the Missouri are far less a problem than they were in the 1980s, but constant diligence is needed to monitor each new operating plan that is unfolded and offered for public debate.

When you fish with Pete, you get accustomed to hearing about his river, how it changes with each season and suffers at the hands of some state and federal agencies. He'll even bend your ear about potential future regulations designed to control use.

For the most part, he still maintains that he and Fish, Wildlife & Parks have an "eye to eye" problem when it comes to certain important issues, but he is satisfied that his ability to impact strategic decisions is greatly enhanced by his advocacy as an outsider, as opposed to what he might have accomplished as a state employee.

Another serious problem that plagues the Missouri River, particularly on its most popular section between the dam and Cascade, is overcrowding by both private and guided fly fishers. It's one of the inevitabilities when rivers become famous. Paralleled by a frontage road extending from Wolf Creek to Ulm, the Missouri is easily accessible. Mile for mile, the Mo offers some of the best wade fishing in Montana, as well as an ample number of public boat launches. This easy access, coupled with the remarkable population of browns and rainbows, makes the Missouri one of the state's most visited fisheries, ranking right up there with the trout-rich Madison and Yellowstone.

In my opinion, the Missouri is a prime example of a river being loved to death. It is often possible to sit on the riverbank and count double-digit boats drifting by each hour, and view wade fishers spread out like age spots on an old fly fisher's hand. It's even common for boat fishers to stack up above certain slots and riffles, waiting in line to fish the same water. The crowding is far more acute on the upper section between the dam and the tiny fishing town of Craig, where a number of outfitters hang their shingles.

The crowding is added to by a host of recreational floaters attracted to its gentle current and interesting landscape.

John Bailey has strong feelings about recreational floaters: "I enjoy seeing people use the river, floating it and such. In my opinion, the more people view the river as an important resource, the more people will come forward in its time of need."

Pete shares Bailey's point of view, but he calls what has happened on the Missouri over the last few years "an explosion of non-fishing use," which includes a public not very familiar with the ethics of multiple use. "Everyone has an equal right to use a river," Cardinal stated. "In fact, diversity adds to those who end up caring about the resource, but it is up to all of us to respect each other's rights and treat people the same way we expect be treated. In the exercise of their enjoyment, some floaters haven't a clue how to respect the domain of trout fishers. It is not uncommon for a bunch of floaters to drift right through a fellow's fishing spot, legs dangling and thrashing in the water, just making it very difficult for everyone to enjoy themselves at the same time. Many of the floaters are in tubes and smaller boats and have almost no control when it comes to managing the current, which usually puts them right in the prime spots for trout fishing without any way to alter their course to avoid fishermen."

Canoes and other more controllable craft are rarely a problem, because in most cases these folks know how to maneuver their vessel, and give a wide birth to other users. The problem comes from more casual floaters out for a warm day's fun, without a care in the world.

I have talked to other fishing guides on the Missouri who tell of inner-tube floaters, two or three at a time, coming right through a riffle to ram smack into the side of a drift boat anchored at the base of a run. How much fun is that for a visiting fly fisher who has traveled to Montana from some other part of the country, and how well does that behavior work into Montana's commitment to developing a competitive fly-fishing industry? Pete thinks Fish, Wildlife & Parks is responsible for ensuring every user learns and follows a code of courtesy in order to avoid chaos and conflict on public waters. I agree. Educating the public may be a huge task for Fish, Wildlife & Parks, but it is their job. The agency must develop a strategy to enable concurrent multiple use on rivers like the Missouri.

Trout fishing is an important growth industry in Montana. It might be interesting to consider that, in this regard, only one user has paid a license fee to be on the river. It is important to those who spend hundreds of dollars a day to enjoy the bounty and peace of our rivers to be allowed a reasonable chance to enjoy themselves, while respecting the right of others to do the same.

In the case of the Missouri, the overcrowding makes it ripe for future regulation. It's a tough call but one that needs to be made, especially here and on a number of other rivers like the Blackfoot, Yellowstone, Bitterroot, Clark Fork, and, of course, the Middle Fork of the Flathead.

Sharing a river all comes down to education and respect. Fly fishers see one side of the story, but other perspectives also have merit. The recreational floaters, spearheaded by the Billings Jaycees, who helped in the fight against the energy industry on the Yellowstone in the 1970s, are a prime example of this. The large service club organized floats and was able to bring public focus to the plight of the river.

A few hours in a drift boat or wading likely spots will prove that the Missouri River fishes great these days. The sporadic overcrowding typically comes during peak season, between the end of June and late September. Thankfully for those of us who like some elbow room, the river saves its best for last. October and early November are my favorite times to fish the Mo, when autumn colors reflect off the gradually cooling water and the river's brown trout start to get active.

A few years back, I found myself waiting early one morning to meet up with Pete and Sandee Cardinal for a day's fishing in their drift boat. I had parked on a rise overlooking the Missouri just across from their house, and was quietly drinking a cup of coffee when a nice trout started to rise in a deep eddy right below me. The trout was gently nosing the edge of a swirling mat of aquatic grass that had gathered in the circulating eddy. Across the river, I could see Sandy walking their hunting dogs in the field behind their house, getting them in shape for bird season, while the trout in the eddy went on harvesting drifting flies.

For the longest time, I sipped my coffee and tried to convince myself every rising trout should not inspire an intuitive signal to fish. Eventually my Zen-like koan failed and I reached for my fly rod and slid down the steep bank. The closer I got, the more I realized the trout beneath the spinning mat was a "Montana lunker."

The brown was feeding on grasshoppers stranded by the chill of autumn. The hoppers rode the edge of the mat like a pack of kids clinging to carved horses on a carousel. The mat was big, maybe twenty feet across, and different trout rose at stations along its perimeter.

I picked out the big brown I had watched from above and counted the seconds between his rises. To temp him, I used a Turck's Tarantula, an ugly attractor that resembles absolutely nothing that exists in the natural world. With a few timely flips of my rod tip, the fly landed about two inches from the edge of the mat, and within a yard of drifting, it vanished inside a loud splash. Until that point the trout had only nosed his food, and I would like to say his reaction had something to do with a special twitch I placed artfully and delicately on the fly, but actually it was a sure sign the trout was ready to spawn and considered the Turck's a stranger in his territory.

As the grass mat bobbed on the wave caused by the rise, the big brown cut directly across the floating circle, pulling a growing V of stringy grass behind. By the time he made the mat's opposite side, the line had to weigh ten pounds. Surprisingly, the tippet held and I eventually was able to get the mess ashore. I had a lot more vegetation than trout. The brown was glowing, attired in his beautiful fall butter-colored belly, bright sides, and piercing red spots spread across his flanks like drops of sparkling red ink. The fish regained his strength and swam back in the direction of the grass mat when released.

As memorable as the catch was, it reveals one of the growing problems on the Missouri: the tremendous mass of aquatic weeds and grass clogging the river, particularly during autumn.

Over the last couple of decades, drifting weeds and grass have grown worse on the Mo, particularly in deep pools, midstream glides, and slower-moving runs. The dense vegetation is compounded by an increase in late-season algae; both create problems for fly fishers.

Some experts say the vegetation results from overabundant nitrogen, and it's likely that much of this nitrogen comes from the three huge reservoirs upstream. The health of those reservoirs ends up affecting the river downstream.

"The amount of nitrogen sources coming artificially from an increasing number of septic systems and man-made fertilizers used on agricultural fields along the waterway, coupled with nitrogen created naturally from the atmosphere, are making the big reservoirs eutrophic," Cardinal said. "That is to say, the vast amount of plant life present literally thrives in the nitrogen-rich atmosphere. We see the proliferation of plant life on the lower tailwater in the form of floating aquatic vegetation.

"I would like to see the state biologists get on the problem today, do some definitive studies, and develop restoration plans to curb the effects of nitrogen buildup before it becomes an overwhelming problem. After all, the health of the river and our fishery hangs in the balance. I believe we should be in a more preventative mode as opposed to our normal reactive posture once problems reach catastrophic levels. The river, the trout, and the entire ecology would be far better served by this type of management approach, and I believe the biologists in the field will agree."

Clearly the problem of excess nitrogen in the Missouri system originates from a number of sources. First and probably foremost are the septic systems from the proliferation of summer homes, resorts, and lodges lining the shores of the three reservoirs, as well as from throughout the entire Missouri Basin as far away as growing towns like Bozeman, Three Forks, and Dillon. On this subject Governor Brian Schweitzer hits the nail on the head: "You don't need to be a rocket scientist to realize that sewage is making its way to the river."

Nitrogen-based fertilizers spread on the fields adjacent to the river and throughout its many tributaries are another source. Man-made nitrogen fertilizer leaches heavily into the ground and eventually enters the river by way of overland flow or through underground aquifers. Significant agricultural operations exist all along the Missouri's course. Nitrogen also enters the system naturally from the atmosphere, but the excessive concentration is clearly due to the area's rapid rate of growth, overdependence on fossil fuels, and the damaging effects of global warming.

The heavy influx of nitrogen makes the reservoirs act as incubators for algae and bacteria capable of upsetting the delicate balance on downstream ecosystems. One school of thought regarding the health of our state's reservoirs places the burden firmly on those responsible for promoting and building the reservoirs: industry and federal government. Many in Montana, including the current governor, believe that when the federal government made decisions to further the development of natural resources within Montana, such as mining, forestry, dam-building, and developing agricultural systems in arid regions, they effectively became partners in those processes. Now, both partners should be accountable for restoration or mitigation.

Today, in many areas across the state—not just the dams on the Missouri—we are paying for some of the previous lack of planning and scientific oversight. Caught in the middle of this larger debate are the underfunded state agencies, and citizen activists like Pete Cardinal.

I asked Pete if he felt that the state biologists on the Missouri took the input of citizens and fishing outfitters to heart. "I think most of the outfitters on the river have a good rapport with the biologists and they take our concerns seriously," he said. "Sadly, decisions are mostly based solely on available funds, and that boils down to politics, especially when the need for biological studies is called for. Money is tight in state government but the future of the trout fisheries in Montana is huge to our state, and we need to be proactive as opposed to reactive. I think field biologists do all they can, but the final word comes from above and we seriously need to take the politics out of fisheries management. The health of Montana fisheries is determined over the long haul by the quality of our water. Without well-protected water we are bound to have trouble in the future."

It is interesting to compare Pete's thoughts to those expressed by Governor

Schweitzer. In a recent interview I conducted with the governor, he said: "Today, more and more people are recognizing that quality water is the most rapidly diminishing natural resource on this planet and when you look at Montana's role in producing clean quality water, you see that we produce 70 percent of all the water that flows in the Missouri River drainage system. It comes from our watersheds, our mountains, our snow, and more than 50 percent of the water that ends up in the Columbia River drainage system is stored in Montana.... I'll tell you I have traveled the length and breadth of Montana and I have had a conversation with more Montanans than just about anybody, and I think there are a few things we share as values and that is, virtually everybody in Montana believes we should have clean places for hunting, for fishing, for camping, and for watershed areas. We're proud in Montana to have healthy places to fish and proud we can still eat the fish we take from our streams. Just today, I heard Washington, D.C. is now having trouble with the fish in the Potomac River. They have lesions on them, they are sterile and not able to reproduce. In Montana we have healthy fisheries because for the most part, we have healthy watershed systems and I think the people in Montana are proud of that."

The governor spoke specifically about two separate visions of urbanization on our public waterways, one from a historical perspective and one a futuristic view. "There are a couple of visions of how we move forward in Montana and one can take a look in our rearview mirror and clearly see two different paradigms: one that works and one that doesn't.

"There were some over the last thirty or forty years who thought it appropriate to crowd a bunch of little houses right down on the riverbank, set a septic in the alluvial gravel, drill a well fifty feet deep, and call it home."

Schweitzer continued, "But then you have some rivers where people decided that we are going to protect the resource a little bit. Take a look at the Blackfoot River, where we have the largest concentration of conservation easements and people recognize how important it is to have a wild river—that is a vision for the future. Compare that to what exists between Great Falls and Helena along the Missouri. I know which vision I like better, and I know which one I would like to see Montana go in the direction of. We don't want to take private property rights away…we think we can continue to bring more people to Montana, but we have to be cognizant of the reason people are coming here in the first place—its clean water, its open spaces, its great viewsheds, and if we are going to put a bunch of little houses along our rivers we may as well move to New York City."

~~~

I was with Pete early one afternoon, right where the river's current slips around a sharp bend bordered by a solid buttress of black rock that rises a hundred feet above a small cove. The current flows to the base of the cliff and suddenly slows, reaching for the far end of the bend. We anchored above the spot and quietly waded downstream. A number of nice trout were rising in the seam just out from the dark wall when we arrived, but within minutes they suddenly stopped feeding. Quietly we waited and, sure enough, the trout started to feed again, but then stopped. Pete smiled at the confusion on my face and remarked, "Watch the pattern of the current as it bounces off the wall. When the seam presses hard against the rocks, the trout won't feed, but when it opens up and moves away from the wall three or four inches, they'll feed again."

Sure enough, he was right. Trout rose when the current's silvery line gently flexed away from the rock wall; when it was tight you would think nothing lived below.

Here we were on a river hundreds of feet across and pushing a tremendous volume of water past us every second, yet we stood with our attention reduced to a narrow slip of current no more than a few inches in width. That is what fishing with an expert outfitter like Pete Cardinal is really all about.

"The trick to fishing a spot like this is patience," said Pete. "You have to wait until everything is just right. But first you have to read the current and try to figure what's happening below, how the narrow feeding lane varies with the current change. What you have to come to terms with is that we humans are impatient and in no way are we going to force trout to feed just by casting into a spot. Neither nature nor trout are to be forced.

"You need to wait, watch, and the surface will tell you when things are right. If you are observant and patient on a river like the Missouri you'll catch trout. If not, you might go away believing trout numbers are down, or the fishery is overrated, overcrowded, or overfished."

Over his long career as a fly-fishing guide on the Missouri, Pete has tailored his approach to different stretches of the river, realizing how hard the upper stretch gets hit. "Sure, it's a lot less difficult to put clients on fish, and plenty of them, on the upper stretch," he said. "But the type of clients I serve, those who return year after year, I think are looking for something special, something more than another day casting to trout right beside others doing the same thing."

Pete's clients are mostly folks who have fished with him for years and are willing to spend the time necessary to create a different kind of fishing experience. For some established guides in Montana, those in the business for a few decades or more, this return list of clients runs high and comes as a result of a quality experience, maybe even a quest for knowledge about rivers and fly fishing as opposed to a race for trout numbers or size.

When Pete fishes the Missouri and teaches others to read the river's intricate moods, he passes on knowledge and intimacy, and each binds a trout fisher to special place like the Missouri.

MADISON RIVER AND CRAIG MATHEWS

"You know many of our rivers today experience angling pressure," said Craig Mathews, owner of Blue Ribbon Flies in West Yellowstone. "I believe some of it comes from the high expectations we fly fishers bring to Montana. We approach a river with a certain notion: it's either a dry fly, nymph, or whatever type of stream. We tend to judge trout fisheries by their reputation as opposed to just getting on them to see what we find. Not enough fly fishers get caught up in the sheer beauty of their surroundings, something I think plays a very important role. We get too busy trying to catch a trout or improve our technique, and tend to miss the circling dive of a bald eagle as it fishes above us, or a mink searching out a meal on the shore beside us. Fishing too hard, we overlook the fantastic mountains hanging above the river, and the golden light as it races across the open benchland just before sunset.

"Montana offers all this, and more, but if we come with only trout fishing on our minds we are ripe to miss the rest. Rivers like the Madison are much more than fantastic trout streams, they demonstrate the awesome force of water as it carves a footprint across a landscape. They are the home for hundreds of mammals, amphibians, and insects on display during a few-hour float.

"We go out of our way to get our clients hooked on the beauty of the Madison or the Gibbon or the Firehole, hooked on the remarkable natural settings through which these rivers flow. We want our clients to truly experience the landscape we fight so hard to safeguard and protect. We have found over the years that the trout fishing will usually take care of itself. After all, Montana offers some of the best fisheries available anywhere. But we feel unless a client gets hooked on the whole experience—the scenery, clean air, wildlife, and the fly fishing—we have missed our mark as guides."

Craig is right about our preset expectations, and the congestion on our most popular rivers. It happens during the salmonfly hatch on the Big Hole, the skwala hatch on the Bitterroot and Clark Fork, and the Mother's Day caddisfly hatch on the Yellowstone. And it happens on the Bighorn, Missouri, and Rock Creek.

I hear a lot of talk about the loss of solitude, the absence of sanctuary on our modern rivers. Perhaps we fly fishers have merely redefined the parameters a little. I often wonder if fly fishing has become more about some sort of competition waged between us and the trout, or us and other anglers. Perhaps we have lost the vision of that sole fisher standing motionless, cradling a rod, watching the final light of sunset cast shadows across the water, or listening to the language of the landscape through which the river flows.

Nothing gives my heart a greater boost than when I see an out-of-state angler put aside a rod to just watch the beauty of Montana, leaning back to drink in a healthy dose of the clean mountain air.

The Madison River holds a special place in both our history and our future. Here, biologists learned that stocking hatchery trout really wasn't needed to maintain trout populations. Here, whirling disease was first detected in Montana in 1994. From the banks of this fantastic river, hundreds of outdoor writers have penned stories that helped define what a world-class trout fishery is all about—but their impressions were usually more about great fishing than embracing landscape and wild neighbors.

The Madison is really a number of linked rivers that originate in varied geography. Fittingly, its headwaters are in the wild and protected lands of Yellowstone National Park. It is named the Madison at the confluence of the Firehole River, spawned by fire and steam, and the Gibbon River, spawned by high-country ice and snow. From Madison Junction the river travels west, cutting a meandering course through meadowlands bordered by stands of tall trees. Here the river is protected by special regulations imposed by the National Park Service. It is graced by abundant insect hatches and a naturally functioning ecosystem. Inside the park, the general fishing season opens the last week of May, a time when cold runoff makes the river hospitable for trout. By the time July rolls around, however, the Firehole's geothermal waters overcome the cooler currents of the Gibbon. Once the thermal scale tips and the river warms, the environment becomes less friendly for trout.

As sometimes happens in nature, a short celebration occurs when change is in the offing. In the case of the Madison, the river's upper sections nourish the early emergence of two insects, the pale morning dun and the salmonfly, which creates a feeding frenzy for trout. As the water temperature hovers between 55 and 65 degrees, trout feed voraciously. The river then slowly grows quiet as water temperatures warm.

By autumn, nights cool the water and the cycle starts afresh, this time enhanced by the annual spawning of brown trout from Hebgen Lake. Once again, the upper river becomes a trout fishing mecca. Outside the tourist town of West Yellowstone, the river eventually enters Hebgen Lake, where it is joined by the South Fork of the Madison.

Hebgen is a man-made impoundment, built in 1916 by the Montana Power Company. It now serves as the rearing grounds for trout working their way into the upper Madison. Joining the browns on their upstream migration are the sizable Eagle Lake rainbows. Here again is demonstrated the symbiotic relationship between a lake and the river upstream.

The river exits Hebgen Lake and picks up water from two protected areas, the Cabin Creek Recreation and Wildlife Management Area and the much larger Lee Metcalf Wilderness. It then hits a second impoundment, this one created by the 1959 earthquake that knocked half a mountain into the canyon below. Fly fishing between Hebgen and Earthquake Lakes can be spectacular, especially during the early salmonfly hatch and the later caddisfly and mayfly hatches.

Below, the Madison moves in a sweeping arc, flows under Three Dollar Bridge, and eventually is joined by the West Fork of the Madison, a great fishery in its own right.

From Three Dollar Bridge downstream, the Madison is known as the famous "fifty-mile riffle." Then it enters a third impoundment, Ennis Lake. Here the water warms and its character changes dramatically due to added nutrients. Below the reservoir, it rumbles and thrashes through Beartrap Canyon, one of Montana's most picturesque and isolated fisheries. At the mouth of the canyon, as if all its energy was spent tumbling over huge boulders, the Madison begins to softly meander through ranch and farmlands. During the hot months of summer, the trout either move out of the lower river or become lethargic, but as soon as the water begins to cool in September, the river below Beartrap Canyon again becomes a quality fishery.

At its mouth, the Madison meets the Jefferson and Gallatin Rivers at Headwaters State Park to form the Missouri River.

There is a wonderful conservation story associated with the fishing access at Three Dollar Bridge. The saga began one morning in 1996 when Madison River rancher Jess Armitage called Hugh Zackheim of The Nature Conservancy. Armitage and his partners owned Candlestick Ranch, a large spread in the upper Madison Valley that included three miles of river frontage with seven square miles of surrounding uplands. Armitage told Zackheim that he would like to work out a conservation deal, but that the alternative was to put the ranch up for sale on the open market. Armitage noted that the property centered on Three Dollar Bridge, a popular fishing stretch of the upper river.

Immediately after his discussion with Armitage, Zackheim placed a call to Craig and Jackie Mathews, long-time supporters of The Nature Conservancy. The Mathews were excited about the prospect of a conservation transaction to preserve the Three Dollar Bridge section and keep it open for public fishing access. From their years of experience on the river, they well understood its great habitat and trout fishing.

For years the river had been prized by fly fishers who were permitted access to the prime water for a three-dollar fee. A previous landowner was particularly dedicated to the fee-to-fish arrangement and was rumored to show up periodically and sit in his pickup with a shotgun prominently displayed in the rear window. According to old-timers in the area, the gent never removed the gun from the rack. He just wanted fly fishers to remember that a deal was a deal, and they were expected at the collection box even if the fishing was lousy, which was seldom.

Candlestick Ranch also provided exceptional wildlife habitat, not only in its wetlands and riparian areas, but also for the vast sagebrush-dotted rangelands. The property's strategic location between the Gravelly and Madison Ranges made it a crucial linkage corridor for elk, moose, bears, and other species dependent on an undeveloped landscape.

Craig cautioned Hugh that they had better move fast or the land would fall prey to developers and more than likely the river access would be lost behind No Trespassing signs. And in the foothills, houses would inevitably take the place of important habitat. The challenge was to come up with a package that would provide a reasonable financial return to the landowners while protecting the river and the upland habitat. The Mathews were convinced that the fly-fishing community would step forward and contribute to public acquisition of the Three Dollar Bridge riverfront. Early on, they demonstrated to Zackheim, and his new conservation employer River Network, the magnetic appeal of Three Dollar Bridge to anglers across the country.

Zackheim recalled the early part of the process: "Craig and Jackie were the key to giving us the confidence to believe we could actually put a deal together and protect the river access. But even at that, it was going to take a bundle of money to keep the river accessible to the public. It was the power of their positive attitudes. Once we went public with the deal, over a thousand individuals from throughout the country generated initially from the client list of Blue Ribbon Flies stepped forward to help the conservation acquisition. These folks loved the Madison and had come to know and trust the folks at Blue Ribbon Flies. That became the essence of our belief that, eventually, the deal would come together."

As another key element of the solution, the project partners needed to find a conservation-minded party to acquire the uplands of the Candlestick Ranch. In 1999 Zackheim began talks with Bob and Annie Graham, who already owned another important ranch in the area. River Network presented the Grahams with their three goals for the project, as the foundation of a proposed partnership: (1) conserve the Madison River frontage, (2) continue the tradition of public access at Three Dollar Bridge, and (3) conserve the adjoining uplands for wildlife habitat and managed livestock grazing. The Grahams shared the vision, and signed on to help.

The Grahams proved to be patient buyers for the uplands, as countless drafts and redrafts of option agreements were exchanged between River Network and the landowners. According to Zackheim, "Not only did they step up in a huge way, they worked effectively with the Montana Land Reliance to protect all the land buffering the Three Dollar Bridge river access."

Locals all along the Madison viewed the proposal favorably. Zackheim and coworker Bob Fitzgerald knocked on doors throughout the valley and the great majority of area residents responded with checks and good wishes.

Trout Unlimited joined the partnership too, extending the project nationwide visibility. The Orvis Company also came on board in 2001 by making the Three Dollar Bridge Project its top conservation priority that year. The National Fish and Wildlife Foundation matched funds raised by Orvis three to one, which proved to be a great incentive for public donations. In June 2007, Montana Fish, Wildlife & Parks came up with the final piece of the puzzle, paying River Network the bargain price of $250,000 to secure public ownership of one hundred acres and three miles of Madison River frontage. The Three Dollar Bridge public fishing access had become a reality.

When you listen to Craig or Hugh tell the story of Three Dollar Bridge, their eyes light up. Here is a project that added immensely to public fishing on one of the state's most important rivers, and it came together via collaboration between agency officials, community leaders, and the fishing public.

Every once in a while I walk into Blue Ribbon Flies and see Craig Mathews sitting behind his fly-tying table with a huge smile on his face. I know what he's thinking about as he perches there surrounded by feathers and fur—another Three Dollar Bridge–type project, this time maybe near Yellowstone National Park or in the Madison Canyon or on some fishery about which he keeps quiet. Or he could be recalling a special brown trout he used to catch year after year around Three Dollar Bridge. Supposedly, the first time Mathews hooked that trout it measured sixteen inches; its upper mandible had been injured by another fly fisher and had a slight but noticeable deformity. The next time Craig caught the brown it measured eighteen inches, and came from behind the same rock in the river. He caught the trout two more times before the property around the bridge went up for sale— excellent incentive for preserving it.

Today, fly fishers of all skill levels line up at Three Dollar Bridge to take their chances on the Madison. A sign tells the story of the ingenious preservation effort and, off to one side, the collection box asks each trout fisher who intends to use the river to donate three bucks; not much compared to a few cans of beer, a bag of chips, or a couple of flies.

One perfect autumn evening I sat on the bank and watched Craig fish the Madison. He waded into the river with a true sense of reverence, like a traveler returning to the place of his birth. On his third cast he took a nice rainbow from a fast run near the bank. The next trout, a little bigger, came from the same run, as did the following two. For a half hour he stayed right there, fishing and watching the water until the sun was finally balanced like a huge orange ball atop the horizon and the rolling benchland to the east was saturated with warm, golden light. For the next half hour we sat on the bank and watched darkness slowly descend on the Madison Valley. Craig finally broke the silence by asking, "Have you noticed we haven't seen another trout fisher, and no boats, all evening?"

I guess in the pleasantness of rising trout, good conversation, and a beautiful sunset, it hadn't struck me that we had been entirely alone. I realized this was not the Madison River to which I had grown accustomed, or the Madison splashed across the pages of so many outdoor magazines.

Surprisingly, it was the river the way Craig knows it best. "By this time in the evening most wade fishers have found a spot like this one and settled into it," he noted. "The boat fishers are all oaring hard for takeouts. So if you know a river like the Madison and the habits of those who fish it, you can almost always find a solitary spot if you're clever about it."

He was right. As we got up to leave, a memory came to mind of when I was traveling through Ennis and had called guide Mike Lum to see if he needed some time away from the shop. "That would be great," he said, "but if you don't mind I'd like a buddy of mine, Joe Dilschneider, to join us." I didn't know Joe but had heard about him from his work on the board of the Fishing Outfitters Association of Montana. Joe owns Montana Trout Stalkers, the outfitter for which Mike works.

"That's fine. What time, and where?" I asked, thinking we would probably put in mid-morning after things warmed up and the surface hatches had begun.

"Let's meet at seven," he answered. "Joe and I don't get a chance to fish together much during the summer, what with guiding and me working the shop. We thought we'd show you another side of the Madison. We'll throw streamers, avoid the rush hour. What do you say?"

Who was I to question these two?

We were bobbing in the drift boat early the next morning. Mike and Joe swapped turns behind the oars while I sat in the back, enjoying the high intensity of these two fishing buddies. Mike caught a trout and almost before the fish was back in the water Joe was in the front of the boat and up for his chance. A minute or so later, Joe was back behind the oars and Mike was working the bank like a steely-eyed predator.

About eight-thirty the fish really started to show up, nice browns right off the bank or taken from the edge of a long run. Joe calls the beefy browns with underbellies the color of maple syrup "the color of the Madison." The browns hit first on streamers thrown by Joe, then Mike, then Joe, and back and forth until I was dizzy. It almost seems unfair to turn Mike Lum and Joe Dilschneider loose to fish together on a morning run.

It was going on ten o'clock when we finally came across another boat. Given the time and distance between put-ins, I realized there were plenty of boats behind us and probably just as many in front, but only one within view.

We had lunch a little after noon, and talked about the crowds on the Madison. "This is the heaviest fished river in the state," said Mike, as he built a four-inch sandwich bulging with roast beef, tomatoes, and purple onions. "There are hundreds of guides somehow connected to this water: old-timers, first-year bucks, and every age in between. This is a fantastic fishery and you just can't expect to have it to yourself most of the time, but there are times, if you plan a day just right, when you have your fishing all done by the time the others are finishing their first cup of morning coffee. That's the fun of it, and definitely that's where the more experienced guides have it over newcomers. We are all going to catch trout, even a few nice ones, but it depends if you want someone else around when you do. The Madison really does offer that type of fly fishing if you plan your day around the crowds.

"I have been on the Madison for a long time, and in the peak of the day it has always seemed crowded. I believe those who really understand the Madison can find times when the river is almost abandoned. Most guides have clients who want to maintain tight schedules, and it seems almost everyone puts in about the same time each day at a variety of locations. Floats take a certain amount of time and that's what makes the river seem congested. The trick is to know those times and get yourself either ahead or between everyone else and stay there. It doesn't take long for the fish to forget the last boat over their heads but they do need a little time. Staying out of the boat clusters can dramatically improve your success, even midday.

"Another thing is, most fly fishers come to the Madison with the expectation that they will either work the surface with dry flies or fish nymphs. Both techniques are really effective on the Madison. A lot of what happens comes as a result of expectations brought to the river. If you are a dry-fly fisher, you are going to search out the hatches, and you just simply have to get used to others doing the same thing. If you think you're going to fish a well-known prime spot alone during a remarkable spinner fall that is simply a myth. Good trout fishers know where to be and when to be there."

I e-mailed Craig Mathews one morning to ask what he thought people could do to protect their favorite trout streams. His response went directly to the heart of the matter: "I believe people should support businesses that support conservation and environmental organizations, and projects that protect, preserve, and enhance what we, our children, and all future generations enjoy and love…wild trout and wild places, clean air, and water! Support businesses like members of One Percent for the Planet, where 1 percent of your purchases will go to support conservation organizations that fight for what we all love: wild trout!"

Craig's answer was right on point because nothing gets done unless financial support is available to "close the deal." Without The Nature Conservancy, River Network, and Blue Ribbon Flies we may not have a Three Dollar Bridge today. But without the support of Orvis, The National Fish and Wildlife Foundation, Montana Department of Fish, Wildlife & Parks, and the generous contributions of thousands of fly fishers, ranchers, and citizens like you and me, the project may have never crossed the goal line. The fundraising effort of organizations like One Percent for the Planet is a vital link to many more projects like the Three Dollar Bridge because, like it or not, a lot of conservation efforts are dependent on financial support.

BIG HOLE RIVER AND FRANK STANCHFIELD

The Big Hole country takes its name from the trappers and mountain men who hunted in the valley before the onslaught of white settlement. Back then they referred to all open valleys as "holes," hence the name Big Hole, Firehole, Jackson Hole, and so on. The Big Hole is Montana's highest and broadest mountain valley, split down the middle by one of the world's most revered trout streams.

Members of President Thomas Jefferson's Corps of Discovery named the Jefferson River's major tributaries for his virtues: Wisdom, Philanthropy, and Philosophy. As with many names that Lewis & Clark bestowed upon the West, those titles didn't hold, and the Wisdom today is called the Big Hole River, the Philanthropy is the Ruby River, and the Philosophy now is the Beaverhead River.

Remarkably, the headwater creeks of the blue-ribbon Big Hole and Beaverhead begin immediately adjacent to one another high in the Beaverhead Mountains, their courses separated by only a narrow ridge. Tiny tributaries of the Beaverhead descend and circle the southeastern edge of the Pioneer Mountains, while its sister river circles the northwestern side and eventually meets its north fork at the ranching town of Wisdom. Here, the river swings east and carves a swath through rich bottomlands beneath the southern flanks of the Anaconda-Pintler Wilderness.

Downstream, at the hamlet of Wise River, the Big Hole merges with the much smaller Wise River. Continuing eastward, the river is suddenly pinched between steep hillsides and rocky outcrops, where the fishery changes from a meandering stream to excellent pocket water pressed between steep canyons. Just below Divide, the river arcs south, and slowly waltzes past the historic ranching towns of Melrose and Glen. At Glen it again changes direction and character, and heads east through the rugged hill country unfolding north of Twin Bridges. Here, after flowing 150 miles, the Big Hole finally meets its sister, the Beaverhead, and the Jefferson River is born.

Renowned fly tier George Grant, a trout-fishing aficionado, considered the guru of the Big Hole from the 1930s on, once remarked that if man were to create the perfect trout stream, the Big Hole could serve as a suitable template. Other fly-fishing greats like Al Troth, Joe Brooks, and Dak Hartke considered the Big Hole their ace in the hole—not the Madison, Missouri, or the Yellowstone.

In addition to a rich cultural history that permeates the agrarian valley, the river itself holds a remarkable history. It was the chosen water for the historic Butte Anglers Club that operated the Columbia Gardens hatchery. They planted feisty brook trout and grayling on the upper section, rainbows throughout the river, and leader-snapping brown trout in places like Maiden Rock Canyon. Today, locals like Frank Stanchfield and visitors from around the world are able to fish for the wild progeny of these species.

Frank owns Troutfitters Fly Shop and Outfitting, located on the river just a few miles west of Wise River. One evening we sat on the riverbank as he talked about his grandfather, who homesteaded in the Big Hole Valley in the 1800s. He was one of the early cattle ranchers who was able to withstand the whiskey-freezing winters common to the Big Hole back then, the days of 50 and 60 degrees below zero, deep snow, and sudden blizzards sweeping in from the mountains. There must have been a staunch determination for survival passed on in the DNA of the Stanchfield clan, because the following four generations made a home in the valley.

While Frank and his son Lance operate the fly-fishing business, Frank's brother runs the family cattle ranch. This combination prompts an unusually diverse perspective on the oftentimes controversial relationship between sportsmen and ranchers. Frank maintains that the first conservationists in the beautiful valley were ranchers, the very people who needed to protect the river, the mountain runoff, the springs, and upland meadows to preserve their way of life. As a sign of this commitment to the landscape, he points to the years of hard work, planning, and collaboration performed by the Big Hole Watershed Committee, as well as a host of other less organized local groups that have worked in harmony with sportsmen and conservationists over the years.

Frank earns his living from the river and is the first to point out that everything is not perfect. But he also will tell you there are plenty of good people from both ranching and trout fishing interests who are engaged in conversation. Frank believes that some of the river's most pressing problems stem from the last seven years of drought, and the likelihood that the cycle will continue, or else get better for a few years only to return in coming decades.

Frank sees another set of problems in extremism on one side or the other. Some groups come in with an "our way or the highway" attitude on important issues. "When one side of the discussion is simply unwilling to bend, there isn't much that can get done on behalf of a resource like the Big Hole," Frank observed. "All you end up with is a shouting match, and in the end, the river suffers."

That night on the riverbank, Frank told me about the first trout he ever caught on the Big Hole. At the age of six his rod was a willow stick, to which his fly-fishing father had tied a long piece of frayed leader and a tattered old fly. Young Frank was shimmying across the pole fence that extended into the river to keep cows off the neighbor's land, when the leader slipped from his hand. Serendipitously, his first cast was made (and one of his best, he added). The fly landed in a riffle at the end of the fence and caught the attention of a nice rainbow, one probably stocked years earlier by the Butte Anglers Club. The ensuing battle was as much an act of balance as it was a fish fight, and it ended only after the boy managed to reach solid ground. The willow rod held and a fat rainbow lay at the feet of a ranch kid. The fishing wizard's spell was cast and a professional fly fisher and prolific storyteller was born.

"Releasing trout was unheard of when I was a kid. If you caught one, you cleaned and ate it, it was just that simple," said Frank. "I believe the first trout I released was in 1973. Phil Wright was one of the first fishing outfitters on the Big Hole. I had lent him a cement mixer, and in trade we went fishing together. I landed a nice four-pound brown trout, and Phil asked, 'Are you going to release it?' and without even thinking, I said, 'Yes.' That was a good day for me, no more cleaning or eating, a good day indeed."

Similar to many Montana rivers that have seen a decline in rainbow trout due to whirling disease, Big Hole brown trout seem to have more than filled the gap. Today on the upper river, where formerly nary a brown trout was found, they are plentiful all the way to Wisdom, with some very large specimens recorded each year.

According to biologists, whirling disease has been in the United States since 1956. It first was uncovered in Montana in 1994, on the Madison. The name comes from the erratic, whirling behavior exhibited by affected trout. The disease is caused by the parasite *Myxobolus cerebralis,* which attacks the cartilage of younger trout and allows severe infections that bring about physical deformities. The affected trout quickly fall prey to natural predators and thus the disease has a severe impact on the affected rivers. To a lesser degree, other trout species like brook, cutthroat, and brown are affected by the parasite, but in Montana, *M. cerebralis* has preyed most heavily on wild rainbows.

When Frank was a boy, rainbows by far comprised the largest trout population. That is not the case today, as a mix of rainbows, browns, and cutthroats make up the average catch. Mountain whitefish have always been present in significant numbers, and a small stock of Arctic grayling remains.

According to George Grant, "The lower Big Hole, extending from Divide to Twin Bridges, is considered by many qualified anglers to be the best wild brown trout stream in the United States. This is a true wild brown trout population that entered the Big Hole about 1925, being part of the original plant in the upper Madison about 1889, eventually working their way up through the Jefferson into the Big Hole."

The upstream migration of browns was obstructed by the old dam at Divide. In 1968, Frank happened to be standing on the silver bridge just above the decrepit dam when a spring icejam took out what remained of it. With the obstruction removed, the browns had a clear shot at the bountiful waters of the upper Big Hole where, over the years, they have flourished.

In the early years, brookies were planted in large numbers on the upper reaches around Wisdom and Jackson. These plentiful, easy-to-catch fish served as a fly-fishing classroom for many youngsters growing up around southwest Montana.

Frank and I were riding back from the Warms Springs settling ponds one evening when the topic of brook trout came up. I told him, as an afterthought, that I needed to get a good photograph of a brookie in full autumn regalia but hadn't caught one of much size for a number of years. In his "I have a handle on these things" attitude, he said he could provide a good brookie without much trouble if I was willing to keep a secret about one of those special places all outfitters tuck up their sleeves.

I agreed, and the next morning we left the fly shop an hour before first light. I was pleased to be allowed to travel without a blindfold. A few hours later I had my picture of a fat sixteen-inch brookie, along with several others. (If you come to fish in Montana without quizzing your outfitter about "special spots," you are likely to miss some of the best action.)

Frank continued our conversation about the early days: "After Phil Wright paid me back for the loan of the cement mixer and I had him convinced I could fly fish, which took some doing, he hired me as a guide. Phil had moved to the Big Hole from Colorado in the mid-1970s. He was a great fly fisher, a good teacher, and a very conscientious outfitter, the perfect man to learn the business from."

At first Frank worked only to pick up some added income during the summer, just like many of Montana's beginning guides. When Wright sold his outfitting business a few years later, Frank started to study for the outfitting test and eventually Troutfitters was born. One important business principle he learned from Wright is evident in the way Troutfitters handles clients today. "Fly fishers come to Montana for the whole experience," Frank said. "Part of it has to do with the western way of life, an ambience that surrounds a place like the Big Hole Valley, with its history, its people, and its attitude toward visitors.

"Sure, our clients come to the river to catch fish, and we make sure that part of it happens, but it usually turns out some of their most pleasurable experience comes from things only the valley can supply, like an appreciation for the ruggedness and beauty of a valley, or a fascination for the high mountains, or even a night out at the Wise River Club—the historic bar down the road."

I had a chance to witness what Frank was talking about one warm autumn evening when the valley was on fire with the colorful change of season. It was that special time of year when the browns run upstream, seeking their old redds. As usual, following the annual migration were a bunch of hungry rainbows well keyed into the event, searching for freed trout eggs.

Rainbows were feeding voraciously in the rapids when a pair of Troutfitters clients came by in the company of their guide. One was a very special fellow in his seventies, who had fished with Frank for more years than he could remember. Each autumn he traveled from his home in California to fish when the colors were just beginning to peak. That evening, as his partner tempted rainbows below the redds and relished in the excitement, the elder angler sat in the shade of a low-hanging tree, expensive rod at his side, eyes fixed on the distant peaks in the Anaconda-Pintler Wilderness. When I walked by, he asked, "I wonder sometimes if you Montanans really know the value of what's here, the beauty of all of this, and the vast quiet that surrounds it."

His words caught me off guard, and as I struggled for a reply he went on. "I just love it every time I come back to Montana, but I have seen it change in a big way over the years. I worry someday we'll lose it all to development."

Here was a man who knew what it was like to live in a congested part of the nation, a fellow who saw Montana as a refuge from a life he could not leave, possibly because his livelihood was there, or his family. But it was clear that his heart was in Montana. He was an avid trout fisher, and a good one; he epitomized Frank's notion that fishing is only a part of the whole experience.

"I grew up in this valley, just like my father did before me," Frank said. "Lance, my son, and his children are following in our footsteps and we all realize it is up to us to make sure the river and the valley are protected for future generations. That commitment didn't start with my generation or Lance's, it goes all the way back to my grandfather, who was a cattle rancher on one hand and a conservationist on the other. If you live in the same place all your life, you begin to realize from the very start just how important it is to protect it. You don't have to be told that if you don't take care of the natural world around you—the water, timber, insect life, wildlife, and the high country pastures and meadows—your whole way of life will be jeopardized, not just a fly-fishing business or a cattle operation."

When outdoor writers spend time with Frank Stanchfield, they learn about the achievements and laws that originated on his homewaters. "If you tramp around here long enough, you'll find, as most ranchers and serious fly fishers have, that the Big Hole Valley is like a huge sponge, one that soaks up a lot of early spring moisture every season," Frank said. "A lot of the irrigation that goes on the streamside fields each year prior to the blazing hot days of summer also soaks into that sponge. Traditionally most of the irrigation done on the Big Hole is flood irrigation delivered from good-sized ditches. That means that a lot of the water, once on the fields, seeps deep into the soil or even into underground aquifers, and is held. The valley holds some of that volume and releases it during the hotter months of the summer in a process we locals call 'trickle back.' The upper Big Hole is prominent for this type of impact on the river.

"Outsiders sometimes don't really fully understand how a valley like the Big Hole works from a natural point of view. We have a tremendous source of clean water coming from the surrounding mountains. It is not only the lifeblood for a remarkable trout fishery, it is the backbone for the entire agricultural industry as well. Both ways of life are extremely important to the Big Hole Valley and both sides have to learn to live alongside one another and really try to understand the dynamics that make our way of life work."

Frank continued, "I feel if we were to do away with the tradition of flood irrigation, as many outside conservationists advocate, and go to a sprinkler system, we'd end up losing the advantage of our time-tested trickle back system, which actually adds water to the river when it's most needed during times of drought and hot summers."

If you have ever walked through the pastures bordering the Big Hole River in spring, you already know the sensation of walking on a big sponge. In order to understand any working ecosystem, it helps if you have spent a lifetime on the land, watching nature adapt to change, human-made or otherwise.

Frank is proud that, in the early 1990s, one of Montana's first watershed committees was formed on the Big Hole. This advisory group still actively works on river issues today. The collaborative group includes local sportsmen, ranchers, recreational property owners, and, in some cases, environmental groups. These stakeholders not only have the most to lose if a watershed is damaged but possess the historic perspective of both the river and the precious wild places from which it comes.

Frank commented on the group, "It was a good idea from the start, and I won't say there haven't been a lot of loud discussions, if that's what you want to call them, but at the end of the day what was agreed on stood, and it was always the best thing for the river and the watershed. After all, that is what is really important."

Over the history of conservation in Montana, the Big Hole River has somehow always been at the forefront, whether for good practices or poor judgment. For example, at one time Big Hole ranchers diverted the free-flowing river with the aid of in-stream diversion wings and dams, excavated with bulldozers. That activity prompted the passage of the Streambed Preservation Act.

The Lower Forty-Eight's last remaining population of fluvial Arctic grayling still clings to existence here even in times of low flow, high temperatures brought on by drought, and heavy irrigation dewatering. Fish, Wildlife & Parks recognized the decline of Arctic grayling and imposed protective measures on the Big Hole to allow these beautiful fish to possibly mount a comeback. This plan relies on the support of the agricultural community to change their irrigation practices. Through the work of the watershed committee, ranchers now are considering drilling wells on their property instead of taking water from the river. Many have partnered with state specialists to evaluate their flood irrigation systems in order to ensure the most efficient use of water.

Frank summed up the attitude of many who live near and love the Big Hole. "It takes a lot of work and time to work on a committee. I have served on it for years and I really don't know how long I'll keep it up, but my family for five generations has taken their living, in one way or the other, from the Big Hole River, and I feel I need to keep giving something back."

BEAVERHEAD RIVER AND TIM TOLLETT

For decades, Tim Tollett of Frontier Anglers in Dillon has watched the Beaverhead and Big Hole Rivers attract fly fishers from throughout the nation, as well as significant numbers of guides and outfitters from across Montana and Idaho. Tim has never been attracted to crowds, so when the state agency imposed controversial use regulations on the two rivers, he approached the idea with mixed emotions. On one side, he sees the regulations as an attempt to decrease the numbers of fly fishers on the rivers, hopefully making the experience better for users of all categories. That would be good for his business in the long run. On the other hand, he believes the agency focused too narrowly on one type of user: resident professional guides and outfitters.

The notion of state-imposed use regulations is perhaps one of the most feared possibilities for people trying to scratch out a living on Montana rivers. For years, these regulations were pretty much on the back burner, until their sudden advent on the Beaverhead and Big Hole.

It is common for the state to set regulations on slot limits, species-related catch-and-release, and even bait restrictions. But this marks one of the few times in history the agency has set absolute use regulations on Montana fisheries. The *2007 Montana Fishing Regulations* lists the new regulations on various sections of the Beaverhead: "Clark Canyon Dam to Anderson Lane, combined trout: 3 daily and in possession, only 1 over 18 inches and only 1 rainbow trout. High Bridge to Henneberry, closed to float fishing by nonresidents and float outfitting on each Saturday from third Sunday in May through Labor Day. Downstream from Pipe Organ Bridge, open entire year. Highway 91 South Bridge to Selway Bridge, closed to float outfitting from third Saturday in May through Labor Day. Anderson Lane downstream to mouth, five trout; five daily and in possession, 1 over 18 inches, only 1 may be a rainbow…"

Use regulations for the Big Hole River read: "Entire river and its tributaries, catch-and-release for grayling and cutthroat trout. Entire river, extended season for whitefish and catch-and-release for trout open December 1 to the third Saturday in May with artificial lures and/or maggots only. All float users are restricted to 2 launches at or near each official access site each day. Headwaters to Muddy Creek, closed to float outfitting from the third Saturday in May through Labor Day…"

According to Tollett, "Just wading through the rules creates a problem for the normal fisherman."

It's hard to argue with the idea that the most famous Montana rivers can be crowded, and at certain peak times, like the salmonfly hatch on the Big Hole, the crowds can grow to obnoxious proportions. But the need for the degree of regulation imposed on the Big Hole/Beaverhead is questionable among many in the fly-fishing industry, including the Fishing Outfitters Association of Montana, which sued the state over it. They lost in district court.

Robin Cunningham was the association's director during the suit, and expressed a strong opinion about the work of Fish, Wildlife & Parks in the years before the regulations were imposed.

"I would have liked to see the agency come at it from a more scientific basis before imposing what might become final use regulations on our important fisheries," said Cunningham. "I don't think anyone will say there isn't a problem on some rivers during peak times, and we all would like to see things better managed, but the use of comprehensive data is necessary, collected over time. It's a critical component, something I don't feel happened in the Big Hole/Beaverhead situation initially, but significant steps have recently been taken by Fish, Wildlife & Parks to come at regulation with a more data-driven model and with far more public participation. I believe we all learned a great deal from the Big Hole/Beaverhead regulations."

Tollett agrees with Cunningham but sees the situation from a broader perspective. "You know, if you stand at the put-ins on both the Big Hole and Beaverhead, you're liable to see rigs parked by professional outfitters licensed from all over Montana, some as far away as the Flathead and Bighorn. So the problem isn't completely the fault of local outfitters. Much of it comes from the popularity of both these rivers, and other guides and outfitters' willingness to travel long distances to service the need of clients.

"The problem of congestion caused by traveling guides and outfitters is in no way restricted to folks making a living in Montana. We get a lot of outfitter traffic from Idaho, and even Wyoming outfitters who have included the Beaverhead and Big Hole on their coverage area, advertised the heck out of it, and add their clients to the hordes on the river. I would have liked the Fish, Wildlife & Parks to aggressively address that serious issue before they let the hammer fall on the local outfitter, the guy who has invested in a Montana business and pays a part of his earnings each year as taxes in Montana. It's only fair."

The success of overuse regulations on the Smith River perhaps laid the groundwork for the Big Hole/Beaverhead restrictions. Whether or not the two programs are comparable is questionable; the restrictions on the Big Hole/Beaverhead fall to a single type of user while the Smith River restricts all floaters—fishing and recreational—during peak times.

The Smith, a tributary of the Missouri south of Great Falls, is a delight, offering 60-odd miles of wilderness float fishing without a road in sight. The river's popularity surged in the late 1970s, when inexpensive rubber rafts began to appear on the market. Multi-day river trips were suddenly accessible to the general public, and overcrowding soon became a serious issue and the resource suffered. In response, Fish, Wildlife & Parks went to a lottery system to limit the number of floaters, a system that works well and has served to protect the canyon.

These days, rafts and drift boats are a common sight on all major Montana rivers, adding to the crowding problem.

George Grant said, "Fishing guides found floating to be a convenient method of accommodating a wide variety of clients, and doing it with a minimum expenditure of time. Perhaps the greatest factor in the proliferation of boats on the major western trout rivers was the increasing number of 'NO TRESPASSING' signs that were beginning to appear."

Access to public rivers continues to raise red flags (and tempers) around the state. Wade fishers are most restricted by new closures on private property; boaters can float right on through. Over the years, this change has led to some overcrowding issues, particularly on smaller rivers like the Beaverhead and Big Hole. (Thankfully, Montana's Stream Access Law still guarantees waders the right to access below the mean high-water mark from public access points like bridges, although this law currently faces challenges from a group that includes wealthy out-of-state landowners hoping to lock up exclusive access to our public waterways. Anyone who takes this law for granted should try fishing in a state where landowners are even allowed to claim ownership of the streambed itself.)

Fisheries managers stationed on Montana trout streams say the answer to overcrowding and consequent resource decimation is to effectively control use. Trout fishers who have grown up fishing the waters of the Big Hole or Beaverhead will tell you the need for restricted use has much to do with protecting solitude.

Sadly, as fly fishers, our entire vision has shifted from the solitary angler with well-worn but cared for gear standing knee-deep in a wild river to one with all the latest gadgets pounding the water from the bow of a custom-built drift boat to maximize the catch.

Whatever regulations will be forthcoming, and whether we get there through scientific data, shooting from the hip, or just plain old common sense, will be influenced by how we all approach rivers. It all boils down to impacts on the resource. We will have crowding as long as there are trout fishers who use the river every day, or guides who stick to only one stretch on a certain river or offer only boat fishing.

According to Tollett, "We all need to evaluate our use of a river like the Beaverhead. We need to look for other ways we can use the resource and still satisfy the growing love for fly fishing. A lot of the problem on the Beaverhead comes as a result of the size of the river, and the fact that much of it is inaccessible without using a boat. Its banks are extremely brushy, which makes for fantastic brown trout fishing, but most of the good water is on private land. Being locals, we have tried to work with landowners in the way of leases on some of this private ground, and use it exclusively as a wade fishery. Our clients seem to love the idea and it gets our boats off the water while still providing a top-notch service. On smaller rivers like the Beaverhead, and especially the Red Rock to the south—which, incidentally, is one of Montana's best trout streams—leased access is the only way we can open up these waters to our clients. We all see the effects of overcrowding but some of us in the outfitting business see any number of ways around the issue, as opposed to just putting another set of regulations on the books."

Rivers in Montana have not changed much on their own. Most always it is humans who bring about the change, and today it is humans who need to change. In George Grant's day, a trout fisher's approach to the river meant one thing. Today it means something entirely different, all because we fly fishers or river users impose our will on the resource.

John Muir once said, "The world, we are told, was made especially for man, a presumption not supported by all the facts. A numerous class of men are painfully astonished whenever they find anything, living or dead, in all God's universe, which they cannot eat or render in some way what they call useful to themselves. They have precise dogmatic insight of the intentions of the Creator."

Pick any river in Montana and sit near it in the quiet of an early morning. Think about its problems and, chances are, you'll find "we" are the problem.

16
WESTERN HUB

}

In Montana...the three fastest-growing counties in the state were all mountain valley counties in the Rockies. The Bitterroot, Flathead, and Gallatin Valleys all registered population gains between 15 and 25 percent during the 1990s.

—Dan Flores, *The Natural West*

For two days I had been camped next to a little blue lake, a brilliant jewel set deep in a glacial cirque on the Continental Divide in the Anaconda-Pintler Wilderness. I began to wonder what southwestern Montana would look like from the 9,498-foot summit of nearby West Pintler Peak, so at dawn on the third day, I doused the last embers in my cobble-lined firepit and ventured for the crest. The clouds seemed stitched to the horizon, the peak sedate under a gray ceiling.

Alone on the climb, I could lollygag, soaking in the terrain along the route. Early morning passed quickly and by the time I was within eyeshot of the summit, the overcast had thickened, marbled by a layer of storm clouds dark as a rifle barrel. The low ceiling pressed on the steep ridges surrounding the peak, partially conceal-ing the rugged facade behind thin veils of mist. A sudden rumble of thunder echoed across the landscape.

At a high point along the cirque's perimeter, maybe ten miles away, a crooked tongue of lightning slammed against the mountains. A closer, more deafening roar of thunder followed, then another, and another. Finally the first raindrops began splashing on the hard talus, their life measured in milliseconds.

Hidden among the scattered rocks at my feet lay a hair-thin line, where the headwaters of three fine trout streams were born. The rain coalesced in pencil-thin streams that flowed into small puddles balanced precariously atop the steep-sided mountain. As the rain continued to surge, the puddles grew larger and larger until a rivulet sprouted from each downward edge, creating a web of moving water that coursed down opposite sides of the summit.

On one side, the water inched southeast, in the direction of Sawed Cabin Lake and Pintler Creek, a tributary of the Big Hole River. This was the first leg of its long journey to the Gulf of Mexico via the mighty Missouri and Mississippi Rivers.

The rivulets spilling off the summit's north rim first headed toward Phyllis Lake and, ultimately, the trout-rich Middle Fork of Rock Creek, en route to the Clark Fork of the Columbia and the misty surf of the Pacific Ocean. A few degrees to the southwest, I watched the runoff trickle toward my campsite at Hidden Lake, where the headwaters of the East Fork of the Bitterroot River originate, another wilderness-born tributary of the Clark Fork.

I sat rain-soaked through the entire storm, watching tiny rivulets form the very first few inches of cherished trout streams.

Everyone who enjoys Montana's streams and rivers should try to gain a real understanding of the vital connection between wild mountain places, clean rivers, and healthy trout. If every fly fisher saw firsthand the headwaters of at least one blue-ribbon trout stream before ever dropping a line into the water, the critical importance of protecting water in high, roadless lands would certainly come into clearer focus.

ROCK CREEK, THE BITTERROOT RIVER, AND DAN SHEPHERD

If you ask Dan Shepherd, owner of Grizzly Hackle and Fly Shop in Missoula, which local trout stream he likes best—the Bitterroot, Clark Fork, or Rock Creek—be prepared to spend some time while the seasoned fly fisher ponders his answer.

Rock Creek burst into the news in the late 1950s when it was singled out as one of Montana's original blue-ribbon trout streams. The prestigious designation brought instant fame along with an invasion of nonresident and resident fly fishers. Shortly, most of the big trout were fished out, numbers in general fell off, and the celebrated trout fishery cried out for management.

In later years, the plentiful population of rainbows on Rock Creek was hit especially hard by whirling disease. The fishery began to rebuild only after implementation of an aggressive management plan that included artificial-lure, catch-and-release-only regulations on cutthroat and bull trout, and strict limits on rainbow and brown trout. Today, it has to be considered one of Montana's best trout waters, an indication of the effectiveness of strong fisheries management supported by the sporting public and conservation groups.

The rainbows that once dominated the catch on the creek have now been replaced by brown trout, with some examples approaching the bragging zone for even the best fly fisher. The exact degree the rainbows were impacted by whirling disease is anyone's guess these days, but if you have fished Rock Creek regularly over the last ten years, the drop in the rainbow population and its replacement by brown trout has been anything but subtle.

The Middle Fork of Rock Creek tumbles through timbered mountains and is joined by Falls Fork and East Fork, all tributaries beginning on the rugged slopes of the Anaconda-Pintler Wilderness. The West Fork has the only non-wilderness origin; it begins on the east-facing shoulder of the Sapphire Mountains in the area of Skalkaho Pass.

"Rock Creek is a quintessential trout stream. It is a wade fisher's paradise, especially after boats are banned on July first each season," said Shepherd. "Rock Creek can be a virtual madhouse during the salmonfly hatch, which usually begins around the middle of June, right during the heaviest spring runoff. We tend to stay away from Rock Creek during the hatch. Most of our clients are looking for a less hurried and tumultuous experience. There are times the fishing can be very good during the hatch if the weather cooperates, but man, the crowds will drive you nuts if you're not ready for it."

Some wags in Montana refer to the salmonfly hatch as "spring break." You know the feeling. After a hard winter of being cooped up in a classroom, college students get ready to turn up the volume a notch or two. The same thing happens to fly fishers at the mention of "the hatch." After being stuffed inside gas-heated offices all winter, suddenly the biggest insect on the river appears. Even hard-wired domestic circuits can break down, sending the angler into an ephemeral state of fishing lust.

If I sound a little irreverent, it probably comes from seeing too many Montana trout streams morph into flowing highways for a couple of weeks each year. Over a half century of life in Montana I have learned to expect events like the salmonfly hatch, Fourth of July fireworks in Troy, and even St. Patrick's Day in Butte. They are part of our western culture, and every now and again I choose to join in just to make sure the kid in me is still alive.

Actually, I believe it vitally important for every fly fisher to experience at least one salmonfly hatch. There really is nothing like the romance of a rising trout mesmerized to stupidity by a drifting fly as large as a small pocketknife. The whole event is visible, splendid, and might just be the apex of dry-fly fishing.

Like all of Montana's great trout streams, Rock Creek shouldn't be judged by its few weeks of youthful spring chaos (thank goodness we weren't either, during college). The blue-ribbon creek's real character, the one for which it is now famous, develops quite differently throughout the rest of the season, starting in spring with the brown drakes.

"Rock Creek is one of those streams where the hatches come one after another, which generally makes for a reliable fishery for all levels of anglers," remarked Shepherd.

The brown drakes are a tribute to the ecological health and natural vitality of Rock Creek, despite the mines operating on its headwaters. Around March or April, during the drake hatch, the current is gentle, shallow, and perfect for comfortable wading. The drakes usually appear for only a short period each day, after the air has warmed. One day an hour's good fishing might be had, the next less, then more. But all the time the trout are keyed into the hatch, and the action can be rewarding.

A similar transformation takes place once the water level drops and boats are banned from use. In July the stream becomes the haunt of wade fishers who move under the full canopy of overhanging cottonwoods, seeking beautiful riffles, deep clear pools, and blinding caddis and mayfly hatches coming in waves in early morning and late evening.

As the dog days of summer slowly bleed into autumn, the creek again changes, as captured on the most beautiful calendars. Dense groves of cottonwood trees are painted gold by chilling air and riparian vegetation changes into maroon, tangerine, and flaming red, creating tunnels of color along the creek. It is in this season that the resident brown trout go on the move in search of old spawning grounds.

There is a reason why Rock Creek was a favorite for famous trout fishermen like Joe Brooks, Dan Bailey, and Charles Waterman and today is the chosen water to thousands of others. Dan Shepherd calls it the quintessential trout stream, others think of it as a summer haven, and to still others it represents the excitement of salmonflies and camaraderie among fly fishers. To fisheries biologists, Rock Creek is a sign of what can happen with hard work and good planning. To many anglers, it is a long list of hatches to match, including golden stonefly, caddis, mayfly, and, as autumn arrives, the October caddis and *Baetis*.

To me, Rock Creek always will be an autumn trout stream, a place where one or two brown trout can be the quarry for an entire day. The rest of the time I can spend watching the wilderness-born water flow while entire mountainsides seem to burst into color.

～✺～

I like to ponder deep questions while standing on the steep, narrow ridge that separates the headwaters of Rock Creek from the East Fork of the Bitterroot River. If ice, wind, and water can break apart entire mountains, then how long will it take to carve away this thin finger of rock? Across the Rockies there are hundreds of such ridges. Someday, long after we're gone, some of these delicate dams will finally be breached by erosion. Will the new watercourse here follow the ancient beds or be drawn elsewhere? Will Rock Creek become the Bitterroot or the Bitterroot, Rock Creek?

It's something to think about when the trout aren't rising. If the answer is the Bitterroot, then the new river will slide around the southern toe of the Sapphire Mountains, then flow through the open bottomland and past the mountain town of Sula. Here it will hook to the north and continue through the tightly folded mountains.

The west branch of the Bitterroot River begins high in the Bitterroot Mountains, adjacent to the Montana-Idaho state line. The West Fork tumbles through the rugged landscape and eventually slows in Painted Rocks Reservoir. Shortly after leaving the reservoir, it is joined by the Nez Percé Fork, which originates beneath Nez Percé Pass just outside the gigantic Selway-Bitterroot Wilderness, at 1.3 million acres one of the largest wilderness areas in the Lower Forty-Eight.

The main stem of the Bitterroot River is formed where the watery bounty from these two different wilderness sources meet near Conner.

The river flows north through rich bottomland, between the spectacular spires of the Bitterroot Mountains to the west and the rolling Sapphire Mountains to the east. The town of Hamilton was built where the Bitterroot Valley broadens. Like the Big Hole, its sister to the southeast, the Bitterroot Valley is deep in the throes of agriculture. Consequently, the river suffers from heavy irrigation withdrawals during the hot months of summer.

Between the irrigation demands, the heavy logging carried on historically in the nearby drainages, and the present runaway urban development, it is amazing the Bitterroot River survives at all. It does so only because of the vigilant work of river advocates and sportsmen, and the addition of water already spoken for by irrigators and stored in Painted Rocks Reservoir.

Over the last hundred years, a mere blink in the valley's geologic life, the water in the Bitterroot River has been a point of contention between those who farm and ranch and those who recreate. Historic water rights filed decades ago had all but dried up the river on several occasions in the past, until sportsmen and agriculturalists began to talk about the future of the river. Through the years, watershed groups, state and federal agencies, environmental groups, and sporting groups worked to devise mutually acceptable water management plans that allow all users an equal voice in water management in the valley. Water from Painted Rocks Reservoir has been allowed to stay in the river through direct purchase and through agreements with hydroelectric companies under the auspices of mitigation paybacks. This activity has kept fish and aquatic life on the Bitterroot River from perishing altogether, and the health of the river has improved over the last few decades.

Aside from its human-caused ailments, the trout fishery has a few natural obstacles with which to contend. One is the result of the geologic makeup of the mountains from which tributary streams originate. The rolling Sapphires are primarily composed of sedimentary strata, generally high in natural nutrients. On the opposite side of the valley, the polished granite face of the Bitterroot Range is almost absent nutrient content. Therefore, the eastern tributaries are far better suited to the development of trout.

The second, and perhaps more important, natural issue faced by the fishery also is a result of the high mountains. Spring runoff on the Bitterroot is one of Montana's most spectacular events, with plenty of media coverage every time the raging snowmelt overflows the riverbanks and floods the valley. But what do we expect when we build homes on a floodplain? Spring is also when heavy silt loads from mismanaged logging projects heavily impact the ecosystem. The same evidence of the ruinous effects of past logging can be witnessed during the seasonal thunderstorms in late May and June. It is not uncommon for the Bitterroot to run as opaque as hot chocolate while it carries tons of silt off deep scars on mountainsides.

The same heavy runoff caused by snowmelt also makes the river hopscotch between channels, opening new ones and sometimes returning to old, abandoned channels. Because of the force of the current, much of the river's riparian zone is littered with downed cottonwood trees.

The switching of stream channels has a negative and positive impact on trout fishing. Newly opened channels may not promote the best trout habitat because important streamside brush and trees might not be well-established, aquatic weed beds are nonexistent, and cover for trout is less available. Often, uprooted cottonwood trees crisscross the river like a spilled box of matchsticks—extremely large matchsticks. Finding an open route through the cottonwood maze can be formidable unless boaters are very familiar with each section of river and how it has changed during seasonal runoff.

Some of the abandoned channels remain water-filled by the underground springs so plentiful in many parts of the valley. Over the years, a number of these old channels and backwater eddies have become my favorite Bitterroot haunts, especially for tempting big brown trout. I learned of them from a college buddy who grew up on a ranch in the Bitterroot Valley, a kid who, when he wasn't stacking hay, mending fence, or repeating a failed geology course, was pulling huge brown trout from backwater holes on the Bitterroot. One thing he did not do is swear me to secrecy.

"You have to fish these spots like the most persnickety spring creek," he told me after I had fished for a few days without much luck. "The lightest tippet, the smallest fly, and the best presentation is required, but done just right the results can be awesome."

A few years ago, I fished the river with Dan Shepherd and his fishing buddy Bob Schroeder. It was one of the most pleasurable and informative trips I've ever been on, simply because Bob is a fourth-generation rancher and owns a large section of river frontage. Not only did I have the chance to learn about how this rancher sees a river flowing through his family's land, but I learned much about how large irrigation systems work and what they might add to the land. I was able to see how important the land and the river are to a man whose ancestors homesteaded in the valley and whose children, hopefully, will continue the family legacy.

Many ranchers are sportsmen, as well as good land and water stewards. As we fished, Bob told me that a lot of Montana ranching families are looking at Block Management, conservation easements, and lease arrangements to allow for a regulated public use of their private land. But allowing a place that has been protected to suddenly become open for public access carries with it a huge risk where stewardship is concerned.

Aside from being responsible for eight thousand acres of Montana, Bob Schroeder is an avid fly fisherman. He knows the section of river that courses through his family's land very well, because he sees it with the dual vision of rancher and angler. He knows full well the amount of land lost to rechanneling each year, and the degree of bank erosion.

We had pulled Dan's drift boat over at the head of a nice run where you could see big trout working the edge of a seam. Shepherd immediately went on point when he saw the size of the trout, and in a matter of minutes was casting to them. Bob lightly tapped me on the shoulder and motioned for me to follow him. We snuck away and headed across a big sandbar. Midway he said, "I want you to try a spot for me, it's just over here."

I was using a light three-weight bamboo rod, one of the masterpieces of Twin Bridges rodmaker Glenn Brackett. As we stepped quietly to the backwater eddy, the tactics of my college chum came roaring back to me. Looking at the deep, slow-moving water, I began to wonder if I had the right rod for what might happen. But by then it was too late. I was already at the edge of the quiet water.

A massive old cottonwood tree, probably taken out by spring runoff decades before, was lying outward from the bank. One of its broken branches formed a nice

V and my guide instructed me to gently land a fly as close to the V as possible. "Quietly," he warned.

The three-weight put the tiny dry fly only inches from the branch, and as soon as it touched down my companion whispered, "Get ready," a phrase that usually starts my heart pounding. The fly drifted through the V. Nothing. With a look of surprise he whispered, "Again." Still nothing.

"He was there last night," Bob said as he turned to leave. I took one more cast. This time, the fly landed five feet upstream from the broken branch and drifted slowly. The eddy exploded in a wild spray, the small tip of the three-weight bent in the direction of the commotion, and in a few seconds recoiled upright. With one jerk, the big brown trout under the cottonwood had freed himself.

We've all had them, strikes so hard and fast that only our imaginations can determine the size of a fish. With a grin and shrug, Bob said, "Yep, that was him. He did the same thing to me just last night. I'm glad he's still there!"

For the next hour, we drifted back and forth in a hole along a steep wall of yellow sedimentary sand rising fifty or sixty feet above the river. I rowed while the two fishing buddies caught one trout after another, rainbows and cutthroats mostly, the grand finale of a nice evening on an outstanding river.

As we fished, we talked about the urban sprawl now taking over the valley, and the likely impact all those new septic systems were having on the important groundwater that feeds the lower river and our favorite backwater eddies. Both fly fishers told me about new neighbors who had come to the valley with an entirely different attitude about stewardship, land ownership, and resource preservation. And both expressed concern for the diminishing legacy of things they cherish: ranching and fly fishing.

There is no getting around it. Montana is quickly changing, and not only the environmentalist, sportsman, and river advocate feels it. A large part of our common heritage in Montana centers on ranching and farming. That heritage requires water from rivers like the Bitterroot, Big Hole, Ruby, Red Rock, and Beaverhead. Like it or not, our future as trout fishers runs parallel to that of ranchers and farmers. Our mutual long-term dedication to conservation easements, watershed committees, subdivision planning, and river partnerships will be the key.

At Stevensville, the river is recharged by significant groundwater originating high in the mountains. As a result, the trout fishing improves. Here the river borders the Lee Metcalf Wildlife Refuge, a refreshing haven from the booming development taking place in other parts of the valley. The refuge is home to migratory birds, white-tailed deer, moose, game birds, and migrating songbirds. It is a peaceful place through which to float and ponder how the valley might have looked back in 1841, when Father Pierre Jean DeSmet established Montana's first white settlement here.

A few miles west of the university town of Missoula, the Bitterroot joins the Clark Fork of the Columbia, and continues its push to the Pacific Ocean.

Dan gave me a ride back to my truck the evening we'd all fished together, and when we shook hands to say good-bye, he finally answered my question about which fishery he likes best. In two short sentences this fine trout fisher summed up what trout fishing is really all about. "One thing I would like you to know," he said, "is that the Bitterroot is my sentimental favorite considering the rivers around me. I am most at peace when I am floating the 'Root or wading it in a lonely stretch by myself or with my son or a good friend."

CLARK FORK RIVER AND BROOKS SANFORD

It was an odd afternoon. For more than an hour I had not come across another angler, even though by then the word had leaked out about the big trout on the Clark Fork below the huge settling ponds at Warm Springs. I was looking upstream, enjoying the warm rays of the low sun, when a quiet voice startled me; I felt as guilty about daydreaming as if I'd been caught stealing apples from a farmer's tree.

"How's the fishing?" The voice belonged to a thin man on the other bank, silhouetted in the bright sunlight. Squinting into the glare, I told the interloper the fishing had been quiet. I tried not to let my penchant for solitude show. "Same here," he answered, while his dog stepped into the water and lapped up a drink.

I was just about to say something about the dog disturbing my fishing spot when I realized the fellow was Mr. Caddis himself, Gary LaFontaine. Gary had made a career for himself by studying the intricacies of fly fishing, trout behavior, and especially the entomology of the tiny caddisfly. Among other publications, he authored *Caddisflies,* a must-read book for any serious fly fisher.

The first time I met Gary was an aggravating event. I was a young fly fisher out for a day on the Big Hole, and had just completed a long walk toward my special spot. I was all keyed up and ready to catch some trout when I spied Gary and one of his entomology buddies standing waist deep in my fishing hole, with funny-looking cylinders attached to their backs. At first I thought someone had drowned and these two were retrieving the remains, which itself would have screwed up the fishing, I guess. But instead, it was Gary and his crew wearing scuba equipment to do their underwater fish studies.

I had a lot less interest in the science of trout fishing then than in the act of trout fishing, and in a less than amiable tone I asked, "What the hell are you doing?"

Gary quietly replied, "Oh, hi," which fell far short of the answer I wanted. There I stood, dust all over my wading boots from walking a fair distance across a hay field, fly rod in hand, and no place to fish. And here was a friendly Frenchman with a smile on his face.

I left in disgust that morning, cussing for the first hundred yards back across the field, and I didn't run into Gary again until that night on the Clark Fork.

He crossed to my side of the river and looked at me carefully, asking, "Haven't we met before?" To which I answered sheepishly, "Yeah, on the Big Hole some time back." With that, I looked away and pretended to make an important cast across the Clark Fork.

I fished with Gary that evening until the last glimmer of light. He started fishing nymphs while I stuck to dry flies—a pretentious thing to do. He caught trout and I didn't, at least until hordes of caddisflies started to emerge.

The hatch started like most others I had experienced—slowly at first, then picking up in steady cadence. The difference here was that the steady cadence came in clouds of insects, swarms. While I grew more and more excited and all but fainted, Gary remained composed and brought a number of bulky trout to the net. He had witnessed this event many times over the years while living in the nearby town of Deer Lodge. But as a neophyte, I just got giddier.

I did manage to catch my share, even staying an hour after the main hatch, fishing cripples on deep corners downstream. That night, as the bushes along the Clark Fork River turned to a mass of silhouetted shadows, I shook Gary's hand and let bygones be bygones, one night of great fly fishing in exchange for one long-ago morning's lost fishing.

Years later, after reading *Caddisflies*, I realized he had studied the insect on that very stretch of the Clark Fork River.

Over the years, biological studies on the upper river have identified between 800 to 1,500 trout per mile. A large share of those are brown trout, due to their higher tolerance for unclean water, a byproduct of mining. As a matter of fact, less than fifteen miles east of where Gary and I fished that night, the waters that eventually enter the Warm Springs settling ponds are void of all aquatic life. Over the past hundred years it's been called a biological desert.

Today, the upper Clark Fork River, from its headwaters on Silver Bow Creek in Butte to Milltown Dam just east of Missoula, makes up one of our nation's most expensive EPA Superfund sites. Over this 120-mile stretch of river, close to one billion dollars already has been spent to clean up pollution caused by copper mining and smelting in Butte and Anaconda.

Locals consider the Clark Fork River to start just below the discharge of the settling ponds, where the flow merges with Warm Springs Creek. From that confluence to Deer Lodge, the river remains fairly productive and generally offers good fishing. It's high in nitrogen content, however, the result of past sewage dumped in from Butte, Anaconda, Opportunity, and Warm Springs. The sewage was historically dumped directly in the river before the construction of the settling ponds in the early 1970s. Then it was dumped for the next few years into the ponds, in the belief that those ponds were just as good as a sewage treatment plant. The nitrogen problems follow the river as far downstream as Drummond and are compounded by the significant load of fertilizer added each season to irrigated fields. The high concentration of nitrogen, coupled with increased water temperature due to significant dewatering, causes an oxygen saturation problem, which not only negatively affects fish but promotes the growth of moss and algae. As the summer wanes, the green blooms at times literally plug the river.

At Garrison Junction, the Clark Fork is joined by the fresh, clean waters of the Little Blackfoot, a stream noted for drawing in plenty of chilly underground springs from throughout the Little Blackfoot Valley. Once the springwater merges with the Clark Fork, aquatic life and trout fishing improve. The stretch of river between Gold Creek and Drummond is touted as some of the best fishing on the upper river. Flint Creek joins the Clark Fork after flowing off the high southern mountains, so the river's habitat remains healthy for a few miles below Drummond. Soon, though, the fishery lags, as if it has to work too hard to stay healthy. It remains lethargic and low in fish numbers until its merger with the wilderness waters of Rock Creek, where once again it springs back to life.

The stretch immediately above Rock Creek was heavily impacted by construction of the interstate highway, which altered the course of much of the natural streambed. It's a tragic sign of what could have happened to many Montana rivers had the Stream Protection Act not been passed in the 1960s.

The Blackfoot River carries a greater volume than the Clark Fork and beefs up the river, but the aquatic habitat can't withstand the toxic water held back by Milltown Dam. In his great guidebook, *Flyfisher's Guide to Montana*, Greg Thomas describes the toxic environment locked behind Milltown Dam: "Seven miles east of Missoula, tailings accumulate behind Milltown Dam, providing a loaded gun effect for Missoula residents and the lower river's excellent rainbow fishery.

"In February 1996, massive releases at Milltown Dam sucked up some of that sediment and deposited it downstream...tests showed high levels of toxic heavy metal...including copper, zinc and arsenic.... Levels of copper ran at 693 parts per billion below Milltown Dam. At the same time, copper levels ran 18 parts per billion in the headwaters of the Clark Fork at Silver Bow Creek, which has been called an industrial ditch and harbors no aquatic life. The state limit on copper is 18 parts per billion."

It should be noted that the author wrote his observations before improvements were made as a result of Superfund efforts on Silver Bow Creek above the settling ponds. Regardless, the evidence of the sedimentary toxicity contained behind Milltown Dam is staggering.

Today, the Montana Department of Environmental Quality and the EPA are in the process of removing the dam at Milltown, in an effort to protect both the massive aquifer under Missoula and the river downstream. The lower Clark Fork's health hangs by a thread while the dam holds back the toxic silt. The only real remedy is for the dam to be removed, but first the engineers have to completely rechannel the river to isolate it from its normal course, which is filled with 150 years of toxic buildup.

The task is tricky, and guide Brooks Sanford of St. Regis has his fingers crossed as the agencies work upriver from the stretch where he and his family make their livelihood. Brooks submitted comments to the EPA prior to the decision to remove the dam, asking what happens if things don't go just right with the removal and the river downstream is heavily impacted for years what would become of his and many other businesses on the lower river? The EPA has only one answer: According to the Comprehensive Environmental Response, Compensation and Liability Act (Superfund Law), there is no reimbursement for private businesses in the event of income lost during a Superfund activity.

At present, the trout fishery, and consequently the health of the Clark Fork, remains stable between the dam and Kelley Island, where it receives the Bitterroot River. Again, this infusion of new water greatly helps the overall condition of the Clark Fork. Fishing on this section is generally good and provides a level of entertainment to local college students and business leaders alike. It's fun to watch them rush from work to their favorite midtown water, ready for the evening's hatch.

Downstream of Missoula the Clark Fork tumbles through Alberton Gorge, where it is rumored that some huge rainbows hang out, hardly ever touched. Fly fishing here is difficult and can be risky. Boating through the gorge should be left to the few whitewater experts who supply the thrilling service. Below Alberton Gorge, the river again relaxes and provides a pleasant float.

"Every river has its quirks," said Sanford. "The Clark Fork is strange, in that the trout seem to pod up and feed in groups. You can drift past some fantastic looking water, fish the heck out of it and find nothing, but look ahead a few hundred feet and there might be a pod of dozens of trout feeding in one little section. It's helpful to spend enough time on a river to figure out where the most likely spots are. You can save a lot of time by not fishing good-looking spots that for some reason don't attract trout. I don't really know why it is that the trout here pod up, but I can tell you it is a huge factor on the Clark Fork."

Brooks is another one of those ex-agency employees, like Pete Cardinal on the Missouri. He has a degree in fisheries, but he put in only a limited amount of time with the government before hanging out his shingle as a fly-fishing guide. If anyone can answer questions about a river like the Clark Fork, it's Brooks.

One of the most fascinating stretches of river in Montana is the lower section of the Clark Fork, where it makes a gigantic meander between St. Regis and its confluence with the Flathead. Here is some of the state's most beautiful trout water, flowing through rocky hill country. Floating the river, seeking its trout, it is easy to get caught up by the narrow image in front of us. If you know the remarkable story of Glacial Lake Missoula, however, an evening on the river as it weaves through the rocky canyon turns into an adventure that complements even the best fly fishing.

Some fifteen thousand years ago, hundreds of miles from today's confluence of the Flathead and Clark Fork, the main stem of the river was pinched closed by an advancing lobe of glacial ice from the gigantic Cordilleran Ice Sheet. The ice dam impounded the Clark Fork where it dumps into present-day Lake Pend Oreille. Once the glacial dam was complete, water backed up hundreds of miles throughout the watershed, flooding all its tributaries and filling the entire valleys of the Bull, St. Regis, Flathead, Bitterroot, Blackfoot, and as far upstream as Deer Lodge.

Experts estimate that as much as five hundred square miles of water was impounded behind the dam, an immense body of water geologists call Glacial Lake Missoula.

One of the natural attributes of ice is that it floats. In what can only be described as another of nature's unique tipping points, just when enough water had been stored to float the colossal ice dam blocking the Clark Fork at the Purcell Trench, it burst, freeing its immense bounty in an act of unfathomable force. A two-thousand-foot wall of water moved through Montana's northwestern tier, taking down everything in its path and scouring entire mountainsides to bedrock. It only took a few days to drain the entire gigantic Glacial Lake Missoula. The torrent carried with it millions of years of sedimentary cover.

Of course, during an event as imposing as a whole Ice Age, the flushing of a glacial lake cannot be considered an isolated event. As the ice sheet continued to flow southward from Canada, the enormous impoundment built up again and again until it had repeated the drama more than forty-three times. Some scientists believe it took only fifty years for each new glacial lake to form, reach its natural balance point, and again burst.

A trip down the Clark Fork River between St. Regis and the Idaho border reveals the magnificent impact of the torrents. In addition, folds of bedrock are plainly visible, denoting the ever-present eastward lean brought about between seventy and ninety million years ago when the new Rockies rose from the ancient prairies.

Once it meets the Flathead River at Paradise, the Clark Fork relaxes and turns into a warmwater fishery. It picks up water from the Thompson River and then is joined by the Vermillion River. A few miles farther, the river enters the backwaters of Noxon Reservoir, where it surrenders its identity as a wild river. Only when it reaches a couple of narrows does it again kick up its heels.

"The Clark Fork, especially the lower section between Superior and Paradise, is one of the most underrated rivers in the state," declared Sanford. "Every season its reputation grows, and we get more and more calls from out-of-state fly fishers who hear about it from one source or another. It's a fun fishery to work, it's not crowded, and the hatches can be fantastic. We get a good skwala stonefly and gray drake hatch early, salmonfly and *Baetis* follow, and then come the grasshoppers, tricos, and another wave of *Baetis*. The lower river is a healthy fishery and its aquatic life demonstrates that. I just hope it makes it through the next wave of human involvement, with the removal of Milltown Dam."

The Clark Fork of the Columbia is one of nature's most enduring specimens. In the past, this resilient river gave and gave until we made it a wasteland. But after we reformed our ways, it somehow found the strength to rebound and continue, fed by some of the state's best wilderness-born trout streams: Rock Creek, Blackfoot, Bitterroot, Flathead, and Thompson. Without these protected waters, it would have stayed a biological desert.

"Rivers are marvelous spirits. Perpetually singing and dancing, they amble merrily toward the ocean, where they rejoin their cradle and their grave, lose their identities, and are mystically transported to the tops of mountains to begin new lives," wrote Constance Elizabeth Hunt.

From the first drops of rain that fall atop the Anaconda-Pintler Wilderness each season comes a part of the bounty of the Clark Fork of the Columbia, a gathering of strong waters that has gone on for millions of years and has, over its course, scraped entire canyons from the bulk of solid mountains. Changing a river almost to the point of its death took humankind just slightly more than a century.

This is a river where ancient history mixes daily with the impacts of recent history. The outcome for the fishery, and the folks who cherish and rely on it like Brooks Sanford, remains to be seen.

EPILOGUE

This star, our own good earth, made many a successful journey around the heavens ere man was made, and whole kingdoms of creatures enjoyed existence and returned to dust ere man appeared to claim them. After human beings have also played their part in Creation's plan, they too may disappear without any general burning or extraordinary commotion whatever.

—JOHN MUIR, *A Thousand-Mile Walk to the Gulf*

It was October, a time for gathering, when ranchers reclaim cattle from high meadows and anglers seek out favorite haunts for one last visit before winter sets in. I had finally finished my field research on Montana's angling heritage, and her future, and was anxious to get back to the Kootenai Valley and the spectacular jade-green currents of my own homewater. As I pulled into the empty campground at Monture Creek in the Blackfoot Valley, where I would spend my last night on the road, I was a little over two hundred miles from the Kootenai. I was edgy as I set up camp, like a racehorse after a hard run. I could almost smell the smoke from my neighbor's fireplace and hear my wife's voice over the murmur of the serene little creek that flows through our front yard.

By the time camp was ready, the afternoon sun already had drifted across the open sky to balance lightly atop the huge trees surrounding the creek. As I had countless times before, in campgrounds from the Yellowstone to the Flathead, I took a book to the bank of the creek, this time George Perkins Marsh's *Man and Nature*.

Monture Creek is a classic western trout stream. It originates in the high mountains bordering the southern Bob Marshall Wilderness. It is not unlike hundreds of other small trout streams that drop from the wilderness—streams still graced with a reliable stock of wild trout.

I pushed through a thick wall of yellow willows and sat on a fallen cottonwood log, watching a quiet pool change colors. The long reflections waved and wrinkled on the surface like a kaleidoscope, as a pair of swallows skimmed and darted above the water. The quick little birds were feeding on a new hatch of mayflies coming off the stream, diving in like fighter planes, picking off their quarry mere inches above the surface.

Midway through a swallow's sweep, it came, just off the tip of a log that was mostly submerged on the opposite bank: the rise of a trout. My focus shifted to the set of perfect concentric circles rippling outward. I marked the exact center in my mind, set the book in the grass, and went to fetch a fly rod.

I returned with the lightest rod I own, a wispy three-weight endowed with the feel of velvet and the sinewy strength only bamboo can offer. To a twelve-foot tippet I tied a small Pale Morning Dun, dressed it, and then slipped downstream. From twenty feet below I waited, crouched on one knee, counting another two rises, then I cast. The little dry fly stood upright on the mirrored pool, like a new dun drying lacey wings, getting ready to leap into the air.

I would get only one chance at the trout under the log, one chance to end a great season. I leaned forward, eyes glued to a single square foot of water, and waited.

This is what fly fishing is for me: the diving swallows, the stained-glass creek, nature's constantly changing scenes—with everything revolving around whether a certain trout would rise at a certain time. Standing ankle-deep in the creek, it seemed my life's fishing experience rode the current with that drifting fly, and again I knew just how lucky I was to have spent a lifetime on Montana trout streams.

Suddenly the water around the fly erupted in chaos, like someone had thrown in a fistful of cat-eye marbles. Minutes later, I carefully slid the thirteen-inch westslope cutthroat trout onto the cobbles and reached down to dislodge the hook. Beautiful black spots sprinkled its sides and tail, and under each jaw, orange as fresh salmon meat, two distinct slashes marked the westslope cutthroat as unique, a species native to Montana waters. There could be no more perfect fish on which to end a season.

Native species are indicator species. The westslope and Yellowstone cutthroats, the redband rainbow, Arctic grayling, and bull trout tell us plainly how healthy our watersheds are. They give us an idea of what is happening throughout an entire ecosystem. Watching the cutthroat fin slowly in the cold mountain water, I recalled the words of Jim Posewitz: "Native species didn't just come back, it took a real effort. Entire careers were spent making it happen."

Our trout streams are what they are today because even though we chased the fantasies of boom and bust economies for decades, we were somehow able to save a portion of our most important gift: water. Pure water is a resource that has no equal. When weighed against all the gold, silver, copper, coal, beaver pelts, logs, and oil taken from our state, water is the only one we cannot live without. It is the real gold Montana can brag about, the solitary component without which nothing lasts very long. Somehow, through the rollicking years of our past, we salvaged at least a portion of our water, probably because we decided to preserve parts of the very fountains from which this water comes, the Rocky Mountains.

Much has been invested in protecting lands in the form of wilderness, national parks, wildlife refuges, and wetlands. Run your finger along the blue lines designating important rivers and streams on any state map, and chances are it will also brush against protected lands that have a tremendous impact on native and wild species and the quality of our trout fisheries.

Yet we must invest in more. Our early commitment to saving homewaters by saving watersheds does not appear to be continuing in the present. This issue goes far beyond Montana, though we are the most immediate beneficiaries of our state's pure water. Any current debate over additional protected lands, whether wilderness or roadless areas, is a national debate. But Congress is standing still on watershed protection, even when proposed by its own government agencies, despite the fact that the lifeblood of troubled rivers like the Columbia and the Mississippi flows from our watersheds. According to John Gatchell of the Montana Wilderness Association, today Montana has more than one hundred thousand miles of roads, but only 3.7 percent of the state is protected as wilderness.

The vital connection between protected lands and healthy fisheries is as straightforward as it gets and, frankly, our future depends on how we address this issue.

Montana Department of Environmental Quality Water Bureau Chief George Mathieus notes that a staggering 73 percent of the water presently being assessed by the department is considered impaired, some beyond the point where swimming or fishing is an option. The department has another five years to complete its assessment of Montana waters, but the early stages of their findings should send up a red flag to trout fishers.

Think back on the historic environmental battles waged over the last century in Montana, battles for rivers like the Yellowstone, Blackfoot, Clark Fork, Flathead, Swan, and Kootenai. Put faces with those battles and you will have the second key component in the fight to save homewaters: the priceless determination and resiliency of individuals committed to saving things wild, free, and healthy, even when that stand is unpopular. River advocates are not radicals or extremists, they simply care about clean water, healthy ecosystems, wild trout, and aquatic life. They are folks accustomed to working within the system when change is needed, but willing to step outside if the system stagnates.

Our water is what it is today only because folks stood up for what is right in our good state. Our homewaters will be tomorrow what we, the people and our leaders, make of it today. Like trout, rivers and mountains have only so much life to give. It is up to each of us to decide when we will start giving back. As our history so clearly demonstrates, we are our own salvation.

SELECTED BIBLIOGRAPHY

Alvord, Bill. *A History of Montana's Fishery Division for 1890 to 1958*. Helena, Mont.: Montana Department of Fish, Wildlife & Parks, 1991.

_____. *A History of Montana's Fishery Division for 1945–2000*. Helena, Mont.: Montana Department of Fish, Wildlife & Parks, 2001.

_____. *History of Montana's Fishery Division, 1890–1983*. Helena, Mont.: Montana Department of Fish, Wildlife & Parks, 1985.

Ambrose, Stephen E. *Undaunted Courage*. New York: Simon & Schuster, 1996.

Barnhill, David Landis, Eds. *At Home on the Earth*. Berkeley: University of California Press, 1999.

"Biennial Reports, Montana Fish and Game Commission." Montana Historical Society Archives.

"Biennial Reports, Montana Fish, Wildlife & Parks Commission." Montana Historical Society Archives.

"Biennial Reports, Montana Game and Fish Commission." Montana Historical Society Archives.

Brooks, Joe. *Complete Book of Fly Fishing*. New York: Outdoor Life, 1958.

Flores, Dan. *The Natural West*. Norman: University of Oklahoma Press, 1984.

Fothergill, Chuck, and Bob Sterling. *The Montana Angling Guide*. Woody Creek, Colo.: Stream Stalker Publishing, 2002.

Fox, Stephen. *John Muir and His Legacy: The American Conservation Movement*. New York: Little Brown and Company, 1981.

Grant, George. *Grant's Riffle*. Butte, Mont.: Big Hole River Foundation, 1977.

"History of Montana Fish, Wildlife and Parks, Centennial Edition." *Montana Outdoors*, 2001.

Hauer, F. R., and J. A. Stanford. "Long Term Influence of Libby Dam Operation on Ecology of Macrozoobenthos of Kootenai River, Montana and Idaho." Report to Montana Fish, Wildlife & Parks, 1997.

Howard, Joseph Kinsey. *Montana: High, Wide, and Handsome.* New Haven, Conn.: Yale University Press, 1948.

Knopp, Malcolm, and Robert Cormier. *Mayflies.* Guilford, Conn.: The Lyons Press, 1997.

LaFontaine, Gary. *Caddisflies.* Helena, Mont.: Greycliff Publishing, 1981.

Leopold, Aldo. *A Sand County Almanac.* New York: Oxford University Press, 1949.

Malone, Michael. *Montana, a Contemporary Profile.* Helena, Mont.: American Geographic Publishing, 1996.

_____. *The Battle for Butte.* Seattle: University of Washington Press, 1981.

Malone, Michael, and Richard B. Roeder. *Montana, a History of Two Centuries.* Seattle: University of Washington Press, 1976.

Marsh, George Perkins. *Man and Nature.* Seattle: University of Washington Press, 2003.

Montana Outdoors. Montana Fish, Wildlife & Parks.

Montana Wildlife. Montana Fish, Wildlife & Parks.

Oelschlaeger, Max. *The Idea of Wilderness.* New Haven, Conn.: Yale University Press, 1991.

Our National Parks. Pleasantville, NY: Readers Digest Books, 1985.

Posewitz, Jim. *Inherit the Hunt.* Guilford, Conn.: Falcon Press, 1999.

_____. Papers.

_____. *Rifle in Hand.* Helena, Mont.: River Bend Publishing, 2004.

Smith, Douglas W., and Gary Ferguson. *Decade of the Wolf.* Guilford, Conn.: The Lyons Press, 2005.

Spence, Clark. *Montana.* New York: W. W. Norton, 1978.

Stiller, David. *Wounding the West.* Lincoln: University of Nebraska Press, 2000.

Stuart, Granville. *Forty Years on the Frontier.* Paul C. Phillips, Ed. Lincoln: University of Nebraska Press, 1977.

Teale, Edwin Way, Ed. *The Wilderness World of John Muir.* Boston: Houghton Mifflin Company, 2001.

Thomas, Greg. *Flyfisher's Guide to Montana.* Belgrade, Mont.: Wilderness Adventures Press, 1997.

Waterman, Charles F. *Mist on the River: Remembrances of Dan Bailey.* Livingston, Mont.: Yellowstone Press, 1986.

Wetzel, Robert G. *Limnology: Lake and River Ecosystems, Third Edition.* New York: Academic Press, 2001.

Zackheim, Hugh. 2006. A History of Montana's Fish, Wildlife & Parks, Fishery Division 1901–2005.

INDEX

{

A

acid mine drainage, 80, 174
agriculture
  in Big Hole Valley, 201–3
  drought influencing, 39–41, 45, 52–53
  Great Depression and, 52–54
  history of, in Montana, 40–47
  irrigated, 29–30, 89, 203
  politics and, 29
  pollution from, 73, 183–84, 220
  trout influenced by, 62–63, 73
  water rights of, 46–47, 104
Alberton Gorge, 222
algae, 184, 220
Allenspur dam proposal, 68–71, 94, 124
Amalgamated Copper, 35–36
American Smelting and Refining Company (ASARCO), 80, 133
Anaconda Mining Company, 30, 75–76, 78–84, 93, 124, 132
Anaconda, MT, 34–37, 75–76, 220
Anaconda-Pintler Wilderness, 35, 196, 200, 209, 211, 224
Anderson, Forrest, 85, 93
Anderson Lane fishing site, 203
aquatic vegetation
  nitrogen influencing, 183–84, 220
  water temperature influencing, 164
aqueducts, 93–94

ARCO. *See* Atlantic Richfield Company
Arctic grayling trout. *See* grayling trout
Armitage, Jess, 190
Army Corps of Engineers, 67–68, 71, 88–89, 91, 146–47, 150, 153–54
arsenic, 18, 28, 221
ASARCO. *See* American Smelting and Refining Company
Atlantic Richfield Company (ARCO), 84, 132–33

B

Baetis, 213, 224
Bailey, Dan, 69–71, 102, 135, 141, 213
Bailey, John, 102, 104, 173–75, 180
Bass, Rick, 39, 146, 156
Baucus, Max, 114
bears, 121–22, 158, 166, 169, 171
Beartooth Mountains, 82
Beartrap Canyon, 190
Beartrap Creek, 80
Beaver Creek, 38
Beaverhead Mountains, 196
Beaverhead River, 41, 63, 67, 114, 139, 196, 217
  conservation of, 203–7
  use regulations for, 203–7
beneficial use, of water, 94–95, 97, 115
Berkeley Pit, 124
Berry, Wendell, 25
Big Belt Mountains, 176
Big Fork, MT, 159